T0321853

Blockchain Technology for Global Social Change

Jane Thomason
University of Queensland, Australia

Sonja Bernhardt
ThoughtWare, Australia

Tia Kansara
Replenish Earth Ltd, UK

Nichola Cooper
Blockchain Quantum Impact, Australia

A volume in the Advances
in Computer and Electrical
Engineering (ACEE) Book Series

Published in the United States of America by
    IGI Global
    Engineering Science Reference (an imprint of IGI Global)
    701 E. Chocolate Avenue
    Hershey PA, USA 17033
    Tel: 717-533-8845
    Fax: 717-533-8661
    E-mail: cust@igi-global.com
    Web site: http://www.igi-global.com

Library of Congress Cataloging-in-Publication Data

Names: Thomason, Jane, 1958- author. | Bernhardt, Sonja, 1959- author. |
   Kansara, Tia, 1983- author. | Cooper, Nichola, author.
Title: Blockchain technology for global social change / by Jane Thomason,
   Sonja Bernhardt, Tia Kansara, and Nichola Cooper.
Description: Hershey, PA : Engineering Science Reference, an imprint of IGI
   Global, [2020] | Includes bibliographical references and index.
Identifiers: LCCN 2019003700| ISBN 9781522595786 (hardcover) | ISBN
   9781522595809 (ebook) | ISBN 9781522595793 (softcover)
Subjects: LCSH: Blockchains (Databases)--Social aspects. | Blockchains
   (Databases)--Economic aspects.
Classification: LCC QA76.9.B56 T46 2020 | DDC 005.8/24--dc23 LC record available at https://
lccn.loc.gov/2019003700

This book is published in the IGI Global book series Advances in Computer and Electrical Engineering (ACEE) (ISSN: 2327-039X; eISSN: 2327-0403)

British Cataloguing in Publication Data
A Cataloguing in Publication record for this book is available from the British Library.

All work contributed to this book is new, previously-unpublished material.
The views expressed in this book are those of the authors, but not necessarily of the publisher.

For electronic access to this publication, please contact: eresources@igi-global.com.

Advances in Computer and Electrical Engineering (ACEE) Book Series

Srikanta Patnaik
SOA University, India

ISSN:2327-039X
EISSN:2327-0403

MISSION

The fields of computer engineering and electrical engineering encompass a broad range of interdisciplinary topics allowing for expansive research developments across multiple fields. Research in these areas continues to develop and become increasingly important as computer and electrical systems have become an integral part of everyday life.

The **Advances in Computer and Electrical Engineering (ACEE) Book Series** aims to publish research on diverse topics pertaining to computer engineering and electrical engineering. **ACEE** encourages scholarly discourse on the latest applications, tools, and methodologies being implemented in the field for the design and development of computer and electrical systems.

COVERAGE

- Digital Electronics
- Applied Electromagnetics
- Power Electronics
- VLSI Design
- Sensor Technologies
- VLSI Fabrication
- Chip Design
- Optical Electronics
- Electrical Power Conversion
- Computer Hardware

IGI Global is currently accepting manuscripts for publication within this series. To submit a proposal for a volume in this series, please contact our Acquisition Editors at Acquisitions@igi-global.com or visit: http://www.igi-global.com/publish/.

Titles in this Series

For a list of additional titles in this series, please visit:
[go here and find specific BS URL: http://www.igi-global.com/book-series/]

Applying Integration Techniques and Methods in Distributed Systems and Technologies
Gabor Kecskemeti (Liverpool John Moores University, UK)
Engineering Science Reference • copyright 2019 • 351pp • H/C (ISBN: 9781522582953)
• US $245.00 (our price)

Handbook of Research on Cloud Computing and Big Data Applications in IoT
B. B. Gupta (National Institute of Technology Kurukshetra, India) and Dharma P. Agrawal
(University of Cincinnati, USA)
Engineering Science Reference • copyright 2019 • 609pp • H/C (ISBN: 9781522584070)
• US $295.00 (our price)

Multi-Objective Stochastic Programming in Fuzzy Environments
Animesh Biswas (University of Kalyani, India) and Arnab Kumar De (Government College
of Engineering and Textile Technology Serampore, India)
Engineering Science Reference • copyright 2019 • 420pp • H/C (ISBN: 9781522583011)
• US $215.00 (our price)

Renewable Energy and Power Supply Challenges for Rural Regions
Valeriy Kharchenko (Federal Scientific Agroengineering Center VIM, Russia) and Pandian
Vasant (Universiti Teknologi PETRONAS, Malaysia)
Engineering Science Reference • copyright 2019 • 432pp • H/C (ISBN: 9781522591795)
• US $205.00 (our price)

Secure Cyber-Physical Systems for Smart Cities
Riaz Ahmed Shaikh (King Abdulaziz University, Saudi Arabia)
Engineering Science Reference • copyright 2019 • 329pp • H/C (ISBN: 9781522571896)
• US $225.00 (our price)

For an entire list of titles in this series, please visit:
[go here and find specific BS URL: http://www.igi-global.com/book-series/]

701 East Chocolate Avenue, Hershey, PA 17033, USA
Tel: 717-533-8845 x100 • Fax: 717-533-8661
E-Mail: cust@igi-global.com • www.igi-global.com

Table of Contents

Foreword

BLOCKCHAIN HYPE, HOPE, AND HARVEST

The book you are now reading takes you on a journey through an exponential technology, scalable distributed ledgers (popularly known as "blockchain"). Jane Thomason and her colleagues examine blockchain applications in both emerging and developed economies, for technology leapfrogging means that the emerging worlds may enjoy some of the benefits of greater transparency, portability, and control over data prior to the G7 countries seeing them realized.

Since people begin seriously commercializing blockchain-related technologies about five years ago, the degree of hype has been extraordinary. Ideological lines were drawn around control of software protocols. People got pretty exercised.

Meanwhile, quietly, a group of researchers and business advocates started less flashy but fundamentally more profound effort. How could this technology address fundamental issues for society and the planet?

I've had the pleasure of meeting Jane Thomason through my online classes which the Saïd Business School, University of Oxford has taken to over 120 countries. Her participation highlighting to my students the applicability of blockchain to more than simply pecuniary advantage, but to global problems, aligns well with our philosophy of global impact around important issues. She elaborates on this philosophy in the book you now possess.

Placing a technology disruption properly in its socioeconomic context, we are given real-world examples of country-scale, and even pan-national, experimentation of delivering blockchain advantage to society.

Most importantly, the authors advocate for a model of Blockchain for Social Change. Rather than simply being offered the chance to marvel at a technology invention, or guided on how to exploit this technology purely for commercial gain, you are given a framework for applying blockchain to humanity's grand challenges. With this gift you've been offered, what will you do next?

David Shrier
Endor, USA
May 2019, Charlestown, MA

Preface

Against the backdrop of major global financial scandals, data and privacy breaches by governments, and large platform providers and significant political events over the last decade, blockchains have risen in the public consciousness. Commonly synonymous with the cryptocurrency bitcoin and its volatile price performance in recent years, blockchains are greeted with a mixed reception.

Bitcoiners, of the libertarian mindset, advocate that blockchains will radically change how industry and governments operate in the years to come. Skeptics believe blockchains are overhyped and present with too few use cases to be considered of any practical value. At the mid-point of these opinions are the entrepreneurs, small businesses and non-government organisations quietly establishing successful proof-of-concepts designed to effect socioeconomic change for the poor and marginalised. For, regardless of one's opinion regarding blockchains' many limitations, there are hundreds of examples of projects across the world making a difference in developing and developed economies. This book showcases but a few of these examples.

The purpose of this book is not one of persuasion. The authors have worked with blockchain technology for many years – they do not wish to contribute to the hype and misunderstanding of blockchains. As researchers, the intent in producing this book is to provide objective information regarding the technology's capability, its application and possible evolution. Blockchain is part of a suite of Web 3.0 technologies – its potential is likely to be realised in the years that follow, coupled with other technologies like artificial intelligence. Thus, the authors see that this book is but an introduction to blockchain technology and, through the use of case studies, serves to demonstrates a way for organisations to achieve social impact, as part of a broader change initiative.

AN INTRODUCTION TO THE BOOK

The first chapter of the text sets the scene for blockchains. In an era of corporate social responsibility, blockchains are contextualised as a method for increasing accountability, transparency and efficiency. The Blockchain for Social Change (B4SC) model is introduced, against which case studies and concepts are mapped.

Chapter 2 introduces blockchains and their limitations on a technical level. Explained in simple terms, the purpose of this chapter is to enable readers unfamiliar with blockchains collectively to understand how they function. This foundation is a platform for Chapter 3, where blockchain utilisation is discussed at a national level. There are several international governments using blockchains to introduce operational efficiencies and social change, this chapter highlights how this is done in dynamic regulatory environments and why some change may happen from the emerging markets first, as seen in Chapter 4.

The features of blockchain in urban environments are discussed in Chapter 5, highlighting how blockchains might support smart cities and how countries like Dubai and India are already implementing them to great effect.

Chapters 6-8 demonstrate the democratic essence of blockchains, describing how they are used to provide healthcare, access to education and financial services; to promote socioeconomic inclusion and equality, to provide digital identity and individual safety. These chapters provide examples of organisations undertaking pilot studies, with proof-of-concepts and extant initiatives which are used to make recommendations for other organisations inspired to follow suit.

Finally, in Chapter 10, "The Emerging Future," the authors aggregate conclusions from the text to lay out the agenda for further research and development. Key challenges are outlined, including how technology might be evaluated and how institutional innovation might be promoted.

CONCLUSION

Blockchains are fascinating. As part of a technology mix, they have the potential to introduce disruptive forms of innovation that take organisations forward into a new era of connected digitisation.

They are not a *solution,* however. They are not a silver bullet or a panacea. They do not replace well-balanced governance nor considered policy intervention. Blockchains will probably not replace banks or governments – but they will force change upon them.

Thus, while the tone of this book is fully positive, it is also pragmatic. The chapters that follow represent but a snapshot in time. Blockchains are fast-evolving technologies. In the time it takes you to read this book there will almost certainly be changes to protocols, nomenclature and data management approaches that invite readers to approach understanding the technology with an open mind and a critical eye.

The authors hope that you enjoy the journey of learning about this dynamic technology as much as they enjoy researching it.

Acknowledgment

It is impossible to name the many people who have made this book possible. It is a community effort.

Blockchain, more than any other technology, brings people together.

Since 2016, when I started understanding, learning, writing and networking in Blockchain circles, I have become a member of an incredible global community of like-minded spirits, who see and are working on the transformative technology that could revolutionise the world that we know.

Firstly, I have to thank my son Jock, who told me in 2016, "Mum, you have to learn about Blockchain, it's going to change everything." He was right, and I did, and it will. I also want to thank my daughter, Georgia, for joining my Blockchain journey, rapidly creating her own journey, and letting me be part of that.

In the early days, it was hard to get traction and I want to thank the Papua New Guinea believers, Rabbie Namaliu, Shane Ninai, David Kavanamur and Satyedra Prasad, who helped create the environment for a use case trial with the Central Bank of Papua New Guinea. The Central Bank Team of Loi Bakani, Elizabeth Genia, Callum Holmes and Naime Kilamanu, who had the courage to join the London Blockchain Week Hackathon in 2017 to see how Blockchain could help solve the financial inclusion problems (85% unbanked) of Papua New Guinea. At that Hackathon, we met many willing collaborators, three of whom need special mention, Luis Carranza the CEO of Fintech Worldwide who supported the first social impact hackathon and has made his organisation available to support many more social impact hackathons since then, including in Lagos, Nigeria on Gender Equity. The two winners of the hackathon Julien Bouteloup and Ish Goel, have become firm friends and continue to inspire me with their ground-breaking work.

Acknowledgment

When I first started accelerating my Blockchain ideas, I was the CEO of Abt Associates Australia, and I was supported by Abt to pursue this work, even though, I am sure many of my US colleagues had little understanding of what it was and where it would lead. First, thanks to Ann Marie Slaughter for raising Blockchain early at an Abt Board meeting, which gave me cover to keep up my exploration. To Hugh McDonough, Mario Bazan, Mira Ahmad, Scott Hefter and Anneke Schmider for being co-conspirators and supporters in my quest to get Abt deeply involved in Blockchain and for Kathleen Flannigan and Jay Knott for turning a blind eye as I increasingly pivoted to a focus on Blockchain and new technologies.

To the whole world of amazing women in Blockchain that have been part of and have enriched my journey in an extraordinary way. First to my great friend and fearless pioneer Loretta Joseph, who has surprised many, including, I am sure, herself, with the incredible progress she has catalysed in Bermuda, Mauritius and Serbia. To many other amazing women in blockchain community, firstly Thessy Mehrain who got it started in the first place and Katrina Donaghy, who has driven this agenda magnificently in the Australia. To Marianne Hahr, Katherine Foster, Cindy Chin, Liz Chee, Jamie Moy, Efi Pylarinou, Amy-Rose Goodey, Akasha Konkoly, Marisol Guzman, Genevieve Lavelle, Helen Disney, Sharon Henley, Michelle Chivunga and so many more driven and passionate women pushing boundaries.

Inevitably there will be many vibrant, progressive founders, researchers and designers championing this technology that I have connected with and have not mentioned here – unfortunately, that will be the case in an area as fast-moving as Blockchains - and I only have but a few pages to express my gratitude and admiration for the time and energy everyone is investing in developing sustainable solutions for social change. Finally, my thanks go to my co-authors, Sonja Bernhardt, Nichola Cooper and Tia Kansara, who, without their tireless effort, this book would not have been possible.

With thanks,

Jane Thomason
University of Queensland, Australia

Chapter 1

Introduction:
How Frontier Technologies Are Changing Our World

ABSTRACT

This chapter introduces Blockchain technology and its potential for social change. It explores the exponential growth of new technologies, highlighting key challenges in Blockchain applications. For context, the authors draw upon management literature for an historical overview of the constructs of social change including charity, stewardship, corporate citizenship, corporate social responsibility, and the triple bottom line. The advent and rise of each construct are presented to explain the dynamics that have contributed to the global focus on social change and the opportunities it creates.

THE BACKGROUND TO BLOCKCHAIN

Today we live in the historical product of successive social impact constructs. They have produced a framework that varies not only over time but also by culture, issue and industry. The framework has not evolved via any unifying principle but has been constructed ad hoc around specific issues at specific points in time and on the prevailing management theories at those times.

It is by deconstructing this historical background that insights into the theories and social influences leading to the more recent calls for greater Social Impact may be framed.

DOI: 10.4018/978-1-5225-9578-6.ch001

It is understanding the narratives of the earlier forms of Social Impact and taking a closer look at their rise (and fall) that has the potential to lend insight into what actually is good practice. That in turn leads to an enhanced framework for the roles and responsibilities of communities, corporations and governments in the overall thrust for greater and beneficial Social Impact.

Blockchain is a word that evokes great excitement and, often, controversy. It is part of a suite of technologies including Artificial Intelligence, the Internet of Things, Big Data and 3D Printing which are rapidly changing the world of today. So rapidly in fact, that the report of the World Economic Forum (2016) foresees that Blockchains could store as much as 10% of global GDP by 2027. Bitcoin, the decentralized digital currency built on Blockchain began to capture global attention in 2008 as Blockchain's first application at scale. Bitcoin was then quickly followed by a plethora of digital currencies such as Ripple, Lite Coin, EOS and Ethereum.

Since then, the world has looked to global leaders in Blockchain such as Estonia (referred to in detail in Chapter 3) for national-level implementations of Blockchain to radically transform staid economies and introduce bold reform for national socioeconomic benefit (Estonian Blockchain Technology, 2019). Indeed, a 2018 report by Stanford University indicates there are now over 193 organisations currently working on Blockchain-enabled social impact projects, 20% of which are solving a problem that would not have been able to be solved without Blockchain (Galen et al., 2018).

PositiveBlockchain.io, an open-source database, media platform and community exploring the potential of Blockchain technologies for social and environmental impact, lists more than 580 projects and start-ups already engaged in this field. Several of which are profiled in Chapter of this book.

Despite the warm reception, there remain, however, questions from the Monitoring, Evaluation and Learning (MERL) community, industry groups and Blockchain advocates alike, regarding the applications of Blockchains, such as:

- *What could each stakeholder group of a project gain from the use of Blockchain across the stages of design and implementation, and would the benefits of Blockchain incentivize them to participate?*
- *Can Blockchain resolve trust or transparency issues between disparate stakeholder groups, for example to ensure that data reported represent reality, or that they are of sufficient quality for decision-making?*

- *Are there less expensive, more appropriate, or easier to execute, existing technologies that already meet each group's needs?*
- *Are there unaddressed needs that Blockchain could help address, or capabilities Blockchain offers that might inspire new and innovative thinking about what is done, and how it gets done?*

Blockchain is a technology that is developing at a rapid pace. This book has been updated almost daily and the day it is published, the information contained within will already be out of date.

This is the nature of exponential growth. Although technology grows in the exponential domain, we humans live in a linear world. So technological trends are not noticed as small levels of technological power are doubled. Then, seemingly out of nowhere, a technology explodes into view. For example, when the Internet went from 20,000 to 80,000 nodes over a two-year period during the 1980s, this progress remained hidden from the general public. A decade later, when it went from 20 million to 80 million nodes in the same amount of time, the impact was rather conspicuous (Kurzweil, 2001).

Blockchain for Social Change is intended as a non-technical overview for readers new to Blockchains and their potential application in emerging markets to reduce socioeconomic inequity through existing use cases. Detailed descriptions of Blockchains in existing use-cases, however, make this book suitable for social and technological researchers and philanthropists.

This chapter frames and contextualises the impacts of the technology through the lens of past social movements that have been precursors to the Blockchain social impact movement and offers a B4SC model depicting the current influences and drivers of change, the enabling shifts required, and an image of the Blockchain-at-scale New World.

THE SOCIAL BUSINESS CASE

The precursors to social change have been defined in a variety of ways and are often subject to broad interpretation. The evolution of such constructs has also been contentious – especially regarding associated corporate rights and responsibilities. Community expectations of social change have also been driven by the rapid socialisation of technology resulting in communities that are able to gather at unprecedented speed with the ability to exert powerful influence through social media, catalyzing physical gatherings. This will inevitably accelerate as connectivity expands exponentially in the age of the 'Internet of Things' (IoT).

The Robber Baron Sets the Robin Hood Scenario

The many incarnations of social impact may be traced back to Andrew Carnegie, the founder of the conglomerate U.S. Steel Corporation, a well-known industrialist, entrepreneur and philanthropist. Carnegie (1901) articulated two principles he believed were necessary for capitalism to work:

1. The charity principle, which required more fortunate members of society to assist the less fortunate, including the unemployed, the disabled, the sick, and the elderly. These 'have-nots' could be assisted either directly or indirectly through institutions such as churches, settlement houses, and other community groups including the Community Chest movement from the 1920s. Initially, charity was considered an individual obligation as opposed to one of business, and wealthy individuals were to decide how much to contribute. However, by the 1920s the perception arose that community needs had outgrown the wealth of even the most generous philanthropists, and the era began wherein business was expected to contribute its resources to charities aiding the unfortunate.

2. The stewardship principle, which required businesses and wealthy individuals to see themselves as the stewards, or caretakers, of their property rather than its owners. Carnegie's view was that the rich hold their money 'in trust' for the rest of society. Carnegie saw the role of business to be that of multiplying society's wealth by increasing its own, through prudent investment of resources under its stewardship; but holding this wealth in trust for the rest of society and using it for any purpose society deemed legitimate.

Both of these views could be described as paternalistic, driving the philosophy that communities lack the capacity to improve their lot independently and require external intervention.

BUSINESS PHILANTHROPIC BEGINNINGS

Crane, Matten & Moon (2008b) flag that "Since medieval times, European business people have engaged in citizenship-like ways through their membership of and participation in their guilds, the forerunners of business associations, which provided systems of governance within individual trades and forms of mutual support." However, business philanthropy as a responsibility was not clearly articulated until by Andrew Carnegie and others in the late 1800s and early 1900s.

Post-Carnegie, business philanthropy was curtailed by the American Civil War and the Great Depression. Commercial philanthropic commitments were generally in response to labour movement pressure and/or legal requirements. However, as wealth later increased, corporations began to need to win legitimacy by societal approval for their existence and success (Crane, McWilliams, Matten, Moon & Siegel, 2008).

Since the Second World War there have been successive waves of new approaches and frameworks to address market weaknesses and renegotiate rights and responsibilities to address issues such as a tendency towards monopoly and the concentration of power and wealth. These waves might be described as fights for the social contract (Waddell, 2000). During the 1950s and 1960s the principles of philanthropy gained global recognition. I.e., if business did not freely accept social responsibilities, it would be forced to accept them by Government (Citeman, 2009). Resulting in the emergence of framing corporations as corporate 'citizens' during the 1980s.

CORPORATE CITIZENSHIP

By the 1980s the terms defining the social role of business such as the charity and stewardship principles and general industrial philanthropy, morphed into the use of the term Corporate Citizenship.

Fundamentally Corporate Citizenship terminology has been in existence since the 1950's (Gossett, 1957), however wider acceptance and use of the construct began in the 1980s, where 'citizenship' is often referred to by a number of attributes, of which 'good corporate citizenship' or 'global citizenship' are the most widely used.

Waddell (2000) explains that "the term is used on the one hand to connect business activity to broader social accountability and service for mutual benefit, and yet on the other it reinforces the view that a corporation is an entity with status equivalent to a person". Crane et al. (2008b) propose that "Citizenship seems to be a desired metaphor in the corporate world to counter notions of impersonal, bureaucratic and inhumane power-players and replace those by the image of the 'good guy' next door who cares for you and looks after the interests."

Crane, Matton & Moon (2008a) provide a more extended view from a more political concept, noting the roles and responsibilities of all the members of a political community: where political communities consist of those who rule (the government) and those who are ruled (the citizens). In this approach, corporations find themselves on both sides of this dichotomy, with economic power considered similar to political power as they increasingly take on some State-like roles, at the same time being subject to voluminous laws and regulations and trying to take on the role of "good citizens" in the community.

The chief issue that this brought to the table was examining corporations through the lens of citizenship, which implies roles and responsibilities. Citizenship rights and responsibilities are described by Waddell (2000) as being "of *all* members of the community, which are mutually interlinked and dependent upon each other" (emphasis the authors' own). Historically Corporate Citizenship sought to expand corporate rights based upon a concept of individual rights.

More specifically, using Corporate Citizenship terminology ultimately treats a corporation in the eyes of the law as an artificial person. Or as defined by Dahl (1985), "the application of the citizen metaphor to corporations can draw on the argument that every large corporation should be thought of as a *social enterprise*; that is, as an entity whose existence and decisions can be justified only in so far as they serve public or social purposes" (Dahl, 1985, p. 17). It is worth noting, however, that this is a dangerous theory of "citizenship": political systems in which the existence and decisions of *individuals* can be justified "only in so far as they serve public or social purposes" in practice put the individual at the mercy of the State and have proved disastrous.

Corporate Citizenship, or more specifically Good Corporate Citizenship, emphasizes the need for people who are often outside the traditional social, political and economic power structures, the marginalized, to become more empowered and influential in development processes (Waddell, 2000).

There are a number of challenging tasks that seek to be resolved under the citizenship framework, e.g. corporations' rights and responsibilities (if any) in reducing the economic inequalities within and between countries in an era of increasing distributed cross border activities, and addressing environmental problems, which may be inseparable from the issues of poverty in most developing countries.

Therefore, for corporate citizenship approaches to encompass developmental concerns, they must address deep power structures and strive for empowerment of partners and stakeholders. As Waddell (2000) argues, "understanding the sectoral differences allows development of more rational and mutually rewarding strategies."

Corporate Citizenship theories therefore opened the pathway to "strategic philanthropy". That is, instead of engaging in the charity principle simply for the sake of it or as an add-on line to 'look good', organisations seek to embed corporate citizenship throughout, based on the insight that a stable social, environmental and political environment ensures profitable business (Windsor, 2001; Wood & Logsdon, 2001).

There has been a resulting debate on the conditions, prerequisites, typical patterns and limitations of corporate participation in power sharing in society. For example, Crane et al. (2008b) argue that aligning corporations with citizenship necessarily results in contestable outcomes: "Since corporations do not fit easily within a single predefined political role, and since citizenship is such a dynamic concept, corporate responsibilities in the field of citizenship are inherently contestable." Indeed, with the shifting dynamics of intersectoral relationships involving corporations, stakeholders, activists, government and the general community, all involved in social, economic and political development, and underscored by differing interpretations, needs and desires (Crane et al., 2008b; Waddell, 2000): high complexity and subjective interpretations seem unavoidable.

Altman (1998) reviewed corporate citizenship models and identified five types. Of most interest for the purposes of this work is: "One of these, referred to as the World Bank Model, aims for social, economic, and political *development*. This model stresses the importance of partnerships between corporations and the rest of society, in contrast to the traditional approaches where the development agenda is under leadership of either the government or business, and usually with outside experts. The growing importance of this approach is demonstrated by a growing number of important institutions involved in development work internationally." This approach is the one reflected in the Blockchain and United Nations SDG projects of 2017, 2018 and onwards.

What we see from the Corporate Citizen reviews and debates is just some of the richness and complexities of aligning corporations into citizenship roles. A wider view that considered the philosophies and nature of rights and government would substantially add to the possibilities.

Now we are again at a point of flux, reconfiguring constructs of citizenship (identity, ecological and cosmopolitan) in an increasingly interconnected and distributed world facing further disruption from the ripple effects of Blockchain and Crypto Currencies. And where corporations' activities, particularly cross-border, cross nation and cross government, are an active part of the mix, with the recognition that "Corporations are not passive players in a stable landscape of citizenship institutions. The dynamics of citizenship are at least partly shaped by the activities of corporations" (Crane et al., 2008b).

CORPORATE SOCIAL RESPONSIBILITY

Corporate Social Responsibility (CSR) has appeared in business and stakeholder terminology since the 1960's (DeGeorge, 2011). Scherer & Palazzo (2007) refer to CSR as "an 'umbrella term' for all those debates that deal with the 'responsibilities of business and its role in society'.

CSR has been defined in often confusing ways (D'Orazio, 2015). A complicating factor leading to multiple definitions of CSR has been its apparent changing nature over time, seemingly driven by the different interests represented. Thus, the authors find CSR has different meanings to a business person, to business shareholders, to an NGO, to an activist, to a government official and to the general community. Hence, we see the same issues of complexity and subjectivity as with its 'Corporate Citizenship' ancestor.

Layering on top of the differing definitions per interest group, there have also been shifts over time that have added to the multiplicity of definitions and expectations. The first shift from the original voluntary basis to self-regulation was followed by a further push for mandated regulatory compliance. This second shift has been fueled by a rising interest in addressing ethical issues, resulting in a move from laws addressing traditional economic and legal responsibilities to ones to impose ethical and philanthropic responsibility (Carroll, 1991).

The second shift has also encompassed a broadening of control. Scherer & Palazzo (2008) describe it as, "a shift in global business regulation from a state-centric model toward new multilateral non-territorial models, with the inclusion of private and non-governmental institution as key actors. On the global level, therefore, non-state actors play an active role in what has been called 'governance without government'."

This has resulted in increasing global pressures for businesses, and in particular Multi-National Corporations (MNC's) to be morally obligated not only to their stakeholders and immediate communities, but to act globally and extend their CSR activity beyond their initial scope and into the wider global community. The extent of that obligation has been debated, including limiting it to within realistic limits. Thus, Hsieh (2004) notes that MNC's based in developed countries have a 'duty to assist' poor countries where they operate, but only as long as such an assistance does not outweigh the benefits obtained these MNC's obtain in those countries. Hsieh further notes that this duty ought to be applicable only when the developed country they are based in is not already fulfilling its 'obligation' to assist those poor countries.

The literature, and indeed communities, approach this with mixed sentiments. Freeman & Liedtka (1991) call for the demise of CSR, naming its failures as chief reasons: "The idea of corporate social responsibility has failed to help create the good society. Long seen by academics and managers alike as the missing link in capitalism, the concept of corporate social responsibility has not delivered on its promise. Furthermore, it has become a barrier to meaningful conversations about corporations and the good life. Corporate social responsibility, in all of its many masks, has outlived its rather limited useful life, and we call for its immediate demise." Later in the article, Freeman & Liedtka (1991) state that "Corporate Social Responsibility is not a useful idea;" in fact they agree with Milton Friedman that CSR is a dangerous idea, which gets in the way of doing good.

This sentiment is shared by others, for various reasons. For example, Hollender & Breen (2010) indicate that failure may be due to CSR being implemented as selective and compartmentalized 'programs' rather than holistic and systemic change. D'Orazio (2015) takes a step back from how to the wider question of why and presents a reality-based argument stating that "the simple fact that corporations possess the capabilities necessary to contribute to the solution of global problems is not enough to put a moral obligation on them to participate in the search for the solution to the problem." Visser (2012) simply states "that CSR, as a business, governance and ethics system, has failed." Visser further argues, "The CSR literature is liberally sprinkled with charming case studies of truly responsible and sustainable projects and a few pioneering companies. The problem is that so few of them ever go to scale. It is almost as if, once the soundbites and PR-plaudits have been achieved, no further action is required. They become shining pilot projects and best practice examples, tarnished only by the fact that they are endlessly repeated on the CSR conference circuits of the world, without any vision for how they might transform the core business of their progenitors."

In other words, some think CSR has failed due to poor implementation, while others think the attempt itself is flawed. Perhaps the latter explains the former.

To resolve the pressures for CSR in the light of its failures, Freeman and Liedtka (1991) offer an alternative of "an ongoing conversation about corporations and the good life. Such an alternative conversation needs to be centrally connected to other conversations about how we human beings can live. In particular, we suggest that reconceptualizing the corporation as a network of relationships makes possible a social world in which 'caring' has primary significance."

The authors support this view of a globalised world where the focus is on relationships and 'caring' is a consequence of personal values not something imposed by laws, and where the overall global governance is based on voluntary trade between independent thinking bodies without the force of 'guns' to impose the opinions of a controlling elite.

THE TRIPLE BOTTOM LINE

The term 'Triple Bottom Line' was coined by John Elkington in 1994. Triple bottom line refers to an accounting framework with three parts, adding social and environmental/ecological to the traditional single, financial bottom line. That is, it is a theory that corporations should do more than make a profit, their worth should be measured by their social and environmental impact as well, and these measures should be incorporated into their accounts.

The late 1990s saw the term take off in the CSR world, driven by a worldwide shift in thinking on human and societal values. It is an attempt to include or embed the frameworks of Corporate Social Responsibility and Sustainable Development into corporate accounting. Elkington is also responsible for developing the 3P formulation, 'people, planet and profits' (Elkington, 2004).

The Triple Bottom Line idea extended the rights and responsibilities demanded by the prior Corporate Citizenship construct and the global societal role driven by the CSR framework, by more formally entrenching further values-based accountabilities in organisations.

Since then there have been corporations that have burned because of values-based crises, such as the Enron and Arthur Anderson scandals (Elkington, 2004). Whether such crises are anything new or would have been prevented by any new construct when they were not by numerous existing laws, is a point worth considering. Nevertheless, the authors propose that the accelerating demand for international transparency will further fuel an ongoing values-based framework, which will be synergistically amplified by the emerging metamorphosis of the old centralized economic powers into a new distributed token and values-based economy.

As early as 2001, Dunham, Freeman, & Liedtka (2001) used the term 'virtual advocacy groups' to describe "a new breed of citizen action group" where "the emergence and maintenance of such groups have been made possible by technological advances facilitating electronic communication among group members. The purposes, tone and tactics of such groups have also been shaped by technology."

A decade later in the Egyptian revolution, it was widely reported that social media had a powerful influence before and after the 'Arab Spring' (Bernhardt, 2014; Bernhardt, Braun, & Thomason 2018). While the final outcomes of such popular movements were usually less than originally hoped, their power to shake up societies and force a response cannot be denied.

Rapid technological growth is opening this up and assisting driving the process, resulting in the collapse of many forms of traditional power bases. A wide range of different stakeholders has streamlined access to increasingly demand information on what businesses are doing and planning to do, from cradle to grave.

The adoption of this approach has fed into the social impact movement and presented further complexities for corporations. The implications according to Elkington are: a shift from current Governance models of Balance Sheets (transparency, accountability, reporting and assurance) to an emerging one of Boards and People (ultimate accountability, corporate governance and strategy), and a shift from a current focus on Brands (engaging investors, customers and consumers directly in sustainability issues) to a fundamental change in Business Models (moving beyond corporate hearts and minds to the very DNA of business: an internal rather than external motivator).

It is within that rapidly changing landscape and that DNA change that Blockchain for Social Impact Activity operates and seeks to generate zealous passion as a driver for business transformation – that is owned by no one, controlled by no one but benefitting everyone.

THE CALL FOR CHANGE: TOWARDS THE EMERGENT FUTURE

We have seen the evolution of constructs of corporate social impact and its limitations. How might it evolve further in the future?

Visser (2012) proposes that to address the Corporate Citizenship and CSR failures what is needed is a new DNA model of responsible business, built around the four elements of value creation, good governance, societal contribution and environmental integrity, further stating that it would be unfair and inaccurate to characterise all business activity as motivated by greed.

There is a close alignment between Tapscott & Williams (2006) 'Wikinomics' and the current Blockchain-based collaboration Web 4.0 enthusiasts are aiming for. More specifically, Tapscott & Williams defined it as "the effects of extensive collaboration and user-participation on the marketplace and corporate world." Wikinomics, they said, is based on four principles:

- *Openness*, which includes not only open standards and content but also financial transparency and an open attitude towards external ideas and resources;
- *Peering*, which replaces hierarchical models with a more collaborative forum, for which the Linux operating system is a quintessential example;
- *Sharing*, which is a less proprietary approach to (among other things) products, intellectual property, bandwidth and scientific knowledge; and
- *Acting globally*, which involves embracing globalisation and ignoring physical and geographical boundaries at both the corporate and individual level.

As our world becomes more connected and global challenges like climate change and poverty loom ever larger, they argue, businesses that still practice CSR 1.0 will, like their Web 1.0 counterparts, be rapidly left behind. By contrast, companies that embrace the CSR 2.0 era will be those that collaboratively find innovative ways tackle our global challenges and be rewarded in the marketplace as a result (Visser, 2014; Tapscott & Williams, 2006).

That argument eerily echoes the sentiment of the Blockchain Web 4.0 movement and the Blockchain technology core operational principles – such as decentralisation, transparency, equality and accountability. The main advantage of the Blockchain Web 4.0 movement is it is bringing with it innovation and creativity resulting in re-perceiving the world. As Visser (2014) points out, "We know from Thomas Kuhn's work on The Structure of Scientific Revolutions that step-change only happens when we can re-perceive our world, when we can find a genuinely new paradigm, or pattern of thinking. This process of 'creative destruction' is today a well-accepted theory of societal change."

Web 4.0 technologies are an evolution of the web paradigm that can broadly be defined as ubiquitous computing (Almeida, 2017), inclusive of the 'Wikinomics' principles cited above: open, shared and global. If the first iteration of the internet (1.0) was read-only, Web, 2.0 brought social platforms like Wikipedia, Facebook, Youtube, Twitter and Instagram. Websites became interactive and user-based content was encouraged. Web 3.0 - or the Semantic Web - extends from 2010 to 2019 and intends to organize content searching based on users' history and interests. Web 3.0 is also called the intelligent Web, since its functionalities can be customized according to each user's behaviour and preferences. Currently, Web 2.0 and 3.0 coexist. The birth of a new phase, Web 4.0, is at an early stage. Web 4.0, ubiquitous or pervasive computing, refers to a new era of computing where devices are integrated: mobiles, desktops, sensors and electronic goods. A crucial element of pervasive computing is the high level of communication between connected devices which ensures a connected, synchronised infrastructure (Almeida, 2017).

As our world becomes more connected and global challenges like climate change and poverty loom ever larger, organisations that do not embrace principles of responsible business will rapidly be left behind. By contrast, companies that embrace corporate social responsibility will find the market rewards them (Visser, 2014; Tapscott & Williams, 2006). Thus, Blockchain for Social Change and the Web 4.0 community advocate a reformed financial and economic system supported by an inherently sustainable and responsible business model, that makes creating a better-distributed world an easy and rewarding process, flagging hopes that a Blockchain future directly manages services for users and does away with reliance on powerful providers and intermediaries (Al-Saqaf & Seidler, 2017)

Permissionless Blockchains (see Chapter 2 for detailed information regarding permissioned, or private, Blockchains) typically rely on open-source code that does not differentiate between users, allocate special privileges or impose conditions before verifying and executing transactions. Thus, the Blockchain offers the promise of a return to some of the earlier spirit of the internet: interactions that are peer-to-peer, governed by the community, that does away with the convenience, and downsides, of centralized commercial services (Al-Saqaf & Seidler, 2017).

This is the uniqueness and power of the emerging Blockchain environment. Adoption of Blockchain "requires a change of mindset that goes beyond a simple technological shift and requires long-term commitments to equip future generations with the knowledge and skills needed to remain relevant in what will be an increasingly automated future" (Al-Saqaf & Seidler, 2017).

Blockchain for Social Impact and Web 4.0 are about a reformed financial and economic system supported by an inherently sustainable and responsible business model, that makes creating a better distributed world an easy, natural and rewarding thing to do. Al-Saqaf & Seidler (2017) flag great hopes for the prospect of a Blockchain future that directly manages services for users and does away with reliance on powerful providers and intermediaries.

It may have other consequences. The theorising and constructs on corporate social responsibility have come from assumptions about the proper roles of governments, companies and individuals. Like social media before it, Blockchain will both create its own "bubbles" but also burst and interpenetrate the bubbles of assumptions we live in. We should not assume that the result will be what we imagine. But if it can evolve according to the thinking of all the individuals around the world who are involved, the result will be what people want and choose.

Blockchain technology is arguably the first ever innovation where the end users are both at the centre as well as the periphery of the network. In fact, they are the network (Al-Saqaf & Seidler, 2017).

Permissionless Blockchains typically rely on open-source code that does not differentiate between users based on social status, ethnicity or any other non-technical characteristics. They do not give nodes special privileges or impose conditions before verifying and executing transactions. This neutrality ensures that all are treated equally and are not abused by a central or more powerful element. Al-Saqaf & Seidler (2017) conclude that Blockchain technology offers the promise of a return to some of the earlier spirit of the internet: interactions that are peer-to-peer, by the community, with a strong do-it-yourself culture that does away with the convenience, and downsides, of centralised commercial services.

This is the uniqueness and power of the potential impact of the emerging Blockchain environment. The outlook is optimistic. As neatly stated by Al-Saqaf & Seidler (2017), adoption of Blockchain "requires a change of mindset that goes beyond a simple technological shift and requires long-term commitments to equip future generations with the knowledge and skills needed to remain relevant in what will be an increasingly automated future."

The Blockchain for social impact use cases presented in the following chapters provide a real-world insight into what can and is happening in our rapidly transforming world. The model in Figure 1 is presented to assist framing the current influences and drivers, the enabling shifts required, the possible barriers, and the New Transformed world that each use case is working within and is rapidly approaching for the rest of the world.

INTRODUCTION TO THE STRUCTURE OF THE BOOK

Katrina Donaghy, CEO of Civic Ledger[1], an Australian civic-focused Blockchain company helping governments digitalise operations and services using Blockchain technologies, said of Blockchain, at a Women in Blockchain Meetup in February 2019, that founders, developers, advocates, entrepreneurs, researchers and bureaucrats alike are impassioned by Blockchain technology for its ability to offer the hope we might begin to solve wicked problems. Wicked problems are commonly understood to be structural problems that are nearly impossible to solve.

Blockchains offer us, for the first time, the technical capability to resolve complex structural problems affordably. This book will introduce the reader both new to and experienced with Blockchains, to how start-ups, non-government organisations (NGOs), international non-government organisations (INGOs) and governments are using them to address large-scale problems, collaboratively. Proponents contend that Blockchain will touch - if not disrupt - every major industry and will even alter the way that people and societies interact. This is because Blockchains increase efficiency, reduce costs, and promote transparency which pose significant implications for sectors dedicated to driving social impact. The potential to transform systems can enable solutions that have previously been thought to be impossible. This mindset, however, has generated a hype around Blockchains that can belie

Blockchains' true functionality. While, certainly, incredible potential exists for this technology, many critics argue its fundamental limitations to scale mean it can only be considered but a fad until coupled with more mature or frontier technologies.

The authors of Blockchain for Social Change are firm believers in the ability for Blockchain technologies to radically change how we resolve previously intractable structural and commercial problems while reducing commercial operating costs and extending the reach and depth of humanitarian efforts. They are not immune to their limitations, however. Blockchain technologists often stand accused of tunnel-vision; guilty of employing a Blockchain when a database might be enough (see Chapter 2 for distinctions). In some environments this attitude might prevail - often consultants are purposely tasked with using a Blockchain. Deloitte found in a 2018 survey that 78% of business owners felt compelled to introduce Blockchains into their business models for competitive advantage, despite feeling the future of the technology was "uncertain".

Blockchains ability to radically disrupt vertical industries has seen its heavy adoption in social impact use cases. As founding Blockchains, Bitcoin and Ethereum have made Blockchains synonymous with fintech however with rising interest in smart contracts entrepreneurs have been intrigued by broader applications for such emergent technologies. Accordingly, there have been a plethora of social impact use cases across diverse sectors blooming since 2016 in the traceability, management, transaction and storage of cash transfers, identity, provenance, supply chain, health care, education and institutional functions across the world (Stanford Graduate Business School, 2018). This book has been organised as follows, to help you in finding information and use cases most relevant to your own interests

INTRODUCTION TO THE MODEL: BLOCKCHAIN FOR SOCIAL CHANGE (B4SC)

The model depicted below, referred to as *B4SC* (Blockchain for Social Change) throughout the book, represents the technology (the design, development and tools) and the chief social impact purpose/goal of the Blockchain projects through three stages from the present day. It is fundamentally constructed from 3 key sections plus noting barriers.

Table 1. Chapter roadmap

Use Case	Chapter Location
Identity Management	Chapter Six Chapter Seven
Cash Transfers and Financial Remittances	Chapter Four Chapter Six Chapter Seven
Asset Management; Supply Chain, Housing, Land & Titles, Provenance	Chapter Four Chapter Six Chapter Seven
Health Care and Service Delivery	Chapter Four Chapter Six Chapter Eight
Financial Integrity & Inclusion	Chapter Four Chapter Six Chapter Seven
Education	Chapter Four
Institutional Functions (voting, record-keeping, process efficiency)	Chapter Three

Section 1 is; Cultural Influences and Drivers; this section outlines factors contributing to and/or driving the emerging environment, grouped by the following areas of influence: Technology, Governments and Communities.

The combination of these factors has resulted in a galvanizing cry for change.

Section 2 is; Enabling Shifts; these are the factors required to transition to an environment that supports a world underscored by Blockchain and a new economy. These are grouped into: Economics, Governments, Hyper Co-Collaboration, Sovereign Identity, Communities and Conversation areas of influence.

Figure 1. Current influences and drivers

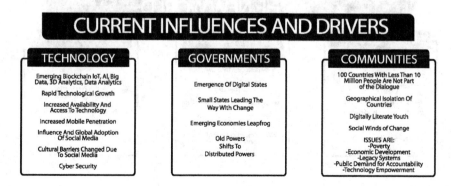

Figure 2. Enabling shifts required

Section 3 is The New World. This presents a picture of the underlying factors of the ideal environment after the transformational shift. These are grouped into: Empowerment, Global Economics and New Data Economy.

The model also includes possible barriers to change that span all the three stages.

These sections are composites of the full Blockchain for Social Change model in figure 5.

Figure 3. The New World

Figure 4. Barriers

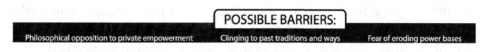

Figure 5. Blockchain for Social Change Model (B4SC)

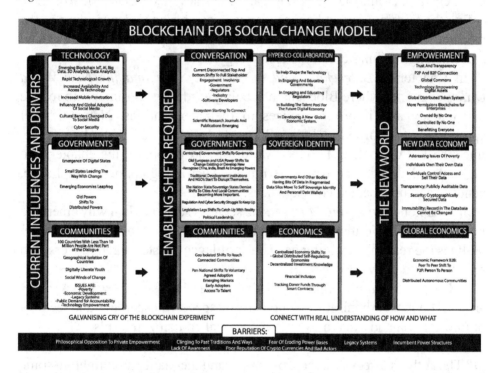

The model is referenced throughout the book to highlight whether the impact is a current influence and driver, an enabling shift that is required or already an element of the new world.

CONCLUSION

This book is a contribution to a growing body of knowledge regarding innovators that are developing applications for Blockchain, specifically around social change. The authors focus on emerging markets for two reasons: this is where the problems are greatest, and where there is the greatest potential to leapfrog. The scope of this book is incomplete, as expected with any study of change, and is not able to answer the many questions being raised. From the authors' combined experience in Blockchains they have pre-emptively addressed as many as they think they can but for reasons of scope and speed of technological development, inevitably there will be much excluded.

The book has been divided into the following chapters;

In Chapter 2, *Blockchain Explained*, the authors summarize the history of Blockchain; explain the technology and the relevance of cryptocurrencies; define the terminology and concepts necessary for an understanding of the mechanisms of Blockchain; and outline the consequences both beneficial and challenging, inherent in the technology.

In Chapter 3, *Blockchain and the Digital State and the New World Order,* examines where Blockchain is being used by governments to reduce inefficiency and improve services to their populations. National level applications are profiled, including Bermuda, Liechtenstein, Gibraltar, Kenya, Iraq, the USA and UK, Finland, Moldova and Estonia. This chapter also highlights challenges faced by governments, such as regulations, compliance, benefits and unexpected consequences.

In Chapter 4, *Emerging Markets*, the scene is set to explain why emerging markets will evolve more quickly than developed economies. This chapter outlines the reasons including need, lack of legacy systems and movers, and profiles some early adopters.

In Chapter 5; *Transforming Cities,* the authors discussion how Blockchains are used for mass urbanisation to increase the speed, transparency and security of information and systems, on both personal and citizen levels.

In Chapter 6; *Can Blockchain Really Help the Poor? If so, who is trying to?* The authors direct the focus to poverty and inequality, highlighting some use cases that have the potential to impact on the lives of the disadvantaged by improving economic opportunity and access to services.

In Chapter 7, *Humanitarian Settings,* the authors reflect on the 70 million globally displaced people. Humanitarian settings have the most rapid adoption of Blockchains as aid agencies must innovate to manage their growing portfolios. This chapter includes discourse regarding Blockchain-enabled remittances, digital identity and digital workforce applications.

In Chapter 8, *Health Care,* the ways in which innovators are iterating the use of Blockchain for the health sector are examined, using pilot projects by the UN, WHO and World Food Programme. Special attention is awarded to the use of frontier technologies in sharing and managing health records, undertaking medical research and health care service delivery.

In Chapter 9, *Donors,* the authors examine engagement with Blockchain technology and the financing of public goods and the solving of global problems.

Finally, in Chapter 10, *The Emerging Future,* the authors aggregate conclusions from the text and lay out the agenda for further research and development. Key challenges are outlined, including how technology might be evaluated and how governments and the development community might be brought to disruption and to *lean in* to fully realize the undoubted potential of Blockchain.

The Blockchain for Social Change use cases presented in the following chapters provide a real-world insight into what is and what can happen in our rapidly transforming world. The authors hope you enjoy your journey through this fascinating technology and its inspiring change objective. Chapter Two that follows introduces readers to the fundamental aspects of Blockchain technology, necessary for understanding its vital contribution to the New World order.

REFERENCES

Al-Saqaf, W., & Seidler, N. (2017). Blockchain technology for social impact: Opportunities and challenges ahead. *Journal of Cyber Policy, 2*(3), 338–354. doi:10.1080/23738871.2017.1400084

Almeida, F. (2017). Concept and dimensions of Web 4.0. *International Journal of Computers and Technology, 16*(7), 7040–7044. doi:10.24297/ijct.v16i7.6446

Altman, B. (1998). Transformed corporate community relations: A management tool for achieving Corporate citizenship. *Business and Society Review, 102-103*(1), 43–51. doi:10.1111/0045-3609.00024

Bernhardt, S. (2014). *Women in IT in the new social era: A critical evidence-based review of gender inequality and the potential for change.* Hershey, PA: IGI Global. doi:10.4018/978-1-4666-5860-8

Bernhardt, S., Braun, P., & Thomason, J. (2018). *Gender inequality and the potential for change in technology fields.* Hershey, PA: IGI Global.

Carnegie, A. (1901). *The gospel of wealth.* London, UK: Nineteenth Century Company.

Carroll, A. B. (1991). The pyramid of corporate social responsibility: Toward moral management of organizational stakeholders. *Business Horizons, 34*(4), 39–48. doi:10.1016/0007-6813(91)90005-G

Citeman. (2009). *Andrew Carnegie and wealth.* Author.

Crane, A., Matten, D., & Moon, J. (2008a). *Corporations and citizenship.* Cambridge, UK: Cambridge University Press. doi:10.1017/CBO9780511488542

Crane, A., Matten, D., & Moon, J. (2008b). The emergence of corporate citizenship: Historical development and alternative perspectives. In A. Scherer & G. Palazzo (Eds.), *Handbook of research on global corporate citizenship* (pp. 25–49). Cheltenham, UK: Edward Elgar. doi:10.4337/9781848442924.00008

Crane, A., McWilliams, A., Matten, D., Moon, J., & Siegel, A. (2008). The corporate social responsibility agenda. In *The Oxford handbook of CSR* (pp. 3–15). Oxford, UK: Oxford University Press.

D'Orazio, E. (2015). *Corporate social responsibility and the politicization of the corporation: Democracy, citizenship, human rights, and global justice.* Academic Press.

Dahl, R. (1985). *A Preface to Economic Democracy.* Berkeley, CA: University of California Press.

De George, R. T. (2010). *Business ethics.* Prentice Hall.

Dunham, L., Freeman, R. E., & Liedtka, J. (2001). *The soft underbelly of stakeholder theory: The role of community* (Working Paper No. 01-22). Retrieved from SSRN website: https://ssrn.com/abstract=284973

Elkington, J. (2004). *Enter the triple bottom line. The triple bottom line: Does it all add up?* Retrieved from chrome-extension: http://www.johnelkington.com/archive/TBL-elkington-chapter.pdf

Freeman, R. E., & Liedtka, J. (1991). Corporate social responsibility: A critical approach. *Business Horizons, 34*(4), 92–98. doi:10.1016/0007-6813(91)90012-K

Gossett, W. T. (1957). *Corporate citizenship.* Lexington, VA: Washington and Lee University Press.

Hollender, J., & Breen, B. (2010). *The responsibility revolution: How the next generation of businesses will win.* Jossey-Bass.

Hsieh, N. (2014). Can for-profit corporations be good citizens? Perspectives from four business leaders. In G. Urban (Ed.), *Corporations and citizenship* (pp. 289–300). Philadelphia, PA: University of Pennsylvania Press.

Scherer, A. G., & Palazzo, G. (2007). Towards a political conception of corporate responsibility: Business and society from a Habermasian perspective. *Academy of Management Review, 32*(4), 1096–1120. doi:10.5465/amr.2007.26585837

Scherer, A. G., & Palazzo, G. (2008). *Handbook of research on global corporate citizenship*. Cheltenham, UK: Edward Elgar. doi:10.4337/9781848442924

Tapscott, D., & Williams, A. D. (2006). *Wikinomics: How mass collaboration changes everything*. New York, USA: Penguin Group.

Visser, W. (2012). *The future of CSR: Towards transformative CSR, or CSR 2.0*. SSRN Electronic Journal; doi:10.2139srn.2208101

Waddell, S. (2000). New institutions for the practice of corporate citizenship: Historical, intersectoral, and developmental perspectives. *Business and Society Review, 105*(1), 107–126. doi:10.1111/0045-3609.00067

Windsor, D. (2001). Corporate citizenship: evolution and interpretation. In J. Andriof & M. McIntosh (Eds.), *Perspectives on Corporate Citizenship* (pp. 39–52). Sheffield, UK: Greenleaf. doi:10.9774/GLEAF.978-1-909493-19-3_4

Wood, D. J., & Logsdon, J. M. (2001). Theorising business citizenship. In J. Andriof & M. McIntosh (Eds.), *Perspectives on Corporate Citizenship* (pp. 83–103). Sheffield, UK: Greenleaf. doi:10.9774/GLEAF.978-1-909493-19-3_7

KEY TERMS AND DEFINITIONS

CSR: Corporate social responsibility. A type of private business self-regulation seeking to do social good outside of and in addition to direct business activities.

IoT: The internet of things. The network of physical devices including vehicles, home appliances, and other items embedded with electronics, software, sensors, actuators, and connectivity which enables these things to connect, collect, and exchange data over the internet.

MNC: Multi-national corporation. A corporation that owns or controls production of goods or services in at least one country in addition to its home country.

Node: A device, such as a computer, that forms an intersection in a computer network.

Permissionless: A public, decentralised Blockchain where all participants can read, write, and participate in the Blockchain. Examples include Ethereum and Bitcoin.

Private Blockchain: A permissioned Blockchain with restrictions on network participation.

SDG: Sustainable Development Goals. A collection of 17 global goals set by the United Nations General Assembly in 2015.

UN: The United Nations. An international organization formed in 1945 to increase political and economic cooperation among its member countries.

ENDNOTE

[1]   https://www.civicledger.com/

Chapter 2
Blockchain Introduced

ABSTRACT

This chapter provides an introductory explanation of Blockchain technology and how it works, concentrating on its potential for social impact. It describes the history of the development of Blockchain, which is a form of distributed ledger technology.

INTRODUCTION

At its essence a Blockchain is a decentralised database. It is a secure chronological record of transactions made on a ledger distributed across multiple computers (called nodes) on a network. The number of nodes on the network may vary; a private Blockchain may have as few as three nodes and a public Blockchain, such as Bitcoin, may have millions. We will go on to explain the function of nodes and the distinctions between private and public Blockchains.

Blockchains are characterised by their distinguishing features of;

1. Transparency; a publicly auditable database
2. Security; cryptographically secured data
3. Immutability; the record of the transaction in the database cannot be changed
4. A decentralised network; thousands of computers validating each record of the ledger
5. Timestamped transactions; confirming the source of truth

DOI: 10.4018/978-1-5225-9578-6.ch002

The following example demonstrates how a transaction might find its way onto the ledger:

You want to send money to your Mother in the Philippines. You check your e-wallet, which has cryptocurrencies like bitcoin in it. Your Mother has given you her wallet ID. You transfer several bitcoins of parts of a bitcoin - to her wallet ID. This process is almost exactly the same as you transferring money to her bank account using internet banking, except this transaction is recorded on the public Blockchain. When you clicked 'Send' on your transaction your bitcoin was sent to the Bitcoin network as a package of data - a block. This block (your transaction) was added to all of the other blocks of data on the Bitcoin network, and as these are organised chronologically, these transactions form a chain known as the block chain.

Blockchain is known as a type of a distributed ledger technology. The distributed ledger is like a spreadsheet or a database, spread across nodes (computing devices) on a peer-to-peer network. Each node is responsible for replicating and saving an identical copy of the ledger every ten minutes. There is no central authority or administrator of the ledger, each node is autonomous. When a ledger update happens with each transaction, each node constructs the new transaction, and then the nodes vote by a consensus algorithm on which copy is correct. Once a consensus has been determined, all the other nodes update themselves with the new, correct copy of the ledger. On a public Blockchain the ledger is public; anyone can view it at any time, and it is encrypted using distinct hash functions. It is therefore said that the Blockchain is unhackable, for alterations to the ledger will easily be detected.

Every ten minutes or so (Tapscott & Tapscott, 2016) all the transactions on the nodes are verified, cleared and stored in a block that links to the previous block in the chain. This structure is time-stamped, preventing anyone from altering the ledger. If you wanted to steal a bitcoin, for example, one would have to rewrite the coin's entire history on the Blockchain in plain view of every person manning a node - practically impossible.

Once private institutions like banks realised that they could use the core idea of Blockchain as a distributed ledger technology (DLT) they began to create permissioned Blockchains (a private Blockchain with far fewer nodes on the network than a public Blockchain) to solve efficiency, security and fraud problems. There are over 200 banks in the world using Blockchains in their business practices at the moment. Some of which include (Mappo, 2018):

- Bank of America
- Bank of America Merrill Lynch

- Bank of England
- Barclays Investment Bank
- Citi Bank
- Commonwealth Bank of Australia
- Credit Suisse
- Deloitte
- Federal Bank of India
- Federal Reserve
- JP Morgan
- Macquarie Group
- Morgan Stanley
- National Australia Bank
- Royal Bank of Canada
- Royal Bank of Scotland

The ledger can record almost anything: birth, death and marriage certificates, deeds and titles to assets, accounts, certificates, insurance documentation and claims made, votes, music, art, the provenance of food, coffee or wine - essentially, anything that can be expressed in computer code. As you will see in Chapter 7, this functionality potentially addresses administrative and logistical hurdles in people migration, cross-border payments or financial inclusion.

BLOCKCHAIN TECHNOLOGY STACK

The Blockchain operates on a protocol-heavy technology stack that includes the following components:

The Internet or the Infrastructure Layer; The Internet is the most foundational technology layer. It relies on the Internet Protocol Suite (TCP/IP) that defines how data should be packeted, addressed, transmitted, routed and received.

The Network and Protocol Layer; In a nutshell, the protocol layer includes the consensus algorithms, participation requirements, Virtual Machines and many more.

The Services Layer; This layer covers all the important tools to create and run the application or the dApps layer. It includes data feeds, Off-chain computing, Governance (DAO's), State channels, and side chains.

The Application Layer; includes the dApp browser, Application hosting, dApps, business logic and User interfaces.

Detailed explanation of the key elements of this stack relating to cryptography, encryption and consensus algorithms now follow.

CRYPTOGRAPHY AND ENCRYPTION

With privacy a central tenet of Blockchains, encryption has become a major focus, but what are cryptography and encryption?

In Blockchain, cryptography is used to secure the identity of the transacting parties and the integrity of the transaction. The type of cryptography Blockchains use is typically public-private key cryptography but some Blockchains use alternative cryptographic algorithms. For example, ZCash uses zero-knowledge proofs and Monero uses Ring Signatures. The Bitcoin Blockchain uses public key cryptography for digital signatures and hashing functions, using elliptic curve cryptography.

Figure 1. Blockchain Technology Stack

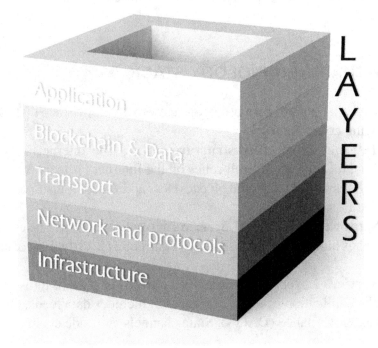

Public-Private Key

Public-private key cryptography, also known as asymmetric cryptography, allows information to be transferred through a public key that can be shared with anyone. A private key, a randomly generated 256-bit integer, is used for the encryption of transactions, while the public key is used for the decryption. The public key is derived from the private key and acts as a locator, like a bank account number. The private key always has to be kept private because it acts as your password to your bank account. The public key is meant to be shared with third parties and ensures that you are the owner of an address that can receive funds.

There is a mathematical relationship between both keys, determined by one-way cryptographic algorithms.

Digital signatures are used to verify who you say you are and are a mathematical function attached to a digital wallet. By attaching a digital signature to a transaction, no one can dispute that that transaction came from the wallet it purports to have come from, and that wallet can't be impersonated by another wallet.

CONSENSUS ALGORITHMS

There are several key algorithms that Blockchains use to ensure the integrity of the distributed ledger. That is, ensure the process by which each node knows they are all holding the same copy of the ledger and different cryptocurrencies use different consensus mechanisms which themselves differ from one another. The Byzantine Generals' Problem is a thought experiment that is intended to illustrate the difficulty of reaching consensus in a distributed system. There is a risk that a distributed system will contain bad actors, that can cause the ecosystem to fall apart. These bad actors may fail to pass on data, or even send inaccurate data to other participants in the computing ecosystem.

Byzantine failures are characterised as the arbitrary ways in which components of a system can fail, which prevents various components of a system from reaching consensus. Byzantine Fault Tolerance is the characteristic of a system - e.g. a distributed system - that is able to tolerate the class of failures belonging to the Byzantine Generals' Problem, with these class of failures being known as Byzantine failures. For example, the incorrect processing of requests, or producing incorrect or inconsistent outputs can be classified as being Byzantine failures. The aim of a Byzantine fault tolerant system is to be able to defend against Byzantine failures.

In the Byzantine General's problem, a group of generals, each commanding a portion of the Byzantine army, encircle a city. These generals must now develop a plan to either attack or to retreat from the city. Some generals may want to attack, whilst others may want to retreat, what is necessary is that every general reaches a collective decision. If a unified decision is not reached, and some generals decide to attack, whilst others choose to retreat, then the uncoordinated attack or retreat will fail. The generals are also physically separated from each other and must communicate their decision to either attack or retreat via messengers. There is a possibility that these messengers may fail to deliver votes, or worse, may forge votes, which would result in an uncoordinated decision taking place. The problem is further complicated by traitorous generals who may send mixed messages about their preferences, leading some generals to believe that they will attack, and others to believe that they will retreat.

The Byzantine Generals' Problem is particularly challenging to a public Blockchain, because there is no central authority to remedy any wrongs in the event of a Byzantine failure. If some members within the community send inaccurate information to others about transactions, then the reliability of the whole environment will break down. Proof-of-work (PoW), the consensus algorithm used by Bitcoin and Ethereum, provides a solution to the Byzantine Generals' Problem, by overcoming Byzantine failures to allow public Blockchains to reach a clear and global view of the system (Asolo, 2018).

Proof of Work (PoW)

The of this proof-of-work is adjusted to limit the rate at which new blocks can be generated by the network to one every 10 minutes.

PoW is criticised for being gratuitously energy intensive; there are lots of reports regarding the annual global mining costs of bitcoin stretching to the equivalent of small countries such as Ecuador (Blockgeeks, 2019). However, the computing power required to produce the PoW provides a protection from DoS attacks – the costs are too high to make a DoS attack worthwhile. A 51 percent, or majority, attack, is a case when a user or a group of users control the majority of mining power which enables them to control most events in the network, monopolise generating new blocks and even reverse transactions

(Tar, 2018). While this might not be that likely, with the concentrating of mining into pools it is possible, which is why Ethereum are considering switching to the proof-of-stake mechanism.

Proof of Stake (PoS)

Where proof-of-work-based cryptocurrencies such as bitcoin use mining - the solving of computationally intensive puzzles to validate transactions and create new blocks - in PoS-based cryptocurrencies the creator of the next block is chosen via various combinations of random selection and wealth or age (*i.e.,* the stake).

What's a stake? In crypto terms, the stake is the cryptocurrency a user owns and pledges in order to partake in validation. Proof-of-Stake algorithms achieve consensus by requiring users to stake an amount of their tokens so as to have a chance of being selected to validate blocks of transactions, and get rewarded for doing so (Thake, 2018).

Since proof of stake must have a way of defining the next valid block in any Blockchain, selection by account balance would result in centralisation, whereby the single richest member would have a permanent advantage. Instead, several different methods of selection have been devised; randomised block selection, coin age-based selection and delegated PoS.

PoS shares many similarities with PoW, but also differs in fundamental ways. While, as with any Blockchain based consensus algorithm, the goal is still to achieve distributed consensus—to create a secure system whereby users are incentivised to validate other peoples' transactions while maintaining complete integrity. In PoS the miner of a new block is called a *forger* and chosen in a semi-random, two-part process. The first element to be considered in this selection process is a user's stake. How much of the currency in question is the user staking? Every validator must own a stake in the network. The more a user stakes, the better their chance of being selected since they'd have more skin in the game—acting maliciously would see them set back by a greater amount than someone who stakes less (Thake, 2018).

The Casper protocol is the PoS protocol that Ethereum has chosen. It works by validators staking a portion of their Ether. They then start validating the blocks. Meaning, when they discover a block which they think can be added to the chain, they will validate it by placing a bet on it. If the block gets appended, the validators get a reward proportionate to their bets. However, if a validator acts in a malicious manner and tries to do a "nothing at stake" (see below), they will immediately be reprimanded, and all of their stake is potentially compromised (Blockgeeks, 2019).

Why is Casper necessary? There are several advantages of implementing proof-of-stake;

- Helps achieve decentralisation better than as demonstrated by these Bitcoin and Ethereum mining pool distribution graphs
- Energy efficiency.
- Economic security.
- Better scaling potential
- Ultimately transitioning to POS.
- The 'Nothing at Stake' Problem

Critics of Proof of Stake point out the economic challenge known as the Nothing at Stake problem. It's a dilemma that allegedly prevents PoS from becoming a viable distributed consensus mechanism because in the event of a fork (the Blockchain splitting in two), block generators have nothing to lose by supporting different Blockchains, essentially preventing the conflict from ever resolving.

Delegated Proof of Stake (DPoS)

DPoS is the next step in the evolution of consensus mechanisms. It builds upon Proof of Stake to drastically increase speed and scalability. Lisk, EOS, Steem, BitShares and Ark (see Platforms) have adopted the Delegated Proof of Stake (DPoS) consensus mechanism to improve scalability without compromising the decentralised incentive structure.

In Proof of Stake a user can put their coins at stake, thereby earning the right to validate transactions, forge blocks, and earn associated rewards. DPoS, reaches consensus by voting on 'witnesses', users they trust to validate transactions. (Ray, 2018).

DISTRIBUTED LEDGERS

As we have already introduced, a Blockchain is an example of a distributed ledger but with additional functionality. All Blockchains are distributed ledgers, but not all distributed ledgers are Blockchains. The difference comes down to governance and data structure.

Figure 2. Blockchain Technology Stack Detail

Both Blockchains and distributed ledgers share a copy of the database across the nodes on the network using a consensus algorithm, however the Blockchain is the only form of distributed ledger technology (DLT) that employs a chain of blocks to reach consensus on the ledger. The blocks in the chain are linked together by cryptographic hashing and become append only. As blocks become sequentially added to the chain data cannot be modified or deleted.

In distributed ledgers, if it is desired, governance can be permissioned to a given number of identified nodes with authority to validate transactions; other nodes may be awarded read permission conferred by the validator nodes. Ultimately, how the network treats the database is determined by the network administrator. Whereas Blockchains aspire to maximal decentralisation to ensure censorship resistance and prevent the centralising of power.

Many Blockchain advocates believe that the inherent principles of a decentralised system lend themselves to greater efficiency and user satisfaction. In fact, the US Department of Defence's original plans for the internet were for it to be decentralised so that if one part of the system fails the rest can still function (this is known as being fault tolerant).

In the early days of trading, people transacted directly without middlemen. Bakers bought wheat from farmers; cobblers bought leather from herders. With the rise of industrialisation and the decline of agrarian societies, the distance between communities grew further apart. Producers and manufacturers began to transact through middlemen, using centralised market places where producers and consumers were aggregated for efficiency. By doing so, producers could access more consumers, and consumers could access more producers. Thus, part of the argument in favour of centralised institutions and processes has been efficiency (Magnr, 2018).

Consider this example; it's Saturday - your errand day - you need to do your food shopping. As you begin to plan your meals for the week and where to shop, there are some criteria that might pop into your head: You probably want to buy local, buy organic, get the best price for your products, the freshest foods, with the lowest carbon footprint and ensure your meat is grass-fed. But, it's Saturday. You only have two hours at your disposal before you must be at your parents for lunch. So, you compromise. Instead of going to four different retailers that specialise in organic, grass-fed, local produce, you go to one: an organic supermarket. This is a highly simplified example of centralisation.

We use banks for the same reasons: efficiency, ease and for a source of passive income in terms of interest paid on credit in the account. However, the proliferation of Blockchains is often connected to the Global Financial Crisis, for, when the first 50 bitcoins (the so-called Genesis block) were mined in January of 2009, he (or she, or they) included this line of text along with the data: "The Times 03/Jan/2009 Chancellor on brink of second bailout for banks" (Gonzalez, 2018). Thus, when Nakamoto refers to the *"inherent weaknesses of the trust based model"* (Nakamoto, 2008, p.1) there is an implied mistrust of financial institutions and how their centralised processes are inherently inefficient, *The cost of mediation increases transaction costs, limiting the minimum practical transaction size and cutting off the possibility for small casual transactions.* (Nakamoto, 2008, p.1).

THE ISSUE OF TRUST

The process of securing the integrity of the ledger on the Blockchain is said to engender trust. What this means is that the process of achieving consensus across the millions of nodes ensures that someone reviewing the transactions on the ledger can *trust* that the record is accurate. Blockchains do not create or increase trust but ensure that the transaction record is *trustworthy* (a seemingly small, but significant difference). Nick Szabo (1999) recognised this in his article regarding *The God Protocols:*

Imagine the ideal protocol. It would have the most trustworthy third party imaginable – a diety who is on everybody's side. All the parties would send their inputs to God. God would reliably determine the results and return the outputs. God being the ultimate in confessional discretion, no party would learn anything more about the other parties' inputs than they could learn from their own inputs and the output. (Szabo, 1999)

The problem with trust occurred as early as 1981 when inventors were trying to solve the problems of privacy, security and inclusion using cryptography on the internet. At the time, making payments on the internet was insecure because of the level of data that users had to divulge and third parties had been plagued by security weaknesses. Then, in 1993, David Chaum created eCash - a "technically perfect product which made it possible to pay over the internet" (Tapscott and Tapscott, 2016, p.4). Fast upon Chaum's work came Szabo (1999) who bemoaned that, instead of a trustworthy, discreet *God, ...we deal with humans rather than deities. Yet, too often we are forced to treat people in a nearly theological manner, because our infrastructure lacks the security needed to protect ourselves. (Szabo, 1999).*
What Blockchains do is minimise the amount of trust required from any single actor in the system by distributing trust among different actors who are incentivised to cooperate with the rules defined by the protocol. In other words, instead of needing to trust one person, one computer or one institution (your bank), one trusts in a whole system that is economically rewarded for ensuring the system is *trustworthy.*

DIFFERENT TYPES OF BLOCKCHAINS

There are many types of Blockchains, which can be categorised into public, private and federated/consortium with slightly different features.

Public Blockchains

A Blockchain network is a distributed, decentralised, peer-to-peer network. There is almost certainly no central authority that monitors, approves or processes transactions, as financial institutions do. Thus, Blockchains are said to *disintermediate* institutions. The two most well-known public Blockchains are Bitcoin and Ethereum.

Bitcoin

Bitcoin, the first Blockchain, is an open source protocol, meaning that its code is freely available for download and modification.

When introducing Blockchains it is often useful to start with Bitcoin[1] (bitcoin.org) for this coin can often be more well-known than Blockchains, collectively. When Bitcoin has a capital 'B", this denotes the protocol and payment network - the Bitcoin ecosystem. Bitcoin with a lower-case 'B' (i.e., bitcoin) usually refers to the digital currency that is part of the Bitcoin network. For example, "I just spent some bitcoin on a coffee at the airport".

While Blockchains have been in use in countries like Estonia since 2007, they weren't more widely known until Satoshi Nakamoto's Bitcoin white paper was released in 2008. What Nakamoto introduced us to in the whitepaper is the notion that Bitcoin, as a distributed ledger technology, can allow *any two willing parties to transact directly with each other without the need for a trusted third party'*. (Nakamoto, 2008, p.1). The 'trusted third party' element of this sentence is crucial to the understanding of Bitcoin and of Blockchains.

Nakamoto created the Bitcoin network as a resolution to the double-spending problem financial institutions encounter. Digital currencies, like bitcoin, are basically a digital file saved to a computer, but with an important difference: being able to *ensure that files cannot be duplicated*, so that the money isn't repeatedly copied. If digital money can be copied, it becomes as worthless as counterfeit money. This is the double-spend problem, which the Bitcoin network prevents by verifying each transaction on the Bitcoin Blockchain using a Proof-of-Work (PoW) algorithm.

The Bitcoin Blockchain - an open and immutable ledger - ensures that all of the transactions are finalised and confirmed by Bitcoin miners (the process of mining is explained further in the chapter) which makes each bitcoin unique and its subsequent transactions legitimate. If one tried to duplicate a transaction, the original block's deterministic functions would change, showing the network that it is counterfeit and it would not to be accepted. Once a transaction is confirmed, it's nearly impossible to double-spend it. The more confirmations that a transaction has, the harder it is to double-spend the bitcoins. Thus, by resolving the double-spend problem, digital currency has now become viable (Bitcoin.com, 2017; Nakamoto, 2008).

Ethereum

Ethereum[2] (www.ethereum.org) – at the time of writing, the second largest cryptocurrency by market cap (Marinoff, 2019) - created their own Blockchain in 2015 with very different properties than Bitcoin. By decoupling the smart contract layer from the core Blockchain protocol, Vitalik Buterin, the founder of Ethereum, offered a radical new way to create online markets and programmable transactions known as Smart Contracts in his 2013 white paper (further details on smart contracts are found throughout this chapter).

With the Ethereum Blockchain, tokens have been moved up the technology stack (see the section on the Blockchain technology stack) and can be issued as DAO or distributed application (dApp) tokens. dApps provide the framework to support more complex services on Ethereum in the form of smart contracts. Smart contract tokens are critical to the continued development of Blockchain based applications (Devan, 2018).

Other types of public Blockchains include:

Monero[3]

Dash[4]

Litecoin[5]

Blockchain protocols are based on the Proof of Work (PoW) consensus algorithm (see Algorithms) which is open source. This means that anyone can participate in a public Blockchain network without permission. Anyone can download the code and start running a public node (a computer) on their local device, validating transactions in the network and participating in the consensus process – the process for determining what blocks get added to the chain and what the current state of the ledger is. Anyone in the world can send transactions through the public Blockchain network and expect to see them included in the Blockchain if they are valid. Anyone can read transactions on the public block explorer (blockexplorer.com - an open source web tool that allows you to view information about blocks, addresses, and transactions on the Blockchain). All transactions on the network are transparent, but anonymous/pseudonymous (Blockchain Hub, 2018).

Private/Permissioned Blockchains

A private Blockchain is an invitation-only network governed by a single entity. Entrants to the network require permission to read, write or audit the Blockchain. There can be different levels of access and information can be encrypted to protect commercial confidentiality. Private Blockchains allow organisations to employ distributed ledger technology without making data public. Popular private Blockchains include: Hyperledger, AWS, IBM and Multichain.

Write permissions on private Blockchains are usually kept centralised to one organisation. Read permissions may be public or restricted to an arbitrary extent, determined by the controlling organisation. Private Blockchains may be used for database management and auditing which are internal to a single company, and so public readability, indeed, in many cases may not be necessary at all. In other cases, public auditability is desired. Private Blockchains are a way of taking advantage of Blockchain technology by setting up groups and participants that can verify transactions internally, however, in such centralisation there is an increased risk of security breaches; as opposed to a public Blockchain which is secured by game theoretic incentive mechanisms and a far greater number of nodes on the network. That said, however, private Blockchains have their uses. By virtue of there being fewer nodes on the network private Blockchains can permit faster transaction throughput and comply with national data privacy regulations (see Chapters 4, 5, 6 and 8 for use cases). When compared to a distributed ledger, private Blockchains have certain security advantages, as with security disadvantages (Blockchain Hub, 2018).

Federated or Consortium Blockchains

Federated Blockchains operate under the leadership of a group, such as R3[6] (r3.com, a consortium of more than 200 firms in research and development of distributed ledger use in the financial system). As opposed to public

Blockchains, they don't allow any person with access to the Internet to participate in the process of verifying transactions. Federated Blockchains have fewer nodes on the network and can, therefore, be faster at processing transactions (which translates into higher scalability). Consortium Blockchains are mostly used in the banking sector. The consensus process is controlled by a pre-selected set of nodes; for example, one might imagine a consortium of 15 financial institutions, each of which operates a node and of which 10 must sign every block in order for the block to be valid. The right to read the Blockchain may be public, or restricted to the participants (Blockchain Hub, 2018).

CRYPTOCURRENCIES AND TOKENS

"What is bitcoin? Can I buy, like, pizza with it?" Asked by sports blogger Dave Portnoy (@stoolpresidente) in his inaugural video as a bitcoin investor. The comment cuts to the core of a truism about the network: while it's been billed as a "digital currency," it's actually not all that useful for payments. While you are increasingly more likely to stumble into a shop that accepts it, you are unlikely to want to spend it given price volatilities. Thus, cryptocurrencies are often said to be a *store of value.*

It is less the case now - after the great bitcoin candlesticks of 2018 - but it certainly used to be that when early adopters of cryptocurrency spoke about their fascination with the digital money in public, listeners would rebut with the bankruptcy of the Mt Gox[7] exchange; or the conviction of Ross William Ulbrecht, founder of the darknet market seized by the FBI for trafficking illegal drugs, child pornography and weapons, who was using the bitcoin Blockchain for payments. Now, countries like Estonia go back and forth on whether they should introduce their own national cryptocurrency, the "estcoin" (Adams, 2018; Alexandre, 2018).

A cryptocurrency is a medium of exchange like *normal* currencies (fiat) like USD and AUD but designed for exchanging digital information by a process made possible by certain principles of cryptography which secure the transactions and control the creation of new coins. The first cryptocurrency to be created was Bitcoin back in 2009. Today there are hundreds of other cryptocurrencies, often referred to as Altcoins.

Cryptocurrencies are legal in most countries but with rising popularity come controls by regulators (see Regulation).

SMART CONTRACTS

Smart contracts are a popular a feature of the Ethereum Blockchain in the Solidity language but can be encoded onto any Blockchain. RootStock (RSK) is a smart contract platform connected to the Bitcoin Blockchain through sidechain technology, however, RSK is also compatible with smart contracts created for Ethereum.

Smart contracts are designed to automate contractual clauses which can be partially or fully enforced depending on they are coded. Smart contracts are traceable and irreversible; the aim is to provide superior security to contract law and reduce the costs of contracting.

Some examples of how smart contracts are used include;

Slock.It[8] automates sharing, payments and rentals. Their most recent work with Share & Charge[9] (shareandcharge.com) is an example of how Slock.It works: Share & Charge uses their smart contract technology to automate the process of paying to rent electric vehicle charging stations.

Buying and selling real estate is a commonly discussed use-case for smart contracts and Propy[10] (propy.com) is one of the first companies to make it happen. They had in September of 2017, when someone purchased a $60,000 apartment in Ukraine (PolySwarm, 2018).

The international real estate marketplace allows owners and brokers to list properties, where buyers can also search and negotiate the sale. Both parties participate in the smart contract together and specific steps are taken throughout the process to ensure fair and legal play. For example, an interested buyer can reserve a property by paying $5K to the escrow company currently holding it—thanks to terms of the smart contract, the buyer will get that money back if the seller refuses to sell the property.

Invoice financing is a way for business owners to get their money from unpaid invoices. Invoice buyers pay up front to take over the invoice for the business and then gets paid the original amount when the debtor pays the invoice. Populous[11] (populous.world) makes it easy for anyone to buy and sell outstanding invoices on the Blockchain using smart contracts.

SMART CONTRACTS AND PLATFORMS

Lisk; Like Ethereum, Lisk[12] (lisk.io) is a platform that allows developers to build, publish, distribute, and monetize their JavaScript-based dApps within a custom-built cryptocurrency-powered system using custom Blockchains, cloud storage, smart contracts, and computing nodes. Lisk has so far produced a long list of products, and what separates it from others is the use of Blockchain apps within their own sidechains.

Hyperledger Fabric; Hyperledger Fabric is a Blockchain framework implementation, intended as a foundation for developing applications or solutions with a modular architecture. Hyperledger Fabric allows components, such as consensus and membership services, to be plug-and-play, leveraging container technology to host smart contracts called "chaincode" that comprise the application logic of the system.

Stellar (XLM); Stellar[13] has been around for a while. Their infrastructure opens a world of financial possibilities for the unbanked, such as opening financial accounts, starting micro-savings, applying for loans, etc. while at the same time allowing fast, reliable, and cost-efficient multi-currency transactions. The network also has a native asset, Lumens (XLM).

EOS (EOS); EOS is dubbed the "Ethereum killer" due to its similarities and competitive advantages over Ethereum, providing operating-system-like set of services and functions that can be used by dApps. It currently boasts over 200 decentralised apps developed with EOS.

Ethereum (ETH); the Ethereum Blockchain not only validates a set of accounts and balances on the ledger but of so-called states. This means that Ethereum can not only process transactions but complex smart contracts. This flexibility makes Ethereum the perfect instrument for Blockchain application. But it comes at a cost. After the hack of the DAO (see DAOS and *The* DAO) – an Ethereum based smart contract – the developers decided to do a hard fork without consensus, which resulted in the emerge of . In addition, there are several clones of Ethereum, and like DigixDAO and Augur. This makes Ethereum more a family of cryptocurrencies than a single currency.

Ethereum support many users right now, it has seen a slew of capacity issues, including that transaction times and interrupt new ICO launches. Sharding[14], (see the section on other chains), [15] (truebit.io and Plasma[16] (plasma.io) have all emerged as ways to ensure future decentralised applications run easily and with the potential change to proof-of-stake in the making.

Ethereum Classic (ETC); After the 2016 hard fork of the Ethereum Blockchain in response to the hack of The DAO, Ethereum Classic[17]'s (ethereumclassic.org) ETC token was created. ETC has attracted a sizeable community thanks to development projects such as the Emerald Software Developer Kit and ETC's implementation of smart contracts, a feature that the currency's developers are pushing in the Internet of Things sector. Ethereum

Classic's largest organisation of developers have been updating a general roadmap that includes ambitious plans for the future, such as introducing scalability through sidechains, IoT and Machine-to-Machine protocol.

Stratis (STRAT); Stratis is a Blockchain-as-a-service platform that allows businesses to build and deploy private chains and Blockchain-based tools securely and quickly.

Ark (ARK); Ark connects different Blockchains through "smart bridges", aimed at obtaining interoperability of the Blockchains. SmartBridges connects two or more Blockchains, allowing them to communicate and giving them the ability to trigger events on other chains.

XinFin (XDCE); first ever hybrid Blockchain platform which can simultaneously handle both public and private Blockchains. With a Blockchain dApp called TradeFinex, they aim to minimise the global infrastructure deficit through retail investor participation and to increase efficiency by workstream automation. XinFin also has a dApp called MyContract.co which delivers automated services for token crowdsale smart contracts. With all these competitive advantages, XinFin surely has a bright future in the industry and is bound to revolutionize Blockchain technology.

Neo (NEO); Dubbed as the "Ethereum of China", NEO provides a dual-layered Blockchain developed by Onchain DNA which is suitable for creating dApps and token sales. Its dual-token, smart-contract ecosystem and Delegated Byzantine Fault Tolerance (DBFT) protocol successfully deal with issues with Ethereum's scalability, making it a powerful competitor.

HOW MINING WORKS

Usually, banks oversee keeping accurate records of transactions - they ensure that money isn't created out of thin air, and that users don't cheat and spend their money more than once. Blockchains, though, introduce an entirely new way of record-keeping - one where the entire network, rather than an intermediary, verifies transactions and adds them to the public ledger. Miners come to a consensus about the transaction history of the ledger while preventing fraud (notably double spending).

For each block of transactions, miners use computers to repeatedly and very quickly guess answers to a puzzle until one of them wins (see Algorithms). More specifically, the miners will run the block's unique header metadata (including timestamp and software version) through a hash function (which will return a fixed-length, scrambled string of numbers and letters that looks random), only changing the 'nonce value'[18], which impacts the resulting hash value.

If the miner finds a hash that matches the current target, the miner will be awarded bitcoin or ether and broadcast the block across the network for each node to validate and add to their own copy of the ledger. If miner B finds the hash, miner A will stop work on the current block and repeat the process for the next block.

It's difficult for miners to cheat at this game. There's no way to fake this work and come away with the correct puzzle answer. That's why the puzzle-solving method is called 'proof-of-work'.

SCALING

What if it was possible for Blockchain-based transactions to avoid using the Blockchain at all? This is an important consideration to ensure efficiency of throughput on the Blockchain network. That's the big idea behind off-Blockchain payment channels which allow two people using any one cryptocurrency to send small payments back and forth, settling to the Blockchain (and dealing with its high fees and slow transaction times) only when necessary. This option is progressing fast with Bitcoin's Lightning network (see below) and Ethereum's Raiden network (raiden.network).[19]

The Raiden Network

Blockchains don't scale well because there needs to be global consensus on the order and outcome of all transfers; every participant needs to learn about all updates to the shared ledger and hardware and bandwidth constraints set a limit on the number of updates per second that can be shared in a decentralised network. The basic idea of the Raiden Network is to avoid the Blockchain consensus bottleneck by not involving the Blockchain for every transaction. Therefore, the Raiden Network is an *off-chain* scaling solution, enabling near-instant, low-fee and scalable payments. It's an infrastructure layer on top of the Ethereum Blockchain and works with any ERC20 compatible token. Developers interface with a simple API to build scalable decentralized applications based on the Raiden Network (Raiden Network, 2018).

The Lightning Network

Rather than updating bitcoin's underlying software, Lightning adds an extra layer to the tech stack, where transactions can be made more cheaply and quickly, but with the same security backing of the Blockchain.

Crucially, the Lighting Network[20] (lightning.engineering) protocol addresses one of the key limitations of Blockchains: it dramatically improves the scalability of Blockchain currencies like bitcoin by streamlining the number of nodes involved in each transaction to a small group of nodes that link sender and receiver. These nodes are connected via "payment channels" established on the underlying Blockchain. Payment channels leverage Blockchain smart contracts to enable virtually unlimited cheap, fast transactions (Lightning Labs, 2018).

DAOs AND THE DAO

A decentralized autonomous organisation (DAO), is an open-source, stateless organisation represented by rules maintained on a Blockchain. A well-known example, intended for venture capital funding, was *The* DAO, instantiated on the Ethereum Blockchain, which launched with $150 million in crowdfunding in June 2016 - setting the record for a token sale at the time - and was immediately hacked and drained of US$50 million in cryptocurrency. This hack was reversed in the following weeks, and the money restored, via a hard fork of the Ethereum Blockchain. This was controversial, and led to a fork in Ethereum, where the original unforked Blockchain was maintained as Ethereum Classic, thus breaking Ethereum into two separate active Blockchains, each with its own cryptocurrency.

REGULATION

As developments to Blockchain technology are moving faster than the regulators can keep up, management approaches to cryptocurrencies, or Digital Financial Assets (DFA),[21] are globally fragmented and reactive. The response to Initial Coin Offerings (ICO's) particularly, has varied across the world from an open-arms approach in creating custom regulatory sandbox licenses to the shutting down of digital exchanges and claims regarding the legitimacy of digital assets.

Regulation consists mainly of issuing guidance and clarification regarding the application of existing regulation on specific DFAs, enforcement action, establishment of regulatory frameworks tailored to some DFAs, e.g. derivative products of DFAs, among other responsibilities, however, some jurisdictions are beginning to develop tailored frameworks for ICOs. The OECD has been one of the leading voices in advocating for regulation and see the top priorities for regulators as being:

1. Addressing legal and regulatory uncertainty
2. Investor protection
3. Operational risks
4. Corporate governance and market integrity
5. AML and cyber-risk
6. Cross-border regulatory arbitrage

The OECD (2018) conclude that *Engaging closely with industry will be critical to realising the benefits of the application of DLTs, such as the Blockchain, while mitigating the risks. A coordinated global approach is likely needed to avoid fragmentation, ensure efficient global financing and scaling for legitimate businesses, while also adequately protecting investors, as DFAs have an international reach and trade across borders* (OECD, 2018).

Liaison with industry enables regulators to understand how to frame standards without limiting the development and invention of interoperability protocols, cryptography, privacy, consensus, management, or other features of Blockchain (Hyland-Wood & Khatchadourian, 2018).

INITIAL COIN/TOKEN OFFERINGS

Initial Coin (or Token) Offerings (ICO/ITOs) are a capital-raising vehicle that work by creating a cryptocurrency that is offered to the community at a discounted rate before it is released to the exchanges. This fundraising method enables start-ups to open source funding for their projects that can stretch into the millions (Thomason, 2019). ICOs raised more money in the first three months of 2018 than the whole of 2017 alone. At $6.3 billion, ICO funding in the first quarter of 2018 was 118 percent of the total for 2017 (Floyd, 2018).

ICOs are currently unregulated, however. The process involves the creation of a digital asset and a value apportioned by consensus of a network of participants rather than by a central authority or government. The absence of traditional financial arbiters in the valuing and regulation of financial assets has created headaches for regulators and criticisms from the community regarding DFA's legitimacy.

As most ICOs don't offer equity in the venture they fall outside of traditional legal frameworks for securities – unless they meet the provisions of the Howey Test[22] and the tokens or coins, actually, are unregistered securities. An ICO typically only offers a discount on the cryptocurrency before its release to the exchanges. Therefore, they do not fit most jurisdictions' definition of a security.

However, tokens that provide dividends or share the same qualities as a typical stock will result in its being classified as a security. Thus, the emerging reality is that not all cryptocurrencies are securities – the US Securities and Exchange Commission, indeed, recently ruled that ether was not a security (Hinman, 2018). Tokens are global instruments, funded using Bitcoin, Ethereum and other cryptocurrencies which are not controlled by any central authority or bank however, regular ping-ponging by regulators regarding their treatment means regulations from 1933 ought to be approached with a modern viewpoint. Chairman of the SEC, Jay Clayton, is quoted by Consensys in March 2019 as saying: "A digital asset may be offered and sold initially as a security because it meets the definition of an investment contract, but that designation may change over time if the digital asset later is offered and sold in such a way that it will no longer meet that definition" (Consensys, 2019).

Table 1 indicates some of the largest capital-raising ICOs to date (Lielacher, 2018).

Table 1. Top performing ICOs in 2018 by US$

	Amount Raised	ICO Dates	Project
EOS	$4.1 billion	6/26/17 - 6/18/18	Blockchain Platform
Telegram	$1.7 billion	01/18-02/18	Encrypted Messaging & Blockchain Ecosystem
Dragon	$320 million	02/15/18 - 03/15/2018	Decentralized Currency for Casinos
Huobi	$300 million	01/24/18 - 02/28/18	Cryptocurrency Exchange
Hdac	$258 million	11/27/17 - 12/22/17	IoT Contract & Payment Platform
Filecoin	$257 million	08/10/17 - 09/10/17	Decentralized Cloud Storage
Tezos	$232 million	07/01/17 - 07/14/17	Self-Amending Distributed Ledger
Sirin Labs	$158 million	12/16/17 - 12/26/17	Open-Source Blockchain Smartphone
Bancor	$153 million	December 6, 2017	Prediction Markets
The DAO	$152 million	05/01/17 - 05/28/17	Decentralized VC

COMMUNITY TOKEN ECONOMIES

Digital financial assets have enabled novel thinking in Community Token Economies (Burke, 2017) that have the potential to form networks and cooperatives through token economies where users would have direct access to token capital, investment and a real interest in the system. The more products and services are used or promoted, the stronger the product and underlying Blockchain becomes while rewarding the user with tokens. This economic model creates active system participants and the incentive structure proactively builds stronger, more rewarding, networks. This is the essence of a DAO. While the first DAO failed, it paved the way for such thinking regarding global connected communities (Santos 2018) using behavioural economics and game theory to incentivise and disincentivise distributed communities to direct behaviour.

Blockchains' 'ability to create new tokens or currencies (monetary policy) and to distribute and allocate these tokens according to economic incentives (mechanism design) will lead to the creation of new forms of commerce & economies' (Chandra, 2018). In so doing, Blockchains may yet scale local solutions for the tragedy of the commons for Blockchain makes it more feasible for individuals to exit political-socioeconomic systems at the level of the system itself and elect to accede freely to institutional systems which formulate, promulgate, keep and verify institutions and public records without a centralised authority (Druzin, 2016).

Thomason (2018) predicts that, over time, small communities of token economies will evolve from purely speculative communities, to sustained and purposeful global collaborations for three reasons:

There is Money: Blockchain based crypto-currencies are increasingly in circulation. From the early days of bitcoin, there now number over 2000 cryptocurrencies (Coin Market Cap, 2019)

There is Motivation: Among the Blockchain community, there is a genuine desire to change the world, using technology and funding to create sustainable social change; whether that be the anti-institutional sentiment of bitcoiners, or the utopian ideals of purist Blockchainers. Social impact is deeply embedded in their personal values, and a driving force behind their actions.

Technology makes it Possible: Digital tools allow large groups of likeminded people to connect, allow members to determine causes worth supporting and to what extent; they improve the way we collaborate and the outcomes of these collaborations for all and enable individuals and groups to support other individuals and groups who pursue causes they believe to be of value to others.

Thus, token economies are the consequence of Blockchain's ability to enable coordinated efforts between similarly motivated actors on a shared infrastructure with the intent of creating a functioning global ecosystem.

LIMITATIONS AND CRITICISMS OF BLOCKCHAIN TECHNOLOGY

We have briefly alluded to some of the main criticisms of Blockchains: scalability, power consumption, high knowledge threshold and limited regulation – there are as many criticisms of Blockchains as there are benefits. These can broadly be categorised according to the following:

"I Can Do That With a Database"

A distributed ledger is, in many cases, the right tool for the job. A Blockchain is simply a database shared across a given number of computers. The number of the computers on the network that hold a copy of the database contributes to the scalability concerns of Blockchains, resulting in the popularity of permissioned Blockchains.

A Blockchain is only necessary, over a distributed ledger, if one needs;

Data to be tamper-proof; one needs evidence a database has not been altered.

Decentralisation; for whatever reason, trust in the network is greater than trust in transacting parties

Transparency; all transactions merit being auditable

"You Shouldn't Store That on Chain"

Privacy is of paramount concern in a digital era. While information *can* be stored on the Blockchain, it is generally not recommended for; privacy (Blockchains are designed to be auditable), storing blocks of data is protocol-heavy and, therefore, expensive (every node on the network has to repeatedly update the same transaction over the period of time you choose to store it). If the stored transaction includes a smart contract, there are yet further transaction fees to consider. Then we need to consider the impact of regulation. The GDPR, for example, includes the 'right to be forgotten', however, by design the Blockchain is append-only – information cannot be deleted.

"Don't Cryptocurrencies Finance Crime?"

As a private, secure, and global network for transactions, cryptocurrencies have provided incredible utility for transferring value in conflict zones, for remittances, retail payments, and, yes, also for dark web transactions for illegal goods. However, analysis by Chain Analysis (2018) shows that bitcoin is no longer the predominant payment mechanism in darknet markets (Chain Analysis, 2018) – cash is still king when it comes to buying drugs (Winstock, Barratt, Ferris & Maier, 2017).

"Blockchains Are Slow and Expensive"

To address throughput concerns, industry looks to permissioned Blockchains and controlling the number of nodes on the network and the development community are looking for ways to reduce the amount of data that's stored or transacted directly on the chain. Plasma, for example, looks to accomplish this using many small Blockchains and the Lightning Network conducts all transactions off-chain, only settling the final transaction on chain.

"Blockchains Don't Scale"

Scaling a decentralized network's ability to handle transactional volume without sacrificing security or speed is undoubtedly a difficult problem to solve. However, layer 1 and layer 2 solutions such as sharding and state channels, respectively, are currently in development and to be launched by the end of 2019. All new technologies require time to mature, especially when Blockchains like Ethereum are working towards becoming the base layer protocol of Web 3.0. Accordingly, the Blockchain ecosystem shows significant growth and clear roadmaps for scalability.

"Blockchains Are Unregulated"

Regulation helps alleviate public concern regarding the future of cryptocurrencies and digital exchanges and the security of digital exchanges and wallets; regulation also has secondary benefits of triggering consumer education. Without it, public Blockchains may struggle on the fringes for longer than is necessary. While it might seem counter-intuitive, many Blockchain advocates are looking forward to greater interest by the regulators, for Blockchains improve the security and functionality of many traditional business processes.

"Blockchains Are Power-Hungry"

Most blogs will compare the power consumption of mining a public Blockchain using a Proof-of-Work algorithm to the equivalent power requirements of a small country, contributing to the environmental destruction of the Earth. However, there are also now as many sources coming forth from leaders in the Blockchain space, like Consensys, disputing the veracity of cited data sets.

A 2018 research report into crypto energy use by Coin Shares, concludes that 77.6% of global bitcoin mining is powered by renewable energy in global regions where there are large, unused supplies of renewable electricity available and, while the algorithm is necessarily energy intensive, its consumption is not as high as is reported. Crypto's carbon footprint is extremely moderate for being the world's largest computer network. Indeed, a highly conservative estimate of the lower bound of renewables in the energy mix powering the Bitcoin mining network at 77.6% makes Bitcoin mining greener than almost every other large-scale industry in the world (Coin Shares Research, 2018).

There are, inevitably, other limitations the authors have not thought of - those relevant to application and particular to certain chains, however, the above are the ones most commonly heard in discussing Blockchains generally. Blockchain developers and advocates tend to be positively-minded, aware of the developments on the bleeding-edge and broad road-maps for larger chains, thus, they can also tend to be patient – aware that what is currently perceived to be a limitation will be addressed in the fullness of time.

CONCLUSION

The purpose of this chapter has been to outline an introduction to Blockchains and its limitations.

A Blockchain has the following components (Crawford Urban & Pineda, 2018):

1. The ability for multiple collaborators to make additions to the Blockchain.
2. A *write-only* design that ensures information can only be added to the Blockchain and never deleted.
3. It is hosted on a decentralized peer-to-peer (P2P) network.
4. It uses a distributed consensus mechanism for automatically reaching decisions on whether to accept or reject proposed additions to the Blockchain
5. An incentive structure integrated into the Blockchain's software that ensures that the nodes maintaining it work together.
6. The use of cryptography to ensure the security, integrity and reliability of the information recorded in the Blockchain and of the systems which manage it

Blockchains are currently used for two purposes; to create new business models and introduce efficiencies to existing models. The auditable nature of ledger improves transparency, enables life-cycle tracing and asset tracking while reducing transaction costs and friction. Functions such as smart contracts allow participants to create and automate contractual agreements when pre-defined conditions are met, reducing operational overheads (Mercy Corps, 2017). These features have made permissioned Blockchains popular in the banking and finance sector, particularly. Accenture (2017) estimate that Blockchains can help banks reduce infrastructure costs by an average $8 to $12 billion a year on reporting, compliance and operating costs.

However, Blockchains are not a silver bullet. There are key barriers to their implementation (Mercy Corps, 2017):

- Best practices, standards and interoperability have yet to be defined. Proven, replicable business models have yet to arise.
- Network dependency is a critical failure point. The technology requires Internet access and robust network infrastructure, and that imposes limitations on viability in some markets.
- Social, legal, and regulatory frameworks are in their early days and remain an area of uncertainty.
- Adequate data storage coupled with an effective means for data retrieval is a necessity. A distributed ledger typically only stores a hash of the transaction data; it is not used for storing the underlying data.

The authors have also outlined the limitations to the nascent technology, such as speed and scalability. As further chapters develop, their application to domain-specific use cases will be outlined and limitations identified. There will also be a number of questions posed that provide fertile ground for future research, including;

Government Mandates for Use of Blockchain and Frontier technologies? Countries need mandates, without which, large-scale digital interventions tend to fail. What kind of digital strategies and policies are necessary for using technologies to create social impact?

Blockchain, big data and data science and artificial intelligence and other frontier technologies: How can these scientific approaches improve human existence? What are some successful examples?

Financing digital interventions at scale? How can we ensure sustained financing for social impact? What are some of the innovations? Innovative financing? Tax incentives? Credits to device manufacturers?

Game changing approach: Enabling hyper-collaboration, to help accelerate the use of digital in solving social impact issues.

Large Technology Firms: What can large technology companies of the world can teach us in reducing inequality?

Where known, these questions will be addressed in the chapters that follow. Chapter 3 introduces the use of Blockchains for social impact at a government level, using Estonia as a model for understanding their full potential.

REFERENCES

Adams, C. (2018). *Estonia, a Blockchain model for other countries?* Retrieved from https://www.investinBlockchain.com/estonia-Blockchain-model/

Asolo, B. (2018). *Byzantine Fault Tolerance and The Byzantine Generals' Problem.* Retrieved from https://www.mycryptopedia.com/byzantine-fault-tolerance-and-the-byzantine-generals-problem/

Bitcoin.com. (2017). *What is Bitcoin double spending?* Retrieved from https://www.bitcoin.com/info/what-is-bitcoin-double-spending

Blockchain Hub. (2018). *Blockchains & Distributed Ledger Technologies.* Retrieved from https://Blockchainhub.net/Blockchains-and-distributed-ledger-technologies-in-general/

Blockgeeks.com. (2019). *What is the Ethereum Casper protocol; Crash course*. Retrieved from https://blockgeeks.com/guides/ethereum-casper/

Burke, J. (2017). *Overview of community token economies*. Retrieved from https://outlierventures.io/research/overview-of-ctes/

Chain Analysis. (2018). *The changing nature of cryptocrime*. Retrieved from https://blog.chainalysis.com/reports/report-the-changing-nature-of-cryptocrime

Chandra, P. (2018). *Crypto-economics: Why Blockchains need computer scientists and economists to come together*. Retrieved from https://medium.com/koinearth/cryptoeconomics-why-Blockchains-need-computer-scientists-economists-to-come-together-fd0eda583834

Coin Market Cap. (2019). *All cryptocurrencies*. Retrieved from https://coinmarketcap.com/all/views/all/

Coin Shares Research. (2018). *The Bitcoin mining network – trends, composition, marginal creation cost, electricity consumption & sources* [white paper]. Retrieved from https://coinshares.co.uk/wp-content/uploads/2018/11/Mining-Whitepaper-Final.pdf

Consensys. (2019). *The 6 biggest misconceptions about Blockchain and cryptocurrency*. Retrieved from https://media.consensys.net/the-6-biggest-misconceptions-about-Blockchain-and-cryptocurrency-aef9c1088e8c?gi=6bec13fb1c4d

Curran, B. (2018, July 13). *What is sharding? Guide to this Ethereum scaling concept explained*. Retrieved from https://blockonomi.com/sharding/

Devan, A. (2017). *The Blockchain technology stack*. Retrieved from https://medium.com/@arun.devan/the-Blockchain-technology-stack-cde66abad791

Floyd, D. (2018). *$6.3 Billion: 2018 ICO funding has passed 2017's total*. Retrieved from https://www.coindesk.com/6-3-billion-2018-ico-funding-already-outpaced-2017

Gonzalez, M. (2018). *Blockchain in Japan*. EU-Japan Centre. Retrieved from https://www.eu-japan.eu/sites/default/files/publications/docs/Blockchaininjapan-martagonzalez.pdf

Hertig, A. (2017, December 9). *Lightning; The Bitcoin scaling tech you really should know.* Retrieved from https://www.coindesk.com/lightning-bitcoin-scaling-tech-really-know

Hertig, A. (n.d.). *How Ethereum mining works.* Retrieved from https://www.coindesk.com/information/ethereum-mining-works

Hinman, W. (2018). *Digital Asset Transactions: When Howey met Gary (plastic).* Retrieved from https://www.sec.gov/news/speech/speech-hinman-061418

Huang, Z. (2018, August 22). *China shuts down Blockchain news accounts, bans hotels in Beijing from hosting cryptocurrency events.* Retrieved from https://www.scmp.com/tech/article/2160805/china-cracks-down-wechat-accounts-offering-Blockchain-and-cryptocurrency-news

Jeffries, A. (2018, March 22). *Inside the bizarre upside-down bankruptcy of Mt Gox.* Retrieved from https://www.theverge.com/2018/3/22/17151430/bankruptcy-mt-gox-liabilities-bitcoin

Kasireddy, P. (2018, February 8). *ELI5: What do we mean by "Blockchains are trustless"?* Retrieved from https://medium.com/@preethikasireddy/eli5-what-do-we-mean-by-Blockchains-are-trustless-aa420635d5f6

Liao, S. (2018, October 22). *China will soon require Blockchain users to register with their government IDs.* Retrieved from https://www.theverge.com/2018/10/22/18008640/china-Blockchain-registration-government-id

Lielacher, A. (2018). *Top 10 biggest ICOs (by amount raised).* Retrieved from https://www.bitcoinmarketjournal.com/biggest-icos/

Lightning Labs. (2018). *The Lightning network.* Retrieved from https://lightning.engineering/technology.html

Magnr. (2016). *Centralized versus decentralized banking.* Retrieved from https://medium.com/@Magnr/centralized-vs-decentralized-banking-5c2a657e94b7

Mappo. (2018). *Comprehensive list of banks using Blockchains.* Retrieved from https://hackernoon.com/comprehensive-list-of-banks-using-Blockchain-technology-97c08fa88385

Marinoff, N. (2019). *Ethereum overtakes Ripple as second-largest cryptocurrency (again).* Retrieved from https://blockonomi.com/ethereum-overtakes-ripple/

Nakamoto, S. (2008). *Bitcoin: A peer-to-peer electronic cash system.* Retrieved from https://bitcoin.org/bitcoin.pdf

O'Leary, R., & Hertig, H. (2018, February 12). *Prices aside; Crypto's tech stack Is steadily improving.* Retrieved from https://www.coindesk.com/prices-aside-cryptos-tech-stack-steadily-improving

OECD. (2018). *Blockchain technology and corporate governance. Technology, markets, regulation and corporate governance.* Retrieved from https://www.oecd.org/officialdocuments/publicdisplaydocumentpdf/?cote=DAF/CA/CG/RD(2018)1/REV1&docLanguage=En

PolySwarm. (2018, March 8). *Five companies already brilliantly using smart contracts.* Retrieved from https://medium.com/polyswarm/5-companies-already-brilliantly-using-smart-contracts-ac49f3d5c431

Raiden Network. (2018). *Home.* Retrieved from https://raiden.network

Ray, S. (2018, April 17). *What is delegated proof-of-stake.* Retrieved from https://hackernoon.com/what-is-delegated-proof-of-stake-897a2f0558f9

Samman, G. (2016, September 11). *The trend towards Blockchain privacy; Zero knowledge proofs.* Retrieved from https://www.coindesk.com/trend-towards-Blockchain-privacy-zero-knowledge-proofs

Szabo, N. (1999). *The God protocols.* Retrieved from https://nakamotoinstitute.org/the-god-protocols/

Taboura, V. (2018, March 25). *The evolution of the internet from centralised to decentralised.* Retrieved from https://hackernoon.com/the-evolution-of-the-internet-from-decentralized-to-centralized-3e2fa65898f5

Tapscott, D., & Tapscott, A. (2016). *Blockchain revolution.* New York: Penguin.

Tar, A. (2018, Jan 17). *Proof-of-work explained.* Retrieved from https://cointelegraph.com/explained/proof-of-work-explained

Thake, M. (2018, July 8). *What is proof-of-stake (PoS)?* Retrieved from https://medium.com/nakamo-to/what-is-proof-of-stake-pos-479a04581f3a

Thomason, J. (2017). *Changing the world crypto style – first UK conference on Initial Coin Offerings.* Retrieved from https://www.linkedin.com/pulse/changing-world-crypto-style-first-uk-conference-initial-thomason/

Thomason, J. (2018). *Hyper co-collaboration for social impact.* Retrieved from https://www.linkedin.com/pulse/hyper-co-collaboration-global-social-impact-dr-jane-thomason/

Token Investor Online. (2018, November 10). *10 smart contract projects that will be huge in 2019.* Retrieved from https://tokeninvestoronline.com/10-smart-contract-projects-that-will-be-huge-in-2019/

Winstock, A., Barratt, M., Ferris, J., & Maier, L. (2017). *Global drug survey.* Retrieved from https://www.globaldrugsurvey.com/wp-content/themes/globaldrugsurvey/results/GDS2017_key-findings-report_final.pdf

KEY TERMS AND DEFINITIONS

Algorithm: A process or set of rules to be followed in calculations or other problem-solving operations, especially by a computer.

Blockchain: One form of distributed ledger technology. A peer-to-peer method of secure data transmission using grouped "blocks" of encrypted data.

Consensus Algorithm: A process used in computer science to achieve agreement on a single data value across distributed networks. A consensus algorithm is designed to solve a consensus problem to achieve network reliability across multiple nodes.

Distributed Ledger Technology: The technology underlying distributed ledgers. This term is most often discussed in the context of enterprise use cases around adoption of distributed ledger technology.

Initial Coin Offering: A type of crowdfunding, or crowdsale, using cryptocurrencies as a means of raising capital for early-stage companies. It has come under fire due to the occurrence of scams and market manipulators.

Know Your Customer (KYC): This process refers to a project's or financial institution's obligations to verify the identity of a customer in line with global anti-money laundering laws.

Monitoring, Evaluation, Resourcing, and Learning (MERL): A process framework used to evaluate the effectiveness of an implemented development program.

Open Source: The original source code has been made publicly available for anyone to modify the code and develop the core product.

Sharding: A method of managing a large database. The Blockchain is separated into different "shards," and each part of the state is stored and processed by different nodes in the network. Each shard only processes a small part of the state and does so in parallel. Blockchain sharding is complicated by the need to maintain security and authenticity amongst a decentralized set of nodes.

ENDNOTES

[1]   https://bitcoin.org/en/

[2]   https://www.ethereum.org/

[3]   https://www.getmonero.org/

[4]   https://www.dash.org/

[5]   https://litecoin.com/en/

[6]   https://www.r3.com/

[7]   Mt. Gox was started in 2010 by Jed McCaleb, a serial entrepreneur, now the founder of Stellar. In 2010, there were few options for buying and selling bitcoin, and the exchange grew fast. It got too big for McCaleb, who sold it to Mark Karpelès, a French entrepreneur who had moved to Japan in 2009. Mt. Gox handled an estimated 70 percent of all bitcoin transactions going into 2014, but the site's rise was never smooth. It suffered hacks, outages, a run-in with the US government, and a $75 million lawsuit. In 2014, customers started to complain that they had requested withdrawals from Mt. Gox but never received the money. Then, the site shut off all withdrawals. Behind the scenes, Karpelès had discovered that an attacker had slowly been draining all of Mt. Gox's bitcoins without being noticed. The company filed for bankruptcy in February 2014, citing $64 million in liabilities (Jeffries, 2018).

8 https://slock.it/

9 https://shareandcharge.com/

10 https://propy.com/

11 https://populous.world/

12 https://lisk.io/

13 https://www.stellar.org/

14 Sharding is much older than Blockchain technology, seen in a variety of systems from business database optimisations to Google's global Spanner database. Essentially, sharding is a method for horizontally partitioning data within a database. The database is broken into little pieces called "shards", that when aggregated together form the original database. A full node in the Ethereum network stores the entire state of the Blockchain, including account balances, storage, and contract code. As the network increases in size at an exponential pace, the consensus only increases linearly. This limitation is due to the communication needed between the nodes needed to reach consensus. Nodes in the network do not have special privileges and every node in the network stores and processes every transaction. As a result, in a network the size of Ethereum's, issues such as high gas costs and longer transaction confirmation times become noticeable problems when the network is strained. The network is only as fast as the individual nodes rather than the sum of its parts. Sharding helps alleviate these issues by providing grouping subsets of nodes into shards which in turn process transactions specific to that shard. It allows the system to process many transactions in parallel, thus significantly increasing throughput (Curran, 2018).

15 https://truebit.io/

16 http://plasma.io/

17 https://ethereumclassic.org/

18 A nonce is an arbitrary number used only once in a cryptographic communication. They are often random or pseudo-random numbers. Many nonces also include a timestamp to ensure exact timeliness. To ensure that a nonce is used only once, it should be time-variant. Some authors define pseudo-randomness (or unpredictability) as a requirement for a nonce

[19] https://raiden.network/

[20] https://lightning.engineering/technology.html

[21] The OECD define DFAs as "cryptography-enabled, digitally-represented financial assets that rely on distributed ledger technologies (DLTs), such as the Blockchain, for the storage and transfer of value (monetary or non-monetary value, such as data or different types of rights)".

[22] According to the US Supreme Court's decision in SEC *v.* Howey Co. the Howey Test determines whether an investment contract is a security and falls under the purview of regulators. For a financial instrument to be deemed a security (and fall under the purview of the SEC), the instrument must meet four criteria: Be an investment worthy of money, with an expectation of profit, in a common enterprise, with the profit generated by a third party.

Chapter 3
Blockchain, the Digital State, and the New World Order

ABSTRACT

Governments across the world are grappling with the emergence and integration of new technologies. Front runner Estonia provides the model for how a country might completely transform their government operations, economy, and society through a purposeful, strategic program of digitization. This chapter considers how such countries are approaching digital transformation, outlining considerations for governments and submitting the new paradigm outlined in the BS4SC model of a citizen-centric, data-driven, and decentralised economy.

INTRODUCTION

Together, governments and stakeholders must shape a common digital future that makes the most of the immense opportunities that digital transformation holds to improve people's lives and boost economic growth (OECD, 2018).

We live in a world where technological advancement is a constant. The recent pace of technological advancement is unprecedented. In fact, it is predicted that by 2020, 1 million new devices will come online every hour. The impact of the Internet of Things (IoT) and digitization is ubiquitous. This is represented by the Technology block in the B4SC Model.

DOI: 10.4018/978-1-5225-9578-6.ch003

Figure 1. Current Influences and Drivers - Technology

The European Commission cites that soon 90% of jobs in careers such as engineering, accountancy, nursing, medicine, art, architecture, and many more will require some level of digital skills (c.f. Cisco, 2018). Technology can transform businesses, governments and drive global innovation. Digitization will enable countries to maintain global competitiveness, increase GDP, foster innovation and create new jobs. Due to the pace and constant advancements in technology, how do countries compete?

An increase in the number of successful government transformations could help solve society's greatest challenges, serve citizens better, and support the more productive use of public resources. (Allas et al., 2018)

Integrating digital technologies and the user experience into the design and delivery of public services yields efficiency and productivity gains for both government and industry, increasing public value and driving broad public sector modernization, thus promoting greater openness, transparency, public engagement and trust in government (OECD, 2016). Estimates from the UK government suggest that by introducing digital tools into government service delivery, their economy can save between GBP1.3-2 billion annually by 2020 (Andrews et al, 2016). In a report commissioned by Adobe, Deloitte (2015) found the economic benefits of digitizing consumer transactions for the Australian government could potentially produce $17.9 billion per annum in cost savings by 2025 if the government digitised only twenty per cent of its current 40 per cent traditional service delivery (Deloitte Access Economics, 2015).

Indeed, many research studies have found a positive relationship between technology penetration and a country's GDP. For instance, the Inter-America Development Bank (IDB) found that a 10% increase in broadband penetration in Latin America was associated with a 3.19% increase in GDP and a 2.61% increase in productivity (Cisco, 2018). Accordingly, governments around the world know that to deliver for citizens, they must transform the services they provide; aging populations are putting pressure on health and social services, education needs to equip young people for a digital future and increased population in cities is placing new demand on urban infrastructure. However, around 80 percent of government efforts to transform government performance don't fully meet their objectives - a key finding of a survey of nearly 3,000 public officials across 18 countries. This failure rate of governments to adapt to a new era is far too high, representing a missed opportunity to address society's greatest challenges more effectively, give citizens a better experience with government and make more productive use of public resources. Indeed, McKinsey estimate if governments matched their more technologically progressive counterparts, they could save as much as $3.5 trillion a year by 2021, while maintaining today's current service quality (Allas et al., 2018).

The Institute for Government (2016) find that where lack of technological development is discernible, the primary hurdle is found to be political will. By upgrading legacy systems that silo data and encourage relay processes, governments are slow to implement change. New technologies are flexible and integrated, working as an ecosystem, that means a digital government with civil servants that work together, can save national economies billions in public funds and increase civic engagement (Andrews et al., 2016).

Transforming a government for economies of scale savings cannot be done iteratively, by doing the same things slightly differently or using waterfall planning methodologies. To create an integrated ecosystem of shared knowledge, governments need to be as agile as start-ups, designing and implementing new systems and responding to users' reactions as IT systems evolve and the complex problems they were designed to address emerge. Failure to change government IT introduces great risk – often core government systems are decades old and hold large amounts of data on citizens in an era of increasing cyber-security risk. It is incumbent on governments and their agents to become comfortable with technology in order to introduce an era of transformation that is resistant to the new technologies that potentially threaten it.

BLOCKCHAIN AND DIGITAL GOVERNMENT

As part of this digital transformation journey, many governments around the world are looking at how Blockchain can be applied to stimulate economic growth, provide better services to citizens and potentially create dividends for the world's poorest people.

As the authors discussed extensively in Chapter 2, Blockchain's fundamental architecture offers users the benefits of security, reduced cyber threat; immutable record-keeping, resource savings; and real time auditability. This chapter details how progressive governments are embracing ambitious digital transformation agendas for the benefit of their citizens. Changing the operations of behemoth Western governments is a tall task, thus the leaders in this space have been small states who are able to pivot more nimbly. Their trail blazing journey is setting a high bar for the traditional states to follow in due course.

This is represented by the Government block and more specifically Small States Leading the Way With Change, and Emerging Economies Leapfrog as represented by the Governments block in the B4SC Model.

Estonia

Named "the most advanced digital society in the world" by Wired (Hammersley, 2017), Estonia started testing Blockchain technology in 2008 as a response to cyber-attacks in 2007 (E-Estonia, 2018b). Since they were the very first nation-state testing Blockchains (E-Estonia, 2018b), Estonians called this

Figure 2. Current Influences and Drivers – Governments

technology "hash-linked time-stamping" at the time. Since then, Blockchain technologies have been in public use in Estonia since 2012 to enforce the integrity of government data and systems. Particularly in their data registries; the national health, judicial, legislative, security and commercial code systems, ultimately with plans to extend into other spheres such as personal medicine, cybersecurity and data embassies (E-Estonia.com, 2018). The Blockchain technology used by Estonia – KSI Blockchain by Guardtime – is also used by NATO and US Department of Defence which, importantly, means it is scalable.

With regards Blockchain, the Estonian model really is the gold-standard. When Estonia gained independence from Russia in 1991, it realised that it needed to find something to set itself apart from its neighbours. Norway had oil, Finland mobile phones and Sweden had design. So, to become distinct, Estonia embarked on a massive technological innovation. In 1991 only half of the country had a phone line, by 1997, 97 per cent of Estonian schools were online. In 2000, cabinet meetings went paperless. By 2002, the government had built a free Wi-Fi network that covered most of the populated areas. By 2007, it had introduced e-voting, and by 2012 huge amounts of fibre-optic cabling were being laid – promising ultra-high-speed data connections – and 94 per cent of the country's tax returns were being made online. Now, every task that can be done with a digital service, is being done. All government services are managed online. Citizens, armed with a chip-and-pin identity card, can manage their affairs from a laptop or phone - anywhere there is connectivity. And from 2015 the Estonian government has offered anyone else the chance to do the same by registering to be a resident of Estonia, with an e-passport. You won't be an Estonian citizen, resident for tax purposes, nor is it a visa or residence permit (Estonian Police and Border Guard Board, 2018). However, your Estonian digital ID card, you can go online, log on to the government portal with your card and PIN, and use it to start an Estonian company, then register with an Estonian bank and start trading. Since the Estonian tax office is digitally connected to Estonian banks, filing taxes is also simple – so too is any bureaucracy involved in keeping the company going.

Furthermore, Estonia is working on linking its tax office with its counterparts in other regions of the world. The Estonians want to offer the option for international citizens to run their companies through the Estonian system, which would in turn, make sure that local tax offices receive all the money it is legally due, too. A UK-based entrepreneur, for example, may open her business in Estonia, use an Estonian bank and pay for some Estonian services, even if the company was only going to be trading in the

UK, because she would find Estonia's national infrastructure far easier to deal with than the UK's. In other words, a nation is now competing with its neighbours based on the quality of its user interface. Just as you might switch your bricks-and-mortar bank to one with a better mobile app or better digital presence, the Estonians hope you'll switch your business to a country with an infrastructure that is easier to use (Hammersley, 2017). Consequently, Estonia is becoming renowned for being a start-up hub and an early adopter of Blockchain technology - there is also much talk about whether it will or won't eventually release its own national crypto token called the "estcoin" (Adams, 2018; Alexandre, 2018).

Every little digital step that Estonia takes has profound social effects. Estonians only need to carry their digital identity card (driving licences, store cards or donor cards have been subsumed into the ID card) so Estonians have complete control over their personal data. The personal data portal accessible with the identity card provides a log of everyone who has accessed it. If you see something you do not like – a doctor other than your own looking at your medical records, for example, you can click to report it to the data ombudsman. A civil servant then must justify the intrusion. Forty percent of Estonians use their ID card for e-banking. If those services are taken down residents must go physically to the bank, and since the banks have optimised according to the need, with 99 per cent of banking transactions happening electronically, they've closed their offices.

Finally, in the event of a national emergency, Estonia wants to be able to turn off the lights and restart the government elsewhere, booting-up from a server farm located outside of Estonia. This way a serious digital attack cannot shut down the government. If this is the case, that emergency copies of their government can be downloaded as back-ups on server-farms elsewhere, there's nothing to say they can't release the code and let another nation upload a new flag gif, change some of the names in the config file and boot themselves up their own version. It wouldn't have to be an officially recognised state, either: fully realised, this would bring down the barrier to entry to effective statehood for the more agile, more entrepreneurial separatist movements, budding caliphates or secessionist offshoots. As the film and music industries have discovered - when something is digitised, it costs nothing to copy it.

Until today, Estonians' digital infrastructure has only been for Estonians but for countries in waiting or insurgent states, Estonia has a roadmap to follow for a fully digital society.

NASDAQ have completed a trial in Estonia that will enable company shareholders to use a Blockchain voting system which allows investors who own shares in companies listed on the Tallinn Stock Exchange to vote online during investor meetings or transfer their voting rights to a proxy (Rizzo, 2016). The Estonian Ministry of Justice is also migrating to digital court files – meaning there is no paper filing to refer back to as the source of truth.

What makes Estonia so successful at implementing digital-first initiatives is support from all levels of society, political commitment from an active government and industry leadership. Estonia is also not burdened by legacy infrastructure – it leapfrogged into its primary spot, progressively developing the technical architecture and the requisite supporting regulatory changes necessary to get to where it is today from the late 1990s.

Singapore

Few governments have had their leaders align themselves with digital efforts as closely and visibly as Singapore's. Estimates suggest that digital transformation will add approximately US$10 billion to Singapore's gross domestic product (GDP) and increase GDP growth at an annual rate of 0.6 per cent by 2021 (Smart Nation Singapore, n.d.).

Singapore established the Smart Nation strategy as a national initiative to solve urban living challenges and improve lives using technology. The strategy covers digitising transport, home and environment, business productivity, health and enabled aging, and public sector services. Singapore's model for establishing innovative initiatives in cross sector government coordination and delivering efficient and effective services is considered world leading. Singaporean Airlines' Krisflyer, for example, restructured its payments and loyalty program this year by adopting Blockchain for its new digital wallet. The digital wallet allows members to use frequent flyer miles to complete point-of-sale purchases both onboard a plane and around an airport. Customer loyalty is fostered due to the ease with which they get to spend their frequent flyer miles. However, Singapore is one of the first nations in the South East Asia region to have announced Blockchain-based initiatives thus far. More extensive Blockchain applications to the airline industry will require regulation and the formation of joint industry guidelines (Lim, 2018).

Singapore's first Blockchain innovation center was established in July 2016 as a partnership between IBM and the Economic Development Board of Singapore. A consequence of which were developments to the higher education sector. In 2017, IBM worked with Singapore's National University

(NUS) to develop a world-leading distributed ledger technology curriculum. The Ngee Ann Polytechnic (NP), a public institution of higher learning in Singapore, is also adopting Blockchain. Together with smart contracts start-up, Attores, NP is using Blockchain to verify the authenticity of the polytechnic's diplomas - the first education institute in Singapore to do so. With a student's Blockchain ID, potential employers can retrieve the person's academic records and education history and their graduation certificates can automatically be posted to their LinkedIn profile with the transaction identification that validates the student genuinely graduated (Lago, 2018).

For the education sector, the benefits of Blockchain technologies are clear; improved productivity, efficient matriculation and graduation, reduced overheads and improved relationships with industry, who can rest assured that claims made by students regarding grades and graduation dates are accurate.

In real estate, online platform Averspace lists properties for sale or rent and conducts transactions using smart contracts. In so doing, Averspace makes it easy for homeowners and tenants to directly enter into a digital tenancy agreement, without having to pay commission fees. Averspace is the first real estate portal in Singapore that allows homeowners and prospective tenants to enter into a digital tenancy agreement on their smartphones, using Blockchain technology to ensure all their transactions are secure (Lago, 2018).

In government services, the Monetary Authority of Singapore (MAS) is partnering with R3, a Blockchain technology company, and other financial institutions on a proof-of-concept called Project Ubin. Project Ubin explores using DLT for the clearing and settlement of payments and securities. The project aims to help MAS and the industry better understand the technology with the eventual goal of developing simpler to use and more efficient alternatives to today's systems based on digital central bank issued tokens. MAS and Singapore Exchange (SGX) announced in August 2018 that it is collaborating to develop Delivery versus Payment (DvP) capabilities for settlement of tokenised assets across different Blockchain platforms. This will allow financial institutions and corporate investors to carry out simultaneous exchange and final settlement of tokenised digital currencies and securities assets, improving operational efficiency and reducing settlement risks. Three companies, Anquan, Deloitte and Nasdaq were appointed as technology partners for this project (Singapore Government, 2018b).

The Public Service Division of Singapore (Singapore Government, 2018) is considering adopting Blockchain to verify vendors' track records on GeBiz, to track a public officer's career moves, and support or even replace certain auditing processes. The Singapore Customs Authority has just launched a national trade platform on Blockchain to connect industry, community systems and platforms and government systems together (Lim, 2018). The platform will replace the current TradeNet and TradeXchange platforms for declaring permits and other services for trade and logistics. Where nowadays there can be dozens of documents exchanged via email or even courier – taking days or weeks – the Networked Trade Platform (NTP) is designed to bring the entire ecosystem to a single online location, where they can trade and transact with each other. Traders will be able to book services such as cargo freight, trade finance, cargo insurance, customs declaration and payment reconciliation. More than 700 companies have signed up as users of the NTP, which will also seek to accelerate innovation in trade finance (Bermingham, 2018).

The Intellectual Property Intermediary (IPI), an organisation established under Singapore's Ministry of Trade and Industry, has been working on *Blockchain Technology for Food,* which tracks and traces materials and products in the food production chain, ensuring food quality, guaranteeing food safety and reducing food waste.

The Singaporean government has also invested in MediLOT Technologies, through SGInnovate, Singapore's government-owned deep technology development firm. MediLOT Technologies is a a Singapore-based Blockchain and healthcare analytics start-up. Using a health data protocol built on the principles "of patient centricity, privacy, and equitable data sharing" (Lago, 2018), MediLOT uses a dual Blockchain with a unique layered architecture which can incorporate Artificial Intelligence (AI) and data analytics capabilities on top of its control and data layers. This allows for machine learning APIs and complex applications to be built on top of MediLOT platform.

Bermuda

Bermuda's micro-state status is a boon to technological innovation for they are unburdened by the weighty bureaucracy of larger governments. Bermuda's proposals and legislative support for Blockchain regulation and development intends to serve as innovative models for other nations to follow.

In 2017, the Bermuda Business Development Agency were engaged by the government to launch a Blockchain taskforce. On their recommendations, the government has built upon the Digital Business Act and Companies Act to pass legislation on ICOs, created a regulatory sandbox for those companies and partnered with BitFury to shift the island's property deeds system to the Blockchain.

Fierce local competition means Bermuda is embedding use cases into public policy, such as youth education and immigration. For example, a memorandum of understanding between Bermuda and Binance reveals that the crypto exchange will not only move its compliance center to Bermuda, but also invest $10 million into Blockchain-related educational programs and $5 million in Blockchain startups over the course of two to three years (Milano, 2018).

Binance will also invest $10 million in education for residents, and $5 million in Bermuda-based Blockchain companies.

Dubai

In 2016, Dubai's crown prince announced the Dubai Blockchain Strategy, which aims to have all government documents on the Blockchain database by 2020. The objective of the Dubai Blockchain strategy is to create the future of Dubai and make Dubai the happiest city on earth, by ushering in economic opportunity for all sectors, and cement Dubai as a global technology leader in the smart economy, fueling entrepreneurship and global competitiveness. The Dubai government estimates that the Blockchain strategy has the potential to save 25.1 million hours of economic productivity each year, and unlock 1.5 billion USD in savings annually in document processing alone. The Dubai Blockchain strategy has three main pillars including: Government Efficiency, create new specialized sectors and achieve global leadership (Smart Dubai, 2018).

Under the first pillar, the new strategy will contribute to increased government efficiency by enabling a paperless digital layer for all city transactions, supporting Smart Dubai initiatives in the public and private sector. Required documentation, such as visa applications, bill payments and license renewals, which account for over 100 million documents each year, will be transacted digitally under the new strategy. Blockchain technology would contribute savings of up to 114 MTons CO_2 emissions in trip reductions and redistribute up to 25.1 million hours of economic productivity in saved document processing time (Smart Dubai, 2018).

Under the second pillar, the Dubai Blockchain Strategy will introduce a system for enabling citizens and partners to create new businesses using the technology. Under the new strategy, Blockchain will enable thousands of business opportunities in the private sector. Industries that will benefit from Blockchain technology including real estate, fin-tech and banking, healthcare, transportation, urban planning, smart energy, digital commerce and tourism.

The third pillar of the Dubai Blockchain Strategy is International Leadership. In line with the third pillar, Dubai will open its Blockchain platform for global counterparts to enhance safety, security, convenience for international travelers to Dubai.

The strategy is underpinned by strong public-private partnerships. Dubai has set up a Global Blockchain Council to explore current and future Blockchain applications. The council currently consists of 47 members from both the public and private sector and launched seven Blockchain proofs-of-concept trails, covering health records, diamond trade, title transfer, business registration, digital wills, tourism engagement and shipping. IBM has also partnered with the Dubai government to trial the use of Blockchain for a trade and logistics solution which transmits shipment data, allowing key stakeholders to receive real-time information about the state of goods and the status of the shipment, replacing paper-based contracts with smart contracts (Smart Dubai, 2018).

Sweden

The Swedish land registry authority, Lantmäteriet, has been testing a way to record property transactions on a Blockchain which is estimated to save $106 million per year in reducing paperwork, eliminating fraud and speeding up transactions. Smart Contracts allow buyers and sellers to sign contracts digitally, and verified automatically, instead of having to do it at an agent's office. The private Blockchain stores records of land authority and banks, and the process is recorded when a land title is transferred from one person to the other.

The underlying technology for this project is ChromaWay's two innovative products. First is Esplix, the smart workflow middleware which enables processes and workflows to be described using code and then enforced by the participants in the system. Second is Postchain, a consortium database technology which combines the capabilities of enterprise databases with private Blockchains. The solution in this project is about streamlining and securing the process leading up the transfer of a property title (Chromaway, 2018)

United Kingdom

In 2015, the UK government committed to spend 10 million pounds to fund research on digital currencies and Blockchain technologies. In 2016, the UK Government Office for Science released a report urging the UK government to test Blockchain Technology (Higgins, 2016).

In June 2016, the Department for Work and Pensions began to trial welfare payments to citizens using mobile phone apps through which citizens can receive and spend their welfare benefits. With the citizens' consent, transactions were recorded on a distributed ledger to support financial management. The UK government is working with GovCoin Systems, Barclays, RWE power, and University College London on the trial, which began in June with 24 users. GovCoin Systems, one of the partners in the project, aims to reduce the $1 trillion loss annually due to friction and fraud costs in the distribution of social welfare and aid, through this project (Higgins, 2016).

In 2016, Credits, a Blockchain startup firm located in the Isle of Man, was awarded the UK Government's first G-Cloud 8 framework agreement for the supply of distributed ledger technology. This means that UK public sector organizations such as central and local governments, health, education, emergency services, defense and certain non-profit organizations, may use the Blockchain platform-as-a-service without having to use time consuming standard procurement procedures to buy services over the existing Digital Marketplace procurement platform (Prisco, 2016).

In 2016, the UK government announced that it would use Blockchain to exert better control and accountability over funds disbursed to research centers, aid organizations or individual students. Examples provided included Student Loans Company tracking money from the Treasury to a student's bank account, and the Department for International Development tracking money to the aid organization spending the money in country (Higgins, 2016a).

One of the risks of Blockchain adoption in the UK government has been dealing with legacy IT systems and associated organizational risk in replacing old systems (Dunn, 2016).

The UK Financial Conduct Authority (FCA) has established a regulatory sandbox so that prospective companies would be able to test innovations and services in a live, protected, business market in 2016. Forty percent of the fourth-round companies accepted were distributed ledger technology (DLT) or Blockchain-based startups. (HM Treasury, 2018)

The FCA recently released the report from the Crypto Assets Task Force, FCA (HM Treasury, 2018) which was tasked with exploring the impact of crypto assets and distributed ledger technology in financial services. The taskforce found that there are examples of crypto assets and other applications of DLT delivering beneficial innovation in financial services. The taskforce also identified three major harms: to consumers, to market integrity and the risk of financial crime. The FCA, HM Treasury and the Bank of England will be taking several steps address these harms and to encourage future beneficial innovation (HM Treasury, 2018).

United States of America

While the US has been grappling with how to regulate cryptocurrencies, several US States have made advanced progress with Blockchain. In 2016, Delaware became the first US state to implement Blockchain technology. Delaware is home to more than 66% of Fortune 500 companies and 85% of initial public offerings, and many private companies and start-ups choose to incorporate in Delaware. Delaware-incorporated companies, with the consent of the state's Legislature, have the option to issue paperless equity shares using Blockchain technology. The Delaware Public Archives will be among the first to use the distributed technology to archive and encrypt government archives. The initiative aims to help companies lower transaction costs while speeding up transaction consummation, automating data processes and reducing fraud, making Delaware an attractive state for Blockchain companies. The initiative also pledges that the state will not create new regulations or laws in the foreseeable future affecting the use of Blockchain technology, which allows individuals and companies to effectuate and verify transactions and then share or distribute the transaction ledger to a self-selected group of entities or the general public.

Illinois has also announced a Blockchain initiative by a consortium of five government agencies including the Illinois Department of Financial and Professional Regulation, the State Department of Commerce and Economic Opportunity (DCEO), the Department of Insurance (DOI), Cook County's Recorders of Deeds and the newly formed Department of Innovation & Technology (DoIT), in addition to private sector players. The inter-agency consortium has three main goals. The first is to create a welcoming regulatory environment for digital currency and Blockchain businesses looking to do business; the second is to invite Blockchain companies to open offices in the state; and the third is to develop specific Blockchain prototypes for use by the Illinois government (del Castillo, 2016).

Then there is the state of Georgia, who are building a permissioned Blockchain for the National Agency of Public Registry to register land titles and validate property transactions. The Georgian government says it expects the system to increase transparency in land title ownership, reduce fraud and create cost savings (Lim, 2018).

THE DIGITAL STATE IS NOT OPTIONAL

These examples show how Blockchain technologies will be an integral part of a suite of solutions to transform governments to digital service providers. Blockchains offer the potential to increase the speed, transparency and efficiency of government processes and improve government accountability to citizens.

Countries like Estonia and Dubai demonstrate the importance of countries striving to remain competitive - it is an imperative that governments look toward innovation and digital technologies to provide the basis for growth in the 21st Century. It is less an option than a necessity. Governments have a critical role to play in crafting policy and regulation to catalyse digital transformation and industry plays a key role in building the eco-system as a primary enabler.

POLITICAL LEADERSHIP

There needs to be a bold political ambition to build digital transformation and the development of policies to attract talent, investors and to be at the forefront of innovation. Governments need to create policy frameworks that foster, and do not hamper, digital innovation. Government interventions that can dramatically affect growth include developing new segments via the digital economy; enhancing public and private sector competitiveness and efficiency; job creation within new segments and greater access to global job markets; attracting foreign investment as digitized economy and diversifying trade using e-commerce and online services. Structural policies should also facilitate innovation and entrepreneurship to foster innovation and technology diffusion, ensure that competitive conditions prevail and avoid erecting barriers to cross border digital markets.

Emerging economy governments can also work with international donors to look at opportunities to digital solutions in aid programmes. Government can promote principles and standards for digital development throughout the aid system, to ensure that more digital products and services reach, empower and improve the lives of poor people, particularly those at risk of being left behind. In relation to inclusion, governments can increase awareness, digital and entrepreneurial literacy in rural and remote areas.

ACCESS TO TALENT

Talent is critical. Governments not only need to grow the talent needed to digitise including, entrepreneurs, programmers, designers, and engineers but develop the internal capability, too. This will only happen through proactive government policy that stresses the importance of IT literacy in education curricula. For example, Code Lagos in Nigeria is an initiative of the Lagos State Ministry of Education aimed at educating Lagos State residents for the future of work – by teaching people how to write code and creatively solve problems. Their ambitious agenda is to train 1 million coders over the next five years, half of them women and 100,000 Blockchain developers (Code Lagos, 2019).

To address a shortcoming of talent at the source, curricula from primary schools to higher education institutions need to be tuned toward digital skills and critical thinking. This shift includes digitisation of the learning process, from equipping classrooms with smart boards and tablets to establishing a truly blended or online learning environment. Coding institutions such as Code Academy provide an inspiring example of how quickly young people can learn programming. Digital curricula starting in basic education can help to narrow the gap. However, holistic approaches should also include dedicated programmes to build digital literacy targeted to specific groups such as the elderly and underprivileged.

ACCESS TO FINANCE AND INFRASTRUCTURE

Governments play a key role in attracting and developing investment instruments like government backed bonds to provide for investment in promising tech companies, and funding for start-ups and incentivising industry to provide accelerator programs for start-ups. Connectivity is key and affordable, secure access to the internet is a fundamental priority. There is also a need to provide physical space for start-ups and an enabling environment to allow young tech entrepreneurs to flourish and build the eco system will enable the digital economy to thrive.

BUSINESS DRIVING DIGITAL

If Government enables the digital economy, business must drive it. Thus, it is imperative for business to proactively form mutually beneficial partnerships to develop the ecosystem and provide opportunities for startups to incubate their ideas. Large corporations struggle to implement innovation as much as large governments do, however a combination of the right policy and regulatory environment, incentive structures, training and skills development, funding and connections among ecosystem actors may provide the fuel for an environment of innovation that many countries seek.

The Government of Malaysia Magic Program (Magic, 2019), the Singapore Smart Nation Strategy (Singapore Smart Nation, n.d.) and Code Lagos (Code Lagos, 2019) are examples of proactive leadership by government to build digital economies. Governments can make it simpler for entrepreneurs to access grants, permits, applications and certifications to enable them to grow their business. Governments can kick start training initiatives and work with business to facilitate the development of co-working spaces, incubator, and accelerator programs to allow their ideas to flourish. Government interventions that can dramatically affect growth include financial inclusion via digital banking and payments; developing new segments via the digital economy; and job creation within new segments and greater access to global job markets.

CONCLUSION

Governments are facing three key trends: the rapid pace of adoption of new technologies and pace of digital transformation; an unprecedented sense of uncertainty; and citizens' trust in their governments is plummeting. This is coupled with the increasing threat of global technology companies dominating in research and development. This is represented by the Technology block in the B4SC Model.

Governments will need to learn how to engage with the new digital issues that cannot be regulated from a single geography. Techno-literacy will prove a key skill for citizen, politician and industry leaders alike. It is a challenging territory because there is a shortage of world class digital experts globally - governments may need to co-invest to fund an elite task force of digital experts who can help multiple governments develop;

Figure 3. Current Influences and Drivers - Communities

- Talent strategy
- Ethical and regulatory strategy
- Data strategy
- Execution and engagement strategy
- Research and Development strategy to foster innovation and develop tech in the context of government.

Policymakers must ensure the capabilities and enablers for digitization are in place, and need to collaborate with industry, consumers, and government to foster an ecosystem in which the uptake and usage of digital applications grow. Just as digitalization enhances the efficiency and competitiveness of businesses, the current technological improvements can also improve efficiency and effectiveness of government functions, thereby enhancing sustainable economic growth.

Mobile connectivity and mobile technology have opened new opportunity to connect people. All economies need affordable, reliable, safe and high-speed digital infrastructure – this will become a basic human right. Digital technologies offer an unprecedented opportunity to change lives, transform economies, and stimulate growth.

Small economies now can play an active or leading role in tech innovation by being open to it. For some economies, disruptive change may bring unique opportunities to leapfrog the legacy issues that advanced economies confront. The digital economy can also enable small business, women and other disadvantaged groups to take part in trade and connect.

Regional collaboration can help address regulation and standards, examine the regulatory fitness of legislation for the digital single market, and to support the sharing of best practices in areas like skills and jobs for the digital change. Regional platforms could allow shared experiences, collaboration and joint investments to be triggered, common approaches to regulatory problems to be explored, and re-skilling of the workforce. Regional platforms could promote best practices, share information and strengthen capacity-building among economies on human resources development in the digital age in cooperation with relevant partners.

Chapter Four will locate some of these themes within the context of emerging markets, clearly demonstrating where governments are using a lack of infrastructure to leapfrog Western democracies approaches to digital innovation.

REFERENCES

Allas, T., Checinski, M., Dillon, R., Dobbs, R., Hieronimus, S., & Singh, N. (2018). *Delivering for Citizens: How to triple the success rate of government transformations.* Retrieved from https://www.mckinsey.com/industries/public-sector/our-insights/delivering-for-citizens-how-to-triple-the-success-rate-of-government-transformations

Andrews, E., Thornton, D., Owen, J., Bleasdale, A., Freeguard, G., & Stelk, I. (2016). *Making a success of digital government.* Retrieved from https://www.instituteforgovernment.org.uk/publications/making-success-digital-government

Bermingham, F. (2018). *Singapore Launches National Platform to Digitise Trade.* Retrieved from https://www.gtreview.com/news/asia/singapore-launches-national-platform-to-digitalise-trade/

Chromaway. (2018). *Future house purchases.* Retrieved from https://chromaway.com/landregistry/

Code Lagos. (2019). *About Code Lagos.* Retrieved from https://codelagos.org/

Del Castillo, M. (2016). *Illinois unveils Blockchain policy in bid to attract industry innovators.* Retrieved from https://www.coindesk.com/illinois-Blockchain-initiative-policy-regulation-bitcoin-Blockchain

Deloitte Access Economics. (2015). *Digital government transformation.* Retrieved from https://www2.deloitte.com/content/dam/Deloitte/au/Documents/Economics/deloitte-au-economics-digital-government-transformation-230715.pdf

Dunn, J. (2016). *Blockchains and the public sector; Distributed Ledger Technology reaches the G-Cloud.* Retrieved from https://www.computerworlduk.com/cloud-computing/Blockchains-public-sector-distributed-ledger-technology-reaches-g-cloud-3644403/

E-Estonia.com. (2018). *Estonian Blockchain technology; Frequently Asked Questions.* Retrieved from https://e-estonia.com/wp-content/uploads/faq-a4-v02-Blockchain.pdf

E-Estonia.com. (2018a). *KSI Blockchain in Estonia.* Retrieved from https://e-estonia.com/wp-content/uploads/faq-ksi-Blockchain-1.pdf

Estonian Police and Border Guard Board. (2018). *Application for E-Residency.* Retrieved from https://apply.gov.ee/

Higgins, S. (2016). *Report urges UK government to test Blockchain tech.* Retrieved from http://www.coindesk.com/report-uk-government-test-Blockchain-tech/

Higgins, S. (2016a). *UK Government could track student loans and grants with Blockchain.* Retrieved from https://www.coindesk.com/uk-government-student-loans-grants-Blockchain

Lago, C. (2018). *How Singapore is using Blockchain outside of cryptocurrencies.* Retrieved from https://www.cio.com/article/3291758/how-singapore-is-using-Blockchain-outside-of-crypto-currencies.html

Lim, C. (2018). *Blockchain to innovate Southeast Asia's airline industry.* Retrieved from https://theaseanpost.com/article/Blockchain-innovate-southeast-asias-airline-industry-0

Magic. (2019). *Malaysian global innovation and creativity centre.* Retrieved from https://mymagic.my/

Milano, A. (2018). *Bermuda's Blockchain strategy goes beyond just winning new business.* Retrieved from https://www.coindesk.com/bermudas-Blockchain-strategy-goes-beyond-just-winning-new-business

OECD. (2016). *Digital government strategies for transforming public services in the welfare areas.* Retrieved from https://www.oecd.org/gov/digital-government/Digital-Government-Strategies-Welfare-Service.pdf

Prisco, G. (2016). *UK Government awards Blockchain framework agreement to Blockchain-As-A-Service.* Retrieved from https://bitcoinmagazine.com/articles/u-k-government-awards-framework-agreement-to-Blockchain-as-a-service-company-credits-1470687028/

Rizzo, P. (2016). *Nasdaq to launch Blockchain voting Trial for Estonian Stock Market.* Retrieved from https://www.coindesk.com/nasdaq-shareholder-voting-estonia-Blockchain

Singapore Government. (2018a). *Project Ubin: Central bank money using Distributed Ledger Technology.* Retrieved from http://www.mas.gov.sg/Singapore-Financial-Centre/Smart-Financial-Centre/Project-Ubin.aspx

Singapore Government. (2018b). *In Blockchain we trust.* Retrieved from https://www.psd.gov.sg/challenge/ideas/deep-dive/Blockchain-trust-public-service

Smart Nation Singapore. (n.d.). *Digital government blueprint; Summary.* Retrieved from https://www.tech.gov.sg/files/digital-transformation/dgb_summary_june2018.pdf

Treasury, H. M. (2018). *Cryptoassets taskforce; Final report.* Retrieved from https://assets.publishing.service.gov.uk/government/uploads/system/uploads/attachment_data/file/752070/cryptoassets_taskforce_final_report_final_web.pdf

Chapter 4
Emerging Markets:
The Innovative First Movers

ABSTRACT

While most of the development and implementation of Blockchains has taken place in Western countries, arguably its greatest potential resides in emerging markets: Argentina, Brazil, Chile, China, Colombia, Czech Republic, Egypt, Greece, Hungary, India, Indonesia, Korea, Malaysia, Mexico, Morocco, Qatar, Peru, Philippines, Poland, Russia, South Africa, South Korea, Taiwan, Thailand, Turkey, and United Arab Emirates – all countries that are evolving and disrupting traditional methods of production like agriculture and the export of raw materials to invest in modern manners of productive capacity. This chapter examines the sectors in which Blockchain is being used to innovate in emerging markets to enable financial inclusion, improved asset and supply chain management, education, and healthcare.

INTRODUCTION

Implementing new technology systems in advanced economies requires massive amounts of change of legacy systems at institutional and structural levels. Change, therefore, typically takes years or even decades. In emerging economies, however, the lack of trusted and effective infrastructure means new technologies are a welcome arrival because they do not mean change to the status quo but the arrival of a functional resolution to a problem.

DOI: 10.4018/978-1-5225-9578-6.ch004

While much of the development and implementation of blockchains thus far has taken place in Western countries, arguably its greatest potential for social impact lies in emerging markets.

An emerging market is an economy in a newly-industrialized country which has not yet fully matured but has, in macroeconomic terms, already outpaced their developing market counterparts by making high levels of investment in commercial productivity capabilities. They could be characterized by indicators of;

- Low income per capita
- Rapid growth
- High volatility
- Low trust in the national government
- Receptivity to innovation

Emerging economies are almost exclusively cash-based (nearly 90% of economic activity occurs by traditional means due to poor trust in local financial institutions and an average of forty percent of residents do not have bank accounts) (Down, 2018).

Most people and small businesses in emerging economies today do not fully participate in the formal financial system; 2 billion individuals and 200 million small businesses lack access to formal savings and credit (Osafo-Kwaako, et al, 2018). Thus, emerging markets are constantly innovating in the field of payments, promoting an increasing shift to digital services (Reuters, 2018; PWC, 2018). The lack of trust in local financial institutions means, however, that the preference for cash prevails, and, indeed continues to increase. The amount of cash in circulation has increased to 9 percent of GDP in 2016 from 7 percent in 2000 yet digital payments are expected to reach a record 726 billion by 2020 with emerging markets leading this trend, at a rate three times that of developed economies. Digital payments in developing markets grew 21.6 percent between 2014 and 2015, compared to a 6.8 percent rise in mature markets. Non-cash payments in Asian emerging markets are projected to grow by almost a third (30.9 percent), led by China and India (Brown, 2017). Accordingly, over the next 10 years or so we are likely to see rapid change in the payments landscape, building on accelerating growth in electronic payments and the advent of new and disruptive market-

Figure 1. Enabling Shifts Required – Communities

players, as Blockchains enable smaller operators to take advantage of more open financial environments.

The emerging markets will be at the forefront of this transformation for they are currently in a sweet spot where demand meets the ability to supply: Millennials respond well to digital-first service delivery and desire financial inclusion, and the legislative environment supports the introduction of a wider array of financial services. Concerted efforts are being directed towards introducing and promoting innovative retail e-payment instruments and systems including e-wallets, mobile payments and one-click payments. For example, in Nigeria, use of mobile-based payment systems has increased due to widespread access to mobile phones both for customer and merchant processes. In India, the central ATM switch that processes all retail ATM transactions has been revamped in preparation for expected demand increase (Osafo-Kwaako et al, 2018).

Providing that technology is efficient, effective and scalable, it is likely emerging markets will see rising numbers of decentralized applications (dApps), blockchains, social media payment platforms (such as Venmo) NFC technology and bluetooth low energy. This is represented in the B4SC Model Enabling Shifts Required (and, indeed, is occurring now), more specifically the emerging markets within the Communities block.

New EU regulations, regarding open banking particularly, will support the growth of digital payments from 2019. Introduced in January 2018, one law is set to allow third-party companies to gain access to banking customers' data with their consent using opened application programming interfaces (APIs). APIs are codes that allow different financial programs to communicate with each other, giving developers access to the software applications of banks. The aim of the EU directive is to open up the payments ecosystem to smaller lenders and non-banking firms and make competition fairer. Mainly intended for developed countries, these directives, in due course, will affect emerging markets such as India and South Korea. The Indian government is promoting sets of APIs via the Aadhaar national identity system which creates an open banking ecosystem with secure biometric identification (Gilbert and Tobin, 2018). With a market structure incapable of dominating the competition, emerging economies can particularly benefit from the advantages provided by open, public Blockchains, namely, greater numbers of competitors delivering a wider range of products and services at more affordable prices for potential consumers. In so doing, emerging market economies might *leapfrog* more developed countries (IFC, 2017; Down, 2018) to follow market-leaders in Blockchain such as Estonia (see Chapter 3 for further information), Mauritius and Bermuda, or leading followers like India.

Countries that traditionally dominated global innovation leadership, notably the U.S. and Germany, are stalling, ceding ground to emerging and developed Asia. Emerging markets are catch up aggressively, and China and Japan have become alternative hotspots for global innovation—confirming that innovation is disrupting the global competitive landscape at the regional as well as industry level (Edelman Intelligence, 2018).

LEAPFROGGING

Leapfrogging involves taking advantage of the absence of developed products, services and infrastructure to establish an advanced method of service delivery. Simply copying systems that have evolved over decades of operational refinement to work well in other countries is not effective in emerging markets. Examples of where leapfrogging has been particularly effective can be found in countries like Kenya and South Africa, which rolled out telephone access on 3G networks first instead of laying copper cables, and provided internet access by smartphone rather than on desktop personal computers; and in Japan, which recovered from World War II by embracing quality control manufacturing in the 1960s and 1970s. One of the most cited examples of leapfrogging is the Safaricom M-Pesa mobile payment system in Kenya and Tanzania launched by Vodafone in 2007, which enabled phone-based banking in the national currency, abandoning traditional banking methods to create a mobile banking revolution. It is now used by over 17 million Kenyans with approximately 25 percent of the country's gross national product flowing through it (Berman, 2018). M-Pesa has boosted economic development by enabling relatively poor farmers to send and receive payments reliably and affordably, fostering economic growth by lowering transaction costs. Research by the Bill & Melinda Gates Foundation has found that mobile money services such as these have lifted 194,000 Kenyans out of poverty (Gupta & Knight, 2017). If M-Pesa could lift thousands of people out of poverty, one can only imagine what a full-scale blockchain transformation could do. The extensive use of mobile-based services, particularly in Africa and Asia, certainly provides an opportunity for a blockchain-based system to extend its service provision, given that mobile penetration in low-income countries is extremely high, at 83 percent among the 16-to-65 age bracket (IFR, 2017).

There are five characteristics of emerging economies that will foreseeably spur rapid innovation and enable leapfrogging:

1. The size and scale of the market
2. The demographic profile, often presenting with a large youth bulge
3. Increasing mobile technology penetration
4. The urgency of wicked problems[1]
5. The ability of their governments to be agile and proactive in the digital space

Size and scale of the market; In 2017, China and India had around 660 million and 400 million smartphone users, respectively. This compared with only 220 million in the US (Currie, 2018).

Demographic profile with large youth bulge; 89.7 percent of people under 30 live in emerging and developing economies, particularly in the Middle East and Africa (UNESCO, 2013; PWC, 2018). Further, the young are increasingly wealthy and tech-savvy, with access to low-cost mobile devices and some of the best network coverage in the world (Currie, 2018).

Mobile technology penetration; The global mobile industry connected over 5 billion people in 2017 (GSMA, 2018). GSMA predicting the number of unique mobile subscribers will reach 5.9 billion by 2025, equivalent to 71 percent of the world's population. Growth will be driven by developing countries, particularly India, China, Pakistan, Indonesia and Bangladesh, as well as Sub-Saharan Africa and Latin America. Kenya has joined three other African countries, Tunisia, Namibia, and Morocco, as the fourth country to cross the 100 percent market in mobile penetration in Africa (CryptoDavid, 2018).

Pressing and urgent problems to solve; Put simply, emerging markets have big problems to solve and this stimulates innovation. (In forthcoming chapters, the nature of these 'big problems' will be covered in greater depth). The GE Global Innovation Barometer (2018) report shows strong innovation momentum in emerging markets, with emerging markets making a virtue out of financial, geographical and other constraints, able to target the inefficiencies of existing business models to deliver greater value. Examples of such start-ups include: BitPesa (Kenya), Bitso (Mexico), Remit.ug (Uganda), Satoshi Tango (Argentina), BitSpark (Hong Kong), OkCoin (China), OkLink/Coinsensure (India), CoiNnect (Mexico/Argentina), Rebit and Coin.ph (Philippines) (International Finance Corporation, 2017).

Small States have traditionally been disadvantaged by geography and knowledge and human resources. Technology can help them overcome some of these barriers. For example, in a Philippines case-study of financial inclusion, the Union Bank has partnered with ConsenSys to develop Ethereum-based banking solutions for the country's rural sector. In the Philippines 77 percent of people remain unbanked, according to a survey conducted by the country's central bank Bangko Sentral ng Pilipinas. Justo Ortiz, the chairman of UnionBank, said that Ethereum's blockchain technology would help them "crack the hole of financial inclusivity". In fragile states, cryptocurrencies are helping resolve issues with hyperinflation. Bitcoin represents an alternative to the banking system for residents of economies such as Venezuela which, in November 2016, had the highest inflation in the world and in the country's history, reaching 833,997 percent (Babayan, 2018).

Governments are agile and proactive in the digital space; the current world-leaders in Blockchain adoption are Estonia and Dubai; the Dubai Blockchain Strategy envisions moving all government documents — more than 100 million documents per year — onto a blockchain by 2020, creating a new platform for innovation (see Chapter 3 for further information).

Start-ups have also begun creating Blockchain-enabled, green-energy electricity solutions that can illuminate households across Africa. An auditable encrypted ledger can record energy consumption, credit histories (to access financing), and facilitate energy trading between households; ensuring consumers have more control of their energy requirements and consumption. In 2017, a non-profit, Energy Web Foundation (EWF), started developing an open source, scalable Blockchain platform to create a market standard for the energy industry to build upon and run their own Blockchain-based solutions. EWF's first use case, EW Origin, creates a marketplace where all smart meters on solar PV can communicate. It also records the provenance of renewable electricity generated, with clear details of source type, time, location and CO_2 emissions. This provides a universal dashboard tracking the energy consumption of the world (Nsikak, 2018). In October 2018 a South African fintech firm partnered with the government of Uganda to develop a Blockchain-based gigawatt-scale clean energy economy to improve the power supply of the country significantly (Emmanuel, 2018).

South Korea also has a plan for developing a voting technology based on Blockchain. Government officials believe a blockchain voting system will increase both security and transparency, thereby improving people's trust in digital voting. The National Election Commission (NEC) initially ran an online voting system dubbed "K-voting" in 2013, but, despite 5.64 million users, trust remained low due to fraud and hacking concerns. Developed by the NEC and South Korea's Ministry of Science and ICT, the distributed ledger system is based on IBM's Hyperledger Fabric and will be used to authenticate voters and save voting results in real time to be ready by the end of 2019 (Marinoff, 2018).

SECTORS INNOVATING IN EMERGING MARKETS

Financial Inclusion and Remittances

The most common use cases for Blockchain initiatives are payments and money transfers (25%) and records and verification (26%). Blockchain's most popular primary benefits are being able to reduce risk and fraud (38%) and increase efficiency (24%) (Stanford Graduate School of Business, 2018). Using Blockchains to secure the end-to-end transaction process is crucial for building trade in developing countries, modernizing bureaucracy and building trust in systems-integrity.

In the financial services sector Blockchain initiatives fall into two categories. The first is process efficiency, which occurs in countries with established financial market leaders (typical in OECD countries). Blockchain projects here use enterprise Blockchains within their own organizations or by consortia such as R3, Hyperledger, and Digital Asset Holdings. The second category is new market creation, whereby new market players target the inefficiencies of existing business models to deliver value in emerging markets, for example in global payments, remittances or digital wallets (IFC,

Figure 2. Enabling Shifts Required – Economics and Sovereign Identity

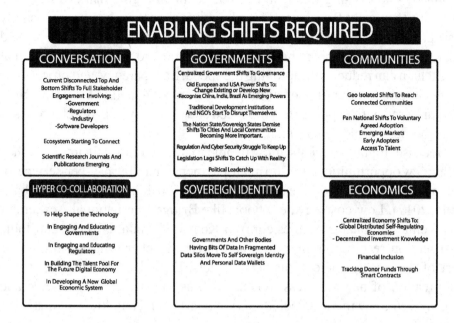

2017). This is represented in the B4SC Model Enabling Shifts Required by the Economics and Sovereign Identity Blocks.

To overcome the preference for traditional cash-based transacting while supporting rapid growth, it is especially important for economic structures in emerging markets to easily integrate with local culture. Large financial solutions-based institutions that are common in mature markets are incongruous and therefore, potentially, ineffective. Small, sometimes home-grown, collectives gather social traction due to better-trusted systems of operation. For example, CrowdForce Solution (token.crowdforce.io) is an African-based start-up using Ethereum to incentivize trusted local and community retailers to act as banks and offer financial services. They offer utility payments, cash deposit and withdrawal accounts, buying and selling of cryptocurrency, and crypto-fiat exchanges on a PayForceMobileApp. This means there is no need for a banking structure - the only start-up capital required is for agent retailers to fund their wallet, with agents earning commission on transactions (Down, 2018).

Shallow banking infrastructure is an advantage for accelerating the adoption of Blockchain in emerging economies. Not only does the lack of financial infrastructure mean reduced social and institutional resistance and lower transition costs for moving from a legacy to a new system; it also means regulators and existing financial institutions in emerging markets have less incentive to prevent Blockchain-based providers, as they do not significantly disrupt existing market conditions (IFC, 2017). International payments and trade finance front-runners have high transaction and verification costs that blockchain can reduce by improving the speed, transparency, and process. As a case-in-point at the time of writing, there are signals that Western Union has partnered with Ripple to test the speed and economy of Blockchain-based cross-border payments (Berman, 2018).

Because digital payments allow people to transact in small amounts, they create new opportunities based on micropayments enabling pay-per-service, or pay-as-you-go, models. For example, AliPay, a subsidiary of China's Alibaba (IFR, 2017). Low-cost private schools like Bridge International Academies (bridgeinternationalacademies.com) in Kenya, Uganda, Nigeria, and India also rely on receiving school fees and paying teacher salaries digitally as part of their cost-efficient business models. Digital payments also enable the creation of new business models such as the rise of e-commerce and sharing-economy models, including ride-sharing and employment matching (Osafo-Kwaako, 2018).

New market creation tends to flourish well in environments of high volatility, where there might be some political or currency instability. In the case of CrowdForce, by operating outside of the regulated banking sector, they are able to leverage the opportunities that political instability provides while ensuring that their economic activity is protected from the effects of rapid political change that can often threaten investment in emerging markets (Down, 2018).

Emerging markets have large population segments that are underserved by traditional financial services, often due to the cost of acquiring these customers. These are known as the 'unbanked'. If Blockchain can provide a scalable proof of concept for a viable mobile banking business model, it could advance financial inclusion by serving previously unprofitable customers and small and medium-sized companies, generating $380 billion in additional revenues (IFR, 2017). Digital finance has the potential to reach over 1.6 billion new retail customers in emerging economies and to increase the volume of loans extended to individuals and businesses by $2.1 trillion. The providers of these products (agents in CrowdForce's terms) stand to gain by having access to potential new revenue streams, and to increase their balance sheets by as much as $4.2 trillion, in aggregate (Osafo-Kwaako, et al, 2018). By building digital finance capabilities, companies will gain the opportunity to develop new business models ranging across new forms of more data-based financial services, micropayments, and entirely new digital businesses. Existing financial services providers also stand to reduce the direct costs of their current businesses by $400 billion annually. Atlas is one such start-up with teams in Ghana and Senegal providing a mobile peer-to-peer application to give to communities in the developing world access to savings and credit through a decentralized solution that lets "the unbanked bank with each other" (Costa, 2016). The app creates a network of people from local communities which cultivates trust while building financial inclusion. In addition, access to capital through savings accounts and loans are offered through the Atlas platform. The Blockchain shows proof of origin for the money and all transactions, ensuring users know exactly where their money is and the latest transactions on their account (Atlas, 2018).

Indeed, lending is a good use case for Blockchain applications since identity verification is crucial, in that, if a person's financial or personal history can be verified, and they have a viable business that needs to be financed, much of the traditional process of securing finance can be eliminated (Wharton, 2018). For mobile finance, the merit of the cause and the scale of the opportunity is clearly understood; However, there are a myriad of unknown factors, and few examples of firms that have achieved scale (Osafo-Kwaako, et al, 2018). Research by McKinsey (2018, c.f Osafo-Kwaako, et al, 2018) indicates that the success of mobile money providers in emerging markets is predicated on preparation for the long-term, adopting new methods of collaborative working - including with regulators - and investing to support scale until the benefits of network effects begin to show (Osafo-Kwaako, et al, 2018).

Kenya's Capital Markets Authority has also proposed the creation of a special unit along with the Central Bank of Kenya, to monitor and facilitate a path for the adoption of digital currencies (Pande & Medikepura Anil, 2019).

Asset Management

India is a front-runner among emerging economies in embracing the Blockchain. The Indian government's policy think tank, the National Institution for Transforming India, has signed a Memorandum of Understanding with the Andhra Pradesh state government for an array of uses, including in land titling, supply chains, health records and Blockchain education.

A ConsenSys Blockchain project in managing land ownership records in Chandigarh city allows for the tracking of all state-level financial services on one platform and prevents corruption once records are entered. In supply chains, Mumbai and Visakhapatnam ports use the Blockchain to create tamper-proof methods for tracking shipments and shippers. The identities of those parties are verified through the government's Know-Your-Customer (KYC) program that was launched a few years ago to combat fictitious accounts and money-laundering. The Mumbai Port Trust has projected savings of $18.2 billion over two years from using blockchain technology in supply chains (Wharton, 2018).

India's north-eastern states of Assam and Sikkim are using the technology to help their tribal people secure ownership titles to lands that the government had promised them at the time of India's Independence in 1947. Land registry case studies are examined further in Chapter Six of this volume.

Supply Chain

To feed their rapidly growing populations, emerging markets have fuelled global growth in agriculture, with estimated markets valued at $2.4 trillion in emerging markets compared to $515 billion in developed economies and contributing 11% to GDP versus only 2% in developed economies. This growth is in no small part due to smallholder farmers, who represent up to 80% of the food supply in Sub-Saharan Africa and Asia. Yet, agriculture is a resource-intensive sector – it accounts for 70% of global freshwater use, 38% of global land area and 14% of total greenhouse gas emissions (Haveson, Lau & Wong, 2017).

Kenya's economy is particularly dependent on agriculture, with it representing one third of national GDP. Of Kenyan farmers, 75% are smallholder subsistence farmers who are highly vulnerable to natural disasters. However, the agricultural insurance market is small, with less than 1% of Kenyan farmers covered by some form of crop insurance. Consumer awareness of modern digital and financial tools is also relatively low – 42% of Kenyans own an account with a formal financial institution while only 26% of the population reporting smartphone ownership (Haveson, Lau & Wong, 2017).

In India, IBM-led artificial intelligence and Blockchain projects are helping improve crop yield for agricultural companies and helping others transition to the unified goods and services tax (GST) system launched in 2017. IBM's Research Lab has completed three pilot projects with Indian companies with use cases including pest and disease prediction, improving yield, and yield prediction on India-specific crops such as potato and sugarcane (Wharton, 2018).

With concerns around climate change and global economic uncertainty rising, there is an increasing need for platforms capable of protecting farmers from volatility while also protecting the environment. Similarly, there are social concerns and trends for which Blockchain technology can offer resolutions in agriculture: 1) supply chain traceability, 2) smart contracts and crop insurance, and 3) micro-financing and bitcoin payments (Haveson, Lau & Wong, 2017). Blockchains' functionality offers consumers reassurance and information regarding the source of their food, coffee and wine, addressing many of the scandals that have beset the food industry in recent times. TraceRegister, ThisFish, and m-Fish are applications that capture and convert physical components into data on the supply chain, from the first to the last-mile (final delivery to consumer). However, each relies on a centralized entity for accountability; Blockchain technology provides the secure and transparent model for traceability. Provenance.org,[2] conducted a pilot study in 2016 using Blockchain, to track tuna from catch to consumer. Their pilot enabled Indonesian fishermen to codify physical assets to a digital identity that can be verified on an open registry. Consequently, suppliers and consumers can access an open suite of proofs that certify a product's quality standards all along the value chain (Haveson, Lau & Wong, 2017). Provenance, a UK-based business, came about because "of a personal frustration for how little we know about the things we buy" (Provenance.org, 2018). In December 2016, Everledger[3] (London) applied similar provenance-tracking technology to wine bottles to combat fraudulent sales.

Smart contracts will also create major improvements in the insurance claims-processing system. Traditionally, the agricultural industry has been slow to adapt with technologies and innovation, so farmers and insurance providers have been using inefficient claims-processing systems built on legacy technologies. Smart contracts will mean that in the event of a natural disaster, weather data could be proactively used to trigger conditions and rules to begin the issuance of capital for claims, and the operational volatility of an agricultural business (inherent because of unpredictable weather) is greatly reduced. Internet of Things (IoT) devices can be used to ensure farmers are buying the correct crop insurance (Wharton, 2018) and embedded within major equipment possessions to feed data back to smart contracts in the event of disaster for verification purposes. SmartCrop, for example, is an Android-based mobile platform leveraging smart contracts and intelligent weather prediction to help farmers hedge against crop volatility. Using weather APIs, SmartCrop provides farmers with the option to initiate crop insurance payouts before natural disasters strike (Haveson, Lau & Wong, 2017).

Health and Education

The health sector has attracted more Blockchain-based start-up initiatives than any other sector. Of catalogued Blockchain initiatives, 25% were focused on health, which is nearly twice as much as the next leading sector, financial inclusion (13%). Energy, Climate, and Environment (12%) and Philanthropy, Aid, and Donors (11%) were the next highest (Stanford Graduate School of Business, 2018).

Autonomous vehicles, such as drones, are actively being used to deliver critical time-sensitive medication between medical camps in Africa (Pande & Medikepura Anil, 2019). Modum.io is a Zurich-based start-up that combines hardware sensors with blockchain technology to track temperatures of medicinal products across the supply chain. Modum.io has completed three pilot projects, and its first-generation sensors are now in mass production, being deployed as part of several new pilots with primarily European-based companies (Stanford Graduate School of Business, 2018).

Prescrypto[4] (prescrypto.com) will provide a digital solution to the lack of electronic prescriptions in developing countries, with a platform that allows medical services providers to view one common history of a patient, and improve the level of care (Unicef, 2018). Statwig[5] (statwig.com) will use blockchain solutions to ensure the efficient delivery of vaccines through an enhanced supply-chain management system.

The Kenyan government is now partnering with IBM to develop a Blockchain solution to counter academic credential fraud. Kenya overall under-indexes as the 92nd most business-friendly country but ranks number 3 for Ease of Getting Electricity and number 8 for Ease of Enforcing Contracts. These conditions suggest that the resource-intensive computational needs of permission-less Blockchains, upon which smart contracts could sit, would be more viable in a low-cost energy environment. Kenya's favorable attitude towards rule of law would also be conducive to supporting smart contract-based programs (Haveson, Lau, Wong, 2017).

CONCLUSION

Emerging markets have become global leaders in the innovative use of technology (Sehgal 2018), transitioning from low value-added services-based economies to strong research and development–driven ecosystems. Decades of private sector innovation and government investment have seen the rise of AI in China, healthcare solutions in Switzerland and drone deliveries in Israel (Pande & Medikepura Anil, 2019). Indeed, in the first India-Russia Strategic Economic Dialogue in November 2018, agreements were made by both countries to invest $30 billion by 2025 into AI and Blockchains for; transport infrastructure, agriculture and agro-processing, small and medium business support, digital transformation and industrial and trade cooperation (Chaudhury, 2018; PTI, 2018).

However, due to public Blockchains' drastic effect on market structure, regulation needs to be addressed in parallel with the discussion of emerging technologies (discussed more fully in Chapters 2 and 10), large-scale digital finance promotes financial inclusion and boosts GDP and in emerging economies financial regulators have the power to ensure economic stability while supporting national policy objectives. Tariff caps, regulation on agent selection and fire-walling of financial and information technology (IT) systems can discourage growth, hamper profitability and prevent organizational viability, critical considerations for emerging economies.

In the next chapter we will discuss the use of Blockchains in cities and their implementation at national scale.

REFERENCES

Adams, C. (2018). *Estonia, a Blockchain model for other countries?* Retrieved from https://www.investinblockchain.com/estonia-blockchain-model/

Atlas. (2018). *About.* Retrieved from https://atlas.money/about

Babayan, D. (2018). *Ethereum adoption in developing countries rising exponentially.* Retrieved from https://www.newsbtc.com/2018/12/02/ethereum-adoption-in-developing-countries-rising-exponentially-lubin/

Berman, A. (2018). *Western Union considers crypto, Partners with Ripple to test Blockchain payments.* Retrieved from https://cointelegraph.com/news/western-union-considers-crypto-partners-with-ripple-to-test-blockchain-payments

Brown, R. (2017). *Digital payments expected to hit 726 billion by 2020 — but cash isn't going anywhere yet.* Retrieved from https://www.cnbc.com/2017/10/09/digital-payments-expected-to-hit-726-billion-by-2020-study-finds.html

Campbell, R. (2017). *How Blockchain technology is helping to clean the River Niger.* Retrieved from https://bitcoinmagazine.com/articles/how-blockchain-technology-helping-clean-niger-river/

Chaudhury, D. R. (2018). *India and Russia to explore new areas of partnership.* Retrieved from https://economictimes.indiatimes.com/news/politics-and-nation/india-and-russia-to-explore-new-areas-of-partnership/articleshow/66780589.cms

Costa, M. (2016). *Economies shared.* Retrieved from https://medium.com/atlas-together/economies-shared-4e14a6e93d0f

Cromley, K. (2019). *Malta to use Blockchain for storing education certificates.* Retrieved from https://www.cointrust.com/market-news/malta-to-use-blockchain-for-storing-education-certificates

CrowdForce. (2018). *Global decentralised network of micro-businesses.* Author.

CryptoDavid. (2018). Mobile phone penetration in Kenya now stands at 100.1. Retrieved from https://bitcoinke.io/2018/12/mobile-phone-penetration-in-kenya-stands-at-100-1-percent/

Currie, M. (2018). Why emerging markets lead the disruption race. Retrieved from https://www.martincurrie.com/corporate/em-disruption/why-em-lead-the-disruption-race

Down, M. (2018). *How blockchain technology can serve emerging market economies.* Hacker.

Edelman Intelligence. (2018). *GE Global Innovation Barometer, 2018; Summary Report.* Retrieved from https://s3.amazonaws.com/dsg.files.app.content.prod/gereports/wp-content/uploads/2018/02/12141008/GE_Global_Innovation_Barometer_2018-Summary_Report.p

Emmanuel, O. O. (2018). *Blockchain Technology Can Solve Africa's Energy Problems.* Retrieved from https://btcmanager.com/blockchain-technology-can-solve-africas-energy-problems/

GE. (2018). *Global Innovation Barometer.* Retrieved from https://www.genewsroom.com/press-releases/2018-ge-global-innovation-barometer-reveals-growing-confidence-business-leaders

Gilbert and Tobin. (2018). *Open Banking Regimes Across the World.* Retrieved from https://www.gtlaw.com.au/insights/open-banking-regimes-across-globe

Green, A. (2018). *Bringing Opportunities to the Emerging Market with Blockchain and Crypto.* Retrieved from https://medium.com/@AnaGreen/ bringing-opportunities-to-the-emerging-markets-with-blockchain-and-crypto-8ee270bc6915

GSMA. (2018). *The Mobile Economy.* Retrieved from https://www.gsma. com/mobileeconomy/wp-content/uploads/2018/02/The-Mobile-Economy-Global-2018.pdf

Gupta, V., & Knight, R. (2017). How blockchain could help emerging markets leap ahead. *Harvard Business Review.* Retrieved from https://hbr.org/2017/05/ how-blockchain-could-help-emerging-markets-leap-ahead

Haveson, S., Lau, A., & Wong, V. (2017). *Protecting Farmers in Emerging Markets with Blockchain.* Retrieved from https://www.johnson.cornell.edu/ Portals/32/EMI%20Docu/Fellows/Blockchain%20Article.v2.pdf

International Finance Corporation. (2017). *Blockchain in Development – Part II: How it can impact emerging markets.* Author.

Marinoff, N. (2018). *South Korea is trialing (sic) Blockchain voting – here's what that means.* Retrieved from https://bitcoinmagazine.com/articles/south-korea-trialing-blockchain-voting-heres-what-means/

Musarura, S. (2018). *The Paradigm Shift: The Future Role of Technology Emerging Markets.* Retrieved from https://by.dialexa.com/the-paradigm-shift-the-future-role-of-emerging-markets-in-technology

Niforos, M. (2017). *Blockchain in Development – Part II: How it Can Impact Emerging Markets.* Retrieved from https://www.ifc.org/wps/wcm/connect/ f12309c5-e625-4ee8-bbd2-0da596419070/EMCompass+Note+41+Blockc hain+in+EM+Part+II.pdf?MOD=AJPERES

Nsikak, J. (2018). *Blockchain can revolutionise the energy industry in Africa.* Retrieved from https://www.weforum.org/agenda/2018/11/blockchain-will-change-the-face-of-renewable-energy-in-africa-here-s-how/

Osafo-Kwaako, P., Singer, M., White, O., & Zouaoui, Y. (2018). *Mobile money in emerging markets; The case for financial inclusion.* Retrieved from https://www.mckinsey.com/industries/financial-services/our-insights/mobile-money-in-emerging-markets-the-business-case-for-financial-inclusion

Pande, S., & Medikepura, A. (2018). *South Asia can become an innovation hub. Here's how.* Retrieved from https://www.weforum.org/agenda/2018/11/here-s-how-south-asia-can-harness-the-power-of-emerging-technologies/

Provenance.org. (2018). *About.* Retrieved from https://www.provenance.org/about

PTI. (2018). *India, Russia to increase cooperation in Artificial Intelligence, Blockchain system.* Retrieved from https://timesofindia.indiatimes.com/india/india-russia-to-increase-cooperation-in-artificial-intelligence-blockchain-system/articleshow/66830031.cms

PWC. (2018). *Emerging markets; Driving the payments transformation.* Retrieved from https://www.pwc.com/gx/en/industries/financial-services/publications/emerging-markets-driving-payments.html

Reuters. (2018). *Cash is far from dead and use is rising.* Retrieved from https://www.reuters.com/article/us-bis-report-cash/cash-is-far-from-dead-and-use-is-rising-bis-idUSKCN1GN0PS

Sehgal, C. (2018). *Today's emerging markets embrace technological innovation.* Retrieved from http://emergingmarkets.blog.franklintempleton.com/2018/03/22/11244/

Smart Dubai. (2018). *Blockchain.* Retrieved from https://smartdubai.ae/initiatives/blockchain

Stanford Graduate School of Business. (2018). *Blockchain for Social Impact; Moving beyond the hype.* Retrieved from https://www.gsb.stanford.edu/sites/gsb/files/publication-pdf/study-blockchain-impact-moving-beyond-hype.pdf

Sustainability International. (2017). *Using the Blockchain to Clean up the Niger Delta.* Retrieved from https://www.sustainability-international.org/using-the-blockchain-to-clean-up-the-niger-delta/

UNESCO. (2013). *Statistics on youth.* Retrieved from http://www.unesco.org/new/en/unesco/events/prizes-and-celebrations/celebrations/international-days/world-radio-day-2013/statistics-on-youth/

UNICEF. (2018). *UNICEF's Innovation Fund announces first cohort of blockchain investments in emerging markets.* Retrieved from https://www.unicef.org/press-releases/unicefs-innovation-fund-announces-first-cohort-blockchain-investments-emerging

Wharton. (2018). *How the Blockchain brings social benefits to emerging economies.* Retrieved from http://knowledge.wharton.upenn.edu/article/ blockchain-brings-social-benefits-emerging-economies/

KEY TERMS AND DEFINITIONS

Decentralised Application (dApp): An application that runs on a decentralised network and uses its resources.

Emerging Market: An economy in a newly industrialized country that has not yet fully matured but is outpacing their developing market counterparts.

Leapfrog: To take advantage of the absence of developed products, services and infrastructure to establish an advanced method of service delivery over existing market offerings.

ENDNOTES

[1] A wicked problem is recognised as a problem that is almost impossible to solve due to complex environments, incomplete information and confounding factors.

[2] https://www.provenance.org/

[3] https://www.everledger.io/

[4] https://www.prescrypto.com/

[5] https://statwig.com/

Chapter 5
Transforming Cities

ABSTRACT

Chapter 5 explores the use of distributed ledger technologies in cities to help improve citizen-centric services: land registries, health care, welfare payments, identity, supply chains, and voting. McKinsey analysts predict that by 2020 the number of smart cities will reach 600 worldwide, and 5 years later almost 60% of the world's GDP will be produced in them. Digital technologies could become an engine of economic progress, and Blockchain could be one of those technologies. This connectivity, however, comes at a cost. How will cybersecurity evolve with Web 3.0 and 4.0 technologies to protect cities from cyber-attacks? This chapter introduces how Blockchains may be used to resolve a range of city-based challenges arising from broader global concerns like national population increases, urban density, anthropomorphic climate change, urban pollution and mobility, local and national citizen services, and infrastructure.

INTRODUCTION

Land consumption and mass urbanisation are concerns world-over (UN, 2016). One in eight people on earth live in slums. By 2050, over 2 billion people will reside in informal settlements without adequate resources to maintain a healthy life. Africa hosts approximately 56% of the globe's slum dwellers, Asia follows with 28%. The number of expanding slums has contributed to a major drive under the UN Habitat Agenda 2030; to provide water, sanitation, secure open spaces, security of tenure and durability of housing structures (UN, 2016).

DOI: 10.4018/978-1-5225-9578-6.ch005

The livability crisis is not contained to the poor, however. The UN approximates that by 2030, over 700 cities will have populations of over 1 million people (UN, 2018a), A further 2.6 billion people are expected to move to cities by 2050 (UN, 2018a). Megacities, like Tokyo, New Delhi, Shanghai, Mexico City and Sao Paulo have still yet more to grow (UN, 2018a). With climate change urgently changing global conditions for everyone, sustainable planning has never been more in demand (IOFM, 2017), yet, notwithstanding the influx, cities appear to be the least prepared for the challenges that urban conglomerations will face in the next two decades (IPCC, 2018).

Governing globally connected cities requires balancing the various demands of soaring levels of poverty, food shortage, corruption, crime, pollution and ill-health including the growing mental stress citizens are under. In progressive countries such as Dubai and China, automated systems and infrastructure sensors using big data and IoT to optimising the efficiency of urban processes and services and connect to residents. In smart cities, Blockchains are being used for more than payment services, but for managing whole cities or encouraging citizens' behaviour change (Social Coin, 2019) - these are the cities of the future (Magas, 2018).

NATIONAL IMPLEMENTATION

Many countries are integrating Blockchains into city services for: increased efficiency, effectiveness and motivating beneficial behavioural change for socioenvironmental benefits. The city transformations detailed below lead the way towards the 'connect with real understanding of how and what' shift, represented by the Government and Conversations blocks in the Enabling Shifts Required section of the B4SC Model.

Dubai

In Dubai unmanned trains, automated sensors, flying taxis, solar panels, and wi-fi benches form part of the Dubai Blockchain Strategy's plans for a 2020 smart metropolis (Magas, 2018). As the authors have discussed in Chapter 3, Dubai plans to be the first country in the world fully operated on the Blockchain (Smart Dubai 2021, n.d). The Smart City program, launched in 2014, involves the phased implementation of more than 545 projects that

Figure 1. Enabling Shifts Required; Governments and Conversation

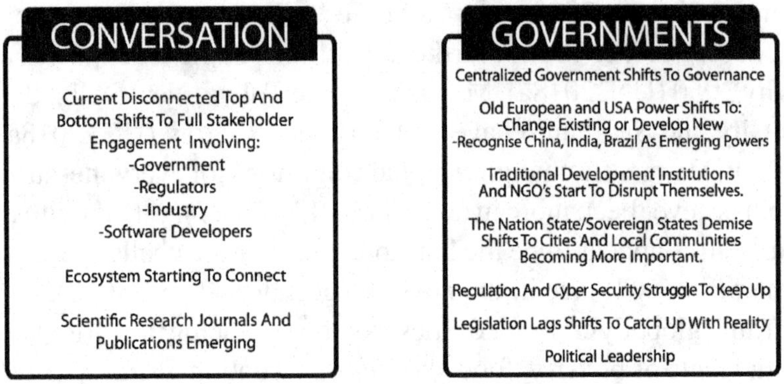

CONVERSATION

Current Disconnected Top And
Bottom Shifts To Full Stakeholder
Engagement Involving:
-Government
-Regulators
-Industry
-Software Developers

Ecosystem Starting To Connect

Scientific Research Journals And
Publications Emerging

GOVERNMENTS

Centralized Government Shifts To Governance

Old European and USA Power Shifts To:
-Change Existing or Develop New
-Recognise China, India, Brazil As Emerging Powers

Traditional Development Institutions
And NGO's Start To Disrupt Themselves.

The Nation State/Sovereign States Demise
Shifts To Cities And Local Communities
Becoming More Important.

Regulation And Cyber Security Struggle To Keep Up

Legislation Lags Shifts To Catch Up With Reality

Political Leadership

will change the way residents and visitors of Dubai interact with the city, with approximately 185 proposed projects in the transport sector holding an estimated value of USD $32bn. These include rail ventures, marine plans, and aviation projects. The implementation of a Blockchain system into the urban structure is projected to save about $1.5 billion and 25.1 million man-hours due to increased efficiency in the processing of documents, which is supposed to set government institutions free from queues. Blockchain will be also applied in logistics and storage. This will help create an entire system of smart unmanned trucks for the transport of products or materials.

China

In April 2017, the Wuzhen Think Tank released a white paper on the development of China's Blockchain industry, introducing global and domestic Blockchain-industry trends. Currently, Chinese authorities are actively studying Blockchain for more orderly data storage. On April 24, the National Audit Office of China discussed the use of the technology to solve problems inherent in centralized storage infrastructure. However, despite the green light given by the government, it is not yet known how soon the discussion of the project will go into the implementation phase.

Nevertheless, this is an official recognition of the beginning of a new digital era in China, which gave a big impetus to the development of Blockchain technology. And again, as in the case of Estonia, Blockchain has become a solution to the security problem of storing citizens' data. In 2014, one of Hong Kong's largest banks, Standard Chartered, lost nearly $200 million as a result of credit fraud. Standard Chartered responded by collaborating with a government agency in Singapore, utilized the Blockchain and developed a unique cryptographic hash for each invoice. Companies can now create an electronic ledger of invoices that uses a parallel platform to the Blockchain employed in Bitcoin transactions. This ensures that no double operations are carried out and banks do not lend money for fake invoices (Magas, 2018).

Alibaba Cloud & Waltonchain also signed a strategic cooperation agreement in 2018 for the use of Blockchain technology to develop smart cities. The results of the partnership are designed to address the problem of limited resources and services caused by the rapidly growing megapolis population of Xiong'an. Merging IoT, AI and Blockchain, the focus areas of this partnership of would be to establish new smart cities in Xiong'an and Yuhang while promoting the Waltonchain for commercial and municipal IoT coverage (Achal, 2018).

The United States

The state of Delaware was the first to announce the Delaware Blockchain Initiative in 2016. This comprehensive program was designed to stimulate the use and development of Blockchain technologies and smart contracts in both the private and public sectors of the state. It's worth noting that the authorities officially recognized electronic transactions recorded in Blockchains as verifiable data, and the bill was signed in order to legalize Blockchain transactions for accounting and other business records for local companies. However, the Carney administration introduced more caution than its predecessor and progress has slowed down of late (Tinianow & Long, 2017).

In the state of Illinois in 2017, the Illinois Blockchain Initiative was convened, which calls on the consortium of state agencies to cooperate in exploring innovations presented in distributed ledger technology.

The state of New York have a Microgrid project being developed specifically for households who want to buy and sell electricity produced by solar panels. Ethereum-based contracts enable on-demand electricity production and sharing. After many years of monopolies dominating the energy market, this kind of citizen-led, Blockchain-enabled energy-sharing system could completely rewrite how humans produce, buy and sell critical utilities.

The US doesn't stop there, however. NASA have just released plans for an air traffic management system on the Blockchain. Using a permissioned Blockchain for secure, anonymous communication (Zmudzinski, 2019).

URBAN CONCERNS

Mobility

Blockchain offers immense possibilities in improving urban transit (also known as mobility-as-a-service) and its attendant physical and digital manifestations. Such as mobility-related transactions and data collection and sharing — bringing siloed data under a single roof (say GPS records from a public bus as traffic ebbs and flows through high-volume corridors). This is due to Blockchain's unique ability to record transactions while establishing secure, nonproprietary identities without the reliance on a centralised intermediary.

Currently, multi-modal transportation requires commuters to pay for different tickets in different places. Take for example the individual who travels on suburban rail (one ticket) to the city, rides the subway downtown (a second ticket), then rents a bike for two hours. The integration of Blockchain technology could both solve, simplify, and potentially eliminate the requirement for multiple purchases and the consequent pain points for the user. Potentially, a transit coin or token could pay fares on public transport - or any kind of mobility service provider - and become a stored value, capable of being used across many different modes of travel. To that end, DOVU, a Jaguar-backed Blockchain startup, has developed a secure marketplace that will let users offset mobility costs in exchange for their transport data (Dovu, 2019). Powered by the Ethereum Blockchain, the DOVU platform empowers individuals to earn tokens for sharing their mobility data or performing rewardable activities defined by a DOVU partner - such as changing drivers' behaviour or undertaking valuable tasks. These tokens then feed back into the ecosystem through mobility related transactions, like offsetting the cost of a car, fuel, paying for a flight, or just riding the bus (Dovu, 2018).

Promoting and maintaining rural, regional and urban mobility is a core concern for cities. With the impact of autonomous vehicles and rising urban emission concerns, cities need to be proactive and responsive, designing for flexible use conditions. Ethereum Blockchain platforms have recently been used to simulate results to show that Blockchain-based distributed network architecture may be used to address autonomous cars in smart cities for sustainable ecosystems. For example, the German energy company RWE is the creation of an Ethereum-based network of charging stations for electric vehicles. Drivers will be able to control the charging process using a special application, and the Blockchain registry will be responsible for calculating the energy spent, making payments and identifying users (Magas, 2018). The app they're using is called <u>Share&Charge</u>. After firstly registering your car and transferring fiat to your wallet, you just find and choose a charging station with the costs transferred from your Share&Charge wallet to the owner of the charging station. To finalize the process, a receipt is automatically sent via e-mail (Trustnodes, 2017).

Greater coordination and collaboration across the different parties involved in the delivery of public services means greater efficiency and better-designed services. In addition to the purely administrative areas, Blockchain can also be very relevant to urban planning and the management of public space, sustainable transportation, public safety, the environment, the circular economy, smart buildings, and much more. One great example of which is Blockchain-based mobility systems. IoMob, a Blockchain-based mobility platform app, is trying to make urban mobility systems more efficient and more user-friendly by placing all transport options in one place for customers.

Similar to CityMapper, IoMob goes one step further by integrating all mobility sharing schemes, all taxi apps, and all public transport options in a city - such as Barcelona - into one single application.

This has several benefits. Not only will citizens be able access any mobility service in their city - whether public or private - and compare it, interoute it, and pay for it on one platform, saving time and money. Mobility companies will also benefit from the efficiencies and increased competition this brings. IoMob will mean that all mobility services - for example, rental scooters - are being used as much as possible within the city, meaning that mobility providers will be able to sell more journeys using fewer resources, making urban transportation not only more sustainable but more profitable. IoMob will also allow companies to make fair and secure agreements between one other through smart contracts, and, furthermore, the app should level the playing-field, allowing a greater diversity of companies to survive and thrive alongside each other.

Security

One of the most powerful attributes of Blockchain is the ability to record all activity on the network in tamper-proof logs. In increasingly connected city infrastructure, the use of Blockchains make it impossible for any potential attackers to hide or erase their attempts to access or misuse information within a secure city network. Further, the instant visibility offered by miners on the network means infected devices can be removed, and access to other devices disabled to prevent any escalation of a cyberattack.

With ever-growing population numbers, digital transformation is the only way to ensure that cities can keep up with the rising demand of residents. Infrastructure cannot be provisioned as quickly as technology progresses, thus there is a risk of cyberattacks unless smart city programs incorporate adequate security provisioning. Emerging technologies, models and methods offer city planners opportunities to secure smart cities in bold new ways, fortifying connected devices, critical infrastructure and complex networks with next-gen security systems. Alternatively, retrofitting software-defined security perimeters around critical infrastructure renders it invisible to prying eyes and helps promote smart city programs as viable solutions for growing urbanisation in a technology-dominated era.

However, the use of IoT to create interdependent and autonomous networks creates currently unfathomable risks for planners, impeding more advanced implementations of smart solutions. The denial of service (DoS) attack on US-based DNS provider Dyn in late 2016, with the Mirai botnet, demonstrated the risk the cyber-attacks on IoT devices. The attack, which brought down Twitter, the Guardian, Reddit, Netflix and CNN, to name but a few websites, was caused by infecting 100,000 connected devices from digital cameras to DVR players. In December 2015 a malware attack on a power grid in Western Ukraine caused a power outage to 200,000 consumers; the government blamed Russian cybercriminals for hacking into Ukraine's infrastructure (DCosta, 2019).

Gartner estimates that by 2020, the number of connected devices could reach 20.4 billion, from 8.4 billion in 2017 (c.f. DCosta, 2019). Smart cities and connected networks raise new security challenges that cannot be addressed by conventional cybersecurity approaches. They will need innovative next generation solutions to ensure that the smart cities of tomorrow are also safe and secure. Blockchains may well be part of that mix.

SMART CITIES

Cities count for more than half of the world's GDP (McKinsey, 2011) hosting more than 54% of the global population and with urban population growth forecasts of 1.5x (World Bank, 2019), cities are deeply concerned about service and infrastructure provision for expanding populations. The shift towards so-called *smart cities* is motivated by the enhanced performance of urban services like resources and transportation that integrated information technologies can provide. Simply put, a smart city, is a city using technology to improve liveability (Tormen, 2011).

Smart cities are the next and inevitable step in urbanization. As more people migrate to large cities in search of employment and a better standard of living, cities are becoming increasingly congested and difficult to manage. Digital transformation enables cities to grow towards generating better social, financial and environmental aspects of urban living, making smart cities more operationally efficient, cleaner and safer.

There are several key use cases for IoT devices across public utilities and public infrastructure in smart cities. For example, automatic lighting control capabilities permit the remote operation of lighting in public spaces; intelligent waste management systems track waste levels in bins and recommend the optimum routes for collection by waste collection trucks. Connected devices on public infrastructure can monitor water supply pipes and alert support staff in the event of a problem. Emergency services can also be triggered and monitored using IoT technology to improve response time and allocate resources efficiently. Sensors connected to devices can help maintain a healthy environment for residents by measuring levels of pollutants and recommending real-time remedial measures (DCosta, 2019).

Thus, smart cities require secure data management and integrated service provision. As a layer - or 'platform' - Blockchain can bring many different public service sectors together, integrating them horizontally into a single cross-cutting system. This is particularly useful for things like government records (laws, expenses, income, contracts, permits, properties, etc.) that are also needed for other areas of public service. With a Blockchain record, for example, these records are naturally interconnected. Interoperable service management systems are crucial to innovating urban ecosystems and services, allowing public services and resources to be both predictively monitored in real-time and for data to be gathered and shared in a way that produces better long-term, evidence-based strategy-making. This kind of system already exists in many smart cities – such as, a standardized platform currently promoted by the European Union, but this platform is based on cloud computing and thus is more vulnerable to cybersecurity threats than Blockchain.

For a truly integrated and collaborative approach to public service management, a secure, transparent system with a common language and rules, like Blockchain, will be needed in future. The benefit of Blockchain, for integrated service provision, is inherent in the shared service; with different service providers, agencies or integrated smart technology systems [street signals, sensors, the Internet of Things] putting their data on a shared Blockchain, it behoves as many agencies as possible to join, because all providers then have access to all the data on the chain. With the ability to share data easily, if residents are willing to surrender their data, the incentive is self-fulfilling: providers receive access to all the data on the chain because it's a public, viewable dataset and beneficiaries (i.e., the residents) gain access to improved, integrated services.

India

India was one of the first countries to release a smart city agenda. The second most populated country in the world, India launched their Smart Cities Mission in 2015 aiming to develop 100 smart cities in the country. While the Indian government has not precisely defined the term "smart city," key features are generally expected to include efficient transportation, energy-efficient buildings and robust digital connectivity, as well as adequate water and electricity supplies, sound governance and affordable housing. The program has the potential to impact around 100 million of the country's 1.25 billion citizens. According to a government statement in May 2018, 1,333 projects under the smart cities program, valued at a total of 506.26 billion rupees had either been completed or were in the implementation/tendering stage, including the development of roads, water, solar networks and public spaces (Sharma, 2018).

Generally speaking, the following areas are how governments typically act to make a city smarter:

- Resolving citizen identity management and citizen participation; counties and some countries are trialling Blockchains for voting purposes. An audit of the Sierra Leonean Presidential election was carried out on the Blockchain in 2018 (del Castillo, 2018) and the US state of West Virginia held their 2018 mid-term elections on a Blockchain platform called Voatz (Wood, 2018).
- Providing payment systems between people and organization; Chapter 6 describes how INGOs are implementing cash transfer systems in Syrian, Jordanian and Pakistan communities to improve financial inclusion.
- Improving employability and access to health care services; e-health services as seen in Estonia are described in Chapter 8.

- Considered public transportation, use of space and the environment; The Netherlands will be the first country to have an active bus line powered by Blockchain technology. The total of 12 buses, are equipped with VMC hardware terminals and VMC wallets, allowing them to receive *VAI* coins from VMC's first users is the first test phase of a bigger project whereby buses, bikes, trams and trains will be connected to the VMC Blockchain (VMC.AI, 2018).
- Energy use, land and waste management; as discussed in Chapter 3, the Swedish land-ownership authority has conducted a successful test between individuals to buy and sell properties through a specific Blockchain. They are now working on scaling this pilot to a national production (c.f. Tormen, 2019).
- Improving public efficiency; By 2021, the UAE plans all government transactions will be based on the Blockchain (Smart Dubai 2021, n.d).

Myanmar

The Myanmar government has partnered with Telenor to overcome laborious birth and death recordings by launching a civil registration system in which is integrated a platform updated by several authorized parties when birth and death of Myanmar's citizens occur. As part of their 2020 agenda, Telenor recommends Myanmar begin with establishing a digital ID for all eligible citizens which should be tied to digital finance services, as modelled by Estonia and planned in Dubai, Canada and Japan, to improve security and lower cost (Telenor, 2018).

BEHAVIOUR CHANGE

Blockchain also facilitates fractional ownership, allowing the tokenization of goods and information that have not previously ever been securitized. This means that urban citizens can own parts (or percentages) of urban infrastructure and initiatives, like local wind turbines, or even urban farms or cooperative food stores, and exchange their shares in these assets (or the outcomes of assets or processes, such as renewable energy) transparently and securely via Blockchain-based smart contracts and token systems. Thus, smart cities represent a win:win solution for residents and providers alike. Members already surrender their data to privately held companies like Lyft and Uber (as well as autonomous vehicle technology companies like Waymo) who are loathe to share the data they've collected; by participating in a Blockchain all parties can share information without compromising users' private information and a parallel token model would reward users financially.

For instance, Fab City launched a partnership with Streamr and Smart Citizen in 2018 to decentralize environmental data in cities. This pilot project, in London, allows citizens to acquire sensors for air-contamination, which they can then use to gather data on local air-quality. This project allows urban residents not only to witness firsthand the impact of air pollution on air quality (hopefully stimulating behavioural change) but also to monetize the data they collect. Through wi-fi citizens' data about air-contamination is transmitted to Streamr's Editor and Marketplace, where it is made available for subscription to whoever needs it most, from government agencies, to environmental bodies, to concerned local parents. By monetizing that data, Streamr hopes that other neighbouring communities will choose to invest in sensors too, in order to make a profit. This initiative promises great things: by the end of 2018, Streamr and Smart Citizen hope to have created a decentralized system, on a not-for-profit platform based on Blockchain, where families, researchers, and local authorities and politicians can subscribe to access the data, again sharing public information across all community stakeholders and ending authoritarian/ corporate monopolies over goods and information.

The fundamental limitations to scale Blockchain suffers becomes of more minor concern in the context of smart cities, for their function is often coupled with other technologies such as IoT or AI which enables scale better. Sensor networks including sensor grids, are widely used in the urban environment whereby any number of devices can be used to scale up or down as appropriate. Advances in AI and image recognition allows for a reduction in the price of increasing reliability of vehicle and pedestrian traffic-flow, queues, density, hyperlocal weather data and circumstantial street closures or work, narrowing or closing lanes. Blockchain solutions can also provide smart contracting for traffic regulations, or more direct measures such as redirections or prohibitive geo-fencing.

CITIZEN SERVICES

Blockchain-based public services have been extensively demonstrated by case studies in Estonia in this book. Estonian citizens have secure digital identities that enable them to access public services easily and securely. For example, the authority to log into the Healthcare Registry records using their digital identities and find out which medical professional has accessed the record and exactly when. If anyone (including government officials) has accessed their data without permission or good reason, this person can be prosecuted. This not only makes government more accountable, and increases citizens' trust in local and national authorities, but also eliminates public service inefficiencies. By having one Blockchain-based medical record system citizens no longer need to waste time explaining their medical history every time they see a new doctor; instead, the medical system is fully integrated, making public medical services more rapid, secure, accurate and efficient.

As cities begin to become more integrated through the blending of frontier technologies with Blockchain, the secure management of public records becomes increasingly more important for ensuring public faith in government integrity and preventing abuse of power. For example, between 1980-90 in Bogota, Colombia, the government confiscated valuable land from its population to give to American companies (Grajales, 2015) in an effort to provide better economic opportunities for itself. Colombian citizens were unable to prove land ownership or occupation of their homes resulting in widespread homelessness and poverty (Grajales, 2015). The Blockchain can address some of these issues through immutability of record-keeping and public auditability. Over 300 cities in Latin America, the Arab States and Africa have helped build a stock of information to expand city-related data (UN Habitat, 2018). The Global Land Tool Network (GLTN) has pioneered the documentation of land rights and certificates of residency for resettlement in over 600 households in the Luhonga community and for the first time in the Democratic Republic of Congo, recording land tenure has helped prepare citizens to show their land provenance (UN Habitat, 2018).

In countries where there are difficult, cumbersome, bureaucratic – and potentially corrupt - systems, Blockchains may introduce innovation effectively and efficiently (Nasulea and Stelian-Mihai 2018). Founded in 2016, OS City, a technology company that creates and curates software technology began to advise governments on building sustainable cities and stronger, innovative institutions. Using an open-source City Manager Platform based on AI, Blockchain and Cloud technologies, OS City helps governments innovate city planning. Its modular architecture allows public institutions to install the apps they need to fast-track their modernization. Currently serving multiple government agencies in Mexico, OS City have demonstrated a 24x increased citizen engagement, effective inter-agency collaboration, and increased trust and transparency. In partnership with Prince Consulting (Argentina), they have implemented multiple Blockchain pilots, including subsidies traceability and university diplomas in Argentina, tamper-proof energy pricings in Chile, improved mobility in Brazil, traceable social support for the *sierras* in Colombia, and alcohol selling permits in Mexico; increasing their presence to 5 major countries in the region (Jesus, Cepeda, CEO OSCity, email, February 2019).

OS City is pioneering AI and Blockchain implementations in the Latin American public sector, to enable the ecosystem to collectively build the capacity and technology to overcome legacy mindsets and speed adoption, building stronger, innovative cities that can face the challenges of unsustainable development, poverty, inequality, crime and corruption (Jesus, Cepeda, CEO OSCity, email, February 2019).

Seso, founded in 2017 (and a case study in Chapter 6), is using Blockchain for land registry use cases in Nigeria and Ghana, helping people collateralise their properties to access capital stored in land titles.

SERVICE PROVISION

Cities are increasingly energy intensive. In the United Arab Emirates (UAE), where temperatures frequently exceed 50°C, there are growing concerns energy demand may soon exceed supply causing frequent blackouts. Thus, the power industry has undergone a transformation over the past several years, with utilities embracing new technologies, new sources of generation, and relying on data to make their operations more efficient

In 2016, the Australian government announced a grant of $8 million for smart utility Blockchain projects. One of which is called Noghi, whereby users can pay their utility bills in bitcoin and the Tokyo Electric Power Company (TEPCO) has invested in UK-based Blockchain firm Electron. Using the Ethereum Blockchain, Electron demoed a platform simulating data from 53 million metering points at individual homes from 60 energy providers and proved that energy supplier switches could be executed up to 20 times faster than current switching rates. Its investment aside, TEPCO has previously established its intent to proactively collaborate with other major energy giants in joining the Energy Web Foundation. Among its partners in the Blockchain initiative is Singaporean counterpart Singapore Power which is looking at deploying Blockchain technology for a number of commercial applications including heating, ventilation and air conditioning, as well as batteries, solar cells and electric vehicles, all of which would be able to 'transact with each other' (Das, 2018).

Rising interest in renewable energy inputs is leading to interest in decentralized power grids and this is opening a real role for the Blockchain in the energy sector, at least in Europe. There is such potential, indeed, a new trend in partnering for faster scaling is discernible. Vattenfall AB, the largest Nordic utility, are considering using a Blockchain to handle both internal and external financial transactions "theoretically". The company, however, intends to trial a Blockchain app that permits customers to purchase and sell electricity independently of the utility. Finland's Fortum aims to enable consumers to control appliances over the internet in connected homes. Grid Singularity is a green distributed energy market, winning the 2018 World Economic Forum 'Technology Pioneer' award (Coin Telegraph, 2016).

The energy market takes time to change, however, not least because of the cost of updating legacy infrastructure. It may take years before Blockchain, which will interact with IoT, artificial intelligence and big data, will be integrated to manage urban services and public infrastructures.

However, many countries in the world have already embarked on the path of a digital economy and very soon we could see qualitative changes in social, economic and environmental aspects of life, without piles of papers, giant traffic jams, documentation errors and double transactions.

CONCLUSION

City management authorities may initially be reluctant to adopt Blockchain technology because for the fear it threatens their position as a centralised third party public intermediator. But, in truth, city governments will not be eliminated by Blockchain: rather, their role will simply change. Rather than public assets and resources being owned and controlled by public authorities and, increasingly, private-sector companies and investors, the increasing presence of Blockchain in cities should means that everybody - including citizens - can invest in their local community and its assets and have more influence over the strategic direction of their local area.

This chapter has described how all levels of government are, and might, respond to the increasing challenges complex environments provide for service provisioning. Currently most governments are only in the research and testing stage of Blockchains for city use but with 70 percent of the world's population expected to be living in cities by 2050 (UN, 2018) many countries have yet to further embark on the path of a digital economy and very soon we could see qualitative changes in social, economic and environmental aspects of life, without piles of papers, giant traffic jams, documentation errors and double transactions as interoperability issues between devices and platforms improves to connect homes, offices and systems.

In the following chapter the authors shift the focus on how Blockchains can be used to help the world's poorest and most vulnerable populations.

REFERENCES

Achal. (2018). *Waltonchain Alibaba cloud partners for smart city in China.* Retrieved from https://coingape.com/waltonchain-alibaba-cloud-partners-for-smart-city-china/

Centre for Cities. (2014). *Smart Cities.* Retrieved from https://www.centreforcities.org/reader/smart-cities/what-is-a-smart-city/1-smart-cities-definitions/

Das, S. (2018). *A decentralised future: Japan's biggest energy giant invests in Ethereum start-up.* Retrieved from https://www.ccn.com/decentralized-future-japans-biggest-energy-giant-invests-ethereum-Blockchain-startup

DCosta, F. (2019). *Making smart cities effective, cleaner and safer.* Retrieved from https://www.entrepreneur.com/article/330089

Del Castillo, M. (2018). *Sierra Leone secretly holds first Blockchain-audited Presidential vote.* Retrieved from https://www.coindesk.com/sierra-leone-secretly-holds-first-Blockchain-powered-presidential-vote

Dovu. (2018). *White paper.* Retrieved from https://dovu.io/index.html

Dovu. (2019). *Home.* Retrieved from https://dovu.io/index.html

Grajales, J. (2015). Land grabbing, legal contention and institutional change in Colombia. *The Journal of Peasant Studies*, *42*(3–4), 541–560. doi:10.1080/03066150.2014.992883

IOFM. (2017). *National labour migration management assessment.* Retrieved from www.iomethiopia.org/publications

IPCC. (2018) *Global warming of 1.5°C.* Retrieved from https://www.ipcc.ch/sr15/

Li, S. (2018) Application of Blockchain technology in smart city infrastructure. 2018 IEEE International Conference on Smart Internet of Things (SmartIoT).

Lopez, D., & Farooq, B. (2018). A Blockchain framework for smart mobility. *Proceedings of IEEE International Smart Cities Conference 2018.* doi:10.1109/SmartIoT.2018.00056

Magas, J. (2018). *Smart cities and Blockchain: Four countries where AI and DLT Exist hand in hand.* Retrieved from https://cointelegraph.com/news/smart-cities-and-Blockchain-four-countries-where-ai-and-dlt-exist-hand-in-hand

Makarevich, A. (2018). *Blockchain powered solutions in smart cities.* Retrieved from https://dzone.com/articles/Blockchain-powered-solutions-in-smart-cities-how-s

McKinsey. (2011). *Urban world; Mapping the economic power of cities.* Retrieved from https://www.mckinsey.com/~/media/McKinsey/Featured%20Insights/Urbanization/Urban%20world/MGI_urban_world_mapping_economic_power_of_cities_full_report.ashx

MedicalChain. (2019). *Home.* Retrieved from https://medicalchain.com/en/

Nam, K., Dutt, C. S., Chathoth, P., & Khan, M. S. (2019). Blockchain technology for smart city and smart tourism: Latest trends and challenges. *Asia Pacific Journal of Tourism Research*, 1–15. doi:10.1080/10941665.2019.1585376

Nasulea, C., & Stelian-Mihai, M. (2018). Using Blockchain as a platform for smart cities. *Journal of E-Technology*, 9(37). doi:10.6025/jet/2018/9/2/37-43

Reilly, E., Maloney, M., Siegel, M., & Falso, G. (2019). *A smart city IoT integrity-first communication protocol via an Ethereum Blockchain light client.* Retrieved from https://cams.mit.edu/wp-content/uploads/A-Smart-City-IoT-Integrity-First-Communication.pdf

Scekic, O., Nastic, S., & Dustdar, S. (2018). Blockchain-supported smart city platform for social value co-creation and exchange. *IEEE Internet Computing*, 23(1), 19–28. doi:10.1109/MIC.2018.2881518

Sharma, K. (2018). *Three years in, India's smart city program has a long way to go.* Retrieved from https://asia.nikkei.com/Spotlight/Cover-Story/Three-years-in-India-s-smart-city-program-has-a-long-way-to-go

Sharma, P. K., Moon, S. Y., & Park, J. H. (2017). Block-VN: A distributed Blockchain based vehicular network architecture in smart city. *Journal of Information Process Systems*, *13*(1), 184–195.

Sharma, P. K., & Park, J. H. (2018). Blockchain based hybrid network architecture for the smart city. *Future Generation Computer Systems*, *86*, 650–655. doi:10.1016/j.future.2018.04.060

Smart Dubai 2021. (n.d.). *Smart Dubai 2021.* Retrieved from https://2021.smartdubai.ae/

Social Coin. (2019). *How does it work?* Retrieved from https://thesocialcoin.com/how-does-social-coin-work/?lang=en

Tapas, N., Merlino, G., & Longo, F. (2018) Blockchain-based IoT-cloud authorization and delegation. *2018 IEEE International Conference on Smart Computing (SMARTCOMP)*, 411-416. 10.1109/SMARTCOMP.2018.00038

Telenor. (2018). *Realising digital Myanmar.* Retrieved from https://www.telenor.com/wp-content/uploads/2018/02/Telenor-Realising-Digital-Myanmar-Report-06-February.pdf

Tinianow, A., & Long, C. (2017). *Delaware Blockchain initiative: Transforming the foundational infrastructure of corporate finance.* Retrieved from https://corpgov.law.harvard.edu/2017/03/16/delaware-Blockchain-initiative-transforming-the-foundational-infrastructure-of-corporate-finance/

Tormen, R. (2018). *Make smarter cities with Blockchain; Outlook and use cases.* Retrieved from https://hackernoon.com/make-smarter-cities-with-Blockchain-outlook-and-use-cases-2ce9112a110b

Trustnodes. (2017). *Germany's energy giant launches 100s of Ethereum based electric cars charging stations.* Retrieved from https://www.trustnodes.com/2017/04/29/germanys-energy-giant-launches-100s-ethereum-based-electric-cars-charging-stations

UN. (2016). *Transforming our world: The 2030 agenda for sustainable development.* Retrieved from www.sustainabledevelopment.un.org

UN. (2018a). *World urbanisation prospects.* Retrieved from https://population. un.org/wup/

UN. (2018b). *The World's cities in 2018.* Retrieved from https://www.un.org/ en/events/citiesday/assets/pdf/the_worlds_cities_in_2018_data_booklet.pdf

UN Habitat. (2018) *Sustainable urban development and agenda 2030: UN Habitat's programme framework participatory slum upgrading programme transforming the lives of one billion slum dwellers.* Retrieved from www. unhabitat.org

UNHCR. (2018) *Donate.* Retrieved from https://donate.unhcr.org/gb/ syria/~my-donation?gclid=Cj0KCQiAvebhBRD5ARIsAIQUmnlDcf2H71 EYHxDYGtKHdohl8u2tXRrBazhX-fSyoMlxgxKZb-_iatwaAmiVEALw_ wcB&gclsrc=aw.ds

VMC.AI. (2018). *World's first Blockchain bus rides in the Netherlands.* Retrieved from https://medium.com/@VMCAI/worlds-first-Blockchain-bus-rides-in-the-netherlands-3c2b11654908

Wood, A. (2018). *West Virginia Secretary of State reports successful Blockchain voting in 2018 mid-term elections.* Retrieved from https://cointelegraph.com/ news/west-virginia-secretary-of-state-reports-successful-Blockchain-voting-in-2018-midterm-elections

World Bank. (2019). *Urban development.* Retrieved from https://www. mckinsey.com/~/media/McKinsey/Featured%20Insights/Urbanization/ Urban%20world/MGI_urban_world_mapping_economic_power_of_cities_ full_report.ashx

Zmudzinski, A. (2019). *NASA publishes proposal for air traffic management Blockchain based on Hyperledger.* Retrieved from https://cointelegraph.com/ news/nasa-publishes-proposal-for-air-traffic-management-Blockchain-based-on-hyperledger

KEY TERMS AND DEFINITIONS

Cyber-Attack: A malicious attempt to breach a computer network to steal or damage its contents.

Cybersecurity: The protection of electronic data from unauthorised or criminal activity.

IoT: The internet of things is the interconnection of computing devices embedded in everyday objects, communicating via the internet.

Chapter 6
Can Blockchain Really Help the Poor?
If So, Who Is Trying To?

ABSTRACT

It is the firm belief of the authors that Blockchain and other frontier technologies will be an important tool for social impact globally. It is now possible, with technology, to envision a world where everyone has an identity, where everyone can be connected to the economic system, where farmers get fair deals for their crops, and land registration is incorruptible. Advances in solar, battery, and digital commerce make it possible to imagine even the smallest village in Africa being able to produce and trade small amounts of energy. The Sustainable Development Goals (SDGs) were a visionary leap to a future state where the world can be a better place for humankind. However, they will not be achieved without harnessing the potential of technology. Nor will they be reached alone. In this chapter, the authors profile innovative case studies in Blockchain, which, if brought to scale, may realise the technology's potential. It is through this learning and experimentation that we will learn how to deploy this technology globally for social impact.

DOI: 10.4018/978-1-5225-9578-6.ch006

INTRODUCTION

One of the great criticisms – and frustrations - for social entrepreneurs, researchers and technologists alike, is the observation that Blockchain has so much potential but so few proven and scalable use cases.

Blockchain is an emergent technology, and many of the social impact projects only started in 2017 (Stanford Graduate School of Business, 2018), so there very few – if any - that are at scale. This means that a case study approach is the most suitable way of understanding how Blockchains can be used.

Through the authors' networks and knowledge, and by expert consultation, we have identified a selection of potential high-impact projects. Specific companies were invited to participate, by email and personal contact. A template tool was designed and presented to each organisation for completion. Data was received, analysed, presented, compared and mapped to the B4SC model identified in Chapter One.

Deployed at scale, there are infinite possibilities for Blockchain to ameliorate challenges faced by the poor and marginalised; providing safe access to critical resources and employment, financial inclusion, health care and education amongst many others. Such opportunity allows us to envision a world where the poor, with an identity on the Blockchain, can secure finance, where the two billion unbanked poor, can access the global financial system through a mobile phone and digital currencies, and where people who live on customary land, have the title secured on a Blockchain and can leverage that title to access finance. Blockchain could resolve complexities in the distribution of foreign aid; ensuring it is delivered directly to targeted beneficiaries using a smart contract, without using a middleman. While the potential for social impact is yet to be fully realised – for there are few use cases at scale in developing countries - those that do exist provide an exciting glimmer of the developments yet to follow and instil hope in the authors that Blockchain could be a revolutionary technology.

Many of the Blockchain applications that have been built in the West are built for smart phones and high infrastructure settings. However, many hard to reach populations have, at best, 2G networks (GSMA, 2018), they live in areas of unreliable mobile service or have limited access to electricity.

In this chapter, we profile two innovative case studies, Hiveonline and IDBox, in which the founders are building for low infrastructure settings in Niger and Papua New Guinea. These projects demonstrate that even in low connectivity settings, it is possible to deploy life changing technology.

The endeavour in this chapter is to profile innovative case studies in Blockchain solutions which may realise the technology's potential if brought to scale. It is thus, through the learning and experimentation of these pioneers that a solution for significant social impact could be developed.

Table 1 outlines the problems being addressed by the 10 case studies.

The vision of the New World is clearly demonstrated though the use cases detailed below, and provide rich evidence of seeking to fulfill the Empowerment, New Data Economy and Global Economics blocks of the B4SC Model and this working to achieve the New World Vision.

It is freely acknowledged, however, that despite these use cases, there remain many practical questions to be answered in settings with little internet access and electricity and that there is yet more to come as capacity, interoperability and scalability limitations are addressed. The case studies below have been purposefully chosen for their application to emerging markets, as argued in Chapter 4, where the greatest number of early adopters will be.

CASE STUDIES IN DETAIL

Shyft

Description: Shyft is building a global trust protocol for the secure sharing and transfer of verified, attested data.

The Problem: Institutions face lengthy compliance requirements (such as KYC, KYB, AML and EDD), involving collecting large amounts of customer data to assess risk. Shyft's technology streamlines data collection, reduces costs, and minimizes the cybersecurity risks inherent in traditional compliance systems. Furthermore, Shyft's "Creditability* system" (Shyft

Figure 1. The New World

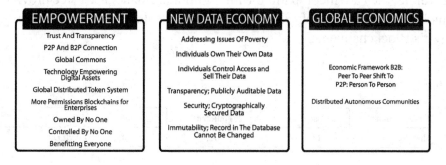

119

Table 1. Case studies and the use cases they address

Problem and Opportunity	Case Study
Identity; More than 1.1 billion people with no identity (World Bank, 2018) and limited or no access to financial institutions.	Shyft Everest
Land Registry; The state of Haryana, India, wants to transition their land registry system from presumptive, i.e., it assumes that the owner or a sale deed was truly the rightful property owner, to a more conclusive system. Further, the state wanted something to ensure data was tamper proof to instil more confidence and trust in the system.	Blockscale Solutions
Microinsurance for farmers	IBISA
Land Registry and Mortgages; Without available access to land and credit information financial institutions cannot lend efficiently and property construction cannot meet the housing demand due to uncertainty in land ownership and credit worthiness.	SESO
Agriculture Supply Chains; AgriDigital solves three key challenges across Agri supply chains. 1) Farmers are not paid for commodities when they deliver them; 2) Buyers don't have access to flexible supply chain finance to pay farmers, as financiers lack visibility and control when financing commodities; and, 3) Consumers don't really know where their food comes from restricting their ability to make informed purchasing abilities.	AgriDigital
Tuna Supply Chains; There is a disconnect between consumers and suppliers in the global seafood industry due to opaque supply chains, cumbersome paper trails and still open to worker exploitation, fraud and environmental destruction.	WWF
Data Analytics; Infrastructure owners, farmers, climate change monitors, and others struggle to survey their land, crops or infrastructure to predict crop failure and see land use degradation, without deploying highly expensive teams.	Flying Carpet
Accountability; Lack of transparency, accountability and long-term quantitative impact measurement in many international developmental projects	SELA
Data Exchange; In emerging economies, government departments are siloed, primarily due to issues of data sensitivity. This leads to double-handling. Lack of a common platform deprives governments of opportunities to improve service delivery.	GovBlocks

Network, 2019) provides users with reputational scores based on compliance and historical transactions. In so doing, Shyft makes the global economy accessible to the approximately 1.1 billion invisible people (World Bank, 2018) without identities.

The Blockchain: Blockchains like Bitcoin and Ethereum display a limited amount of information regarding the origin, volume, and destination of data. Therefore, they are incompatible with traditional financial service providers which require this to satisfy KYC/AML requirements. To solve this challenge, Shyft's Blockchain enables:

Table 2.

Organisation	Use Case	Founded	URL
Shyft Network	Identity	2017	https://www.shyft.network/

- The collection of users' data off-chain, using traditional databases and collection strategies, with the capacity to provide attestation points on Blockchain for third-party utilization.
- The onboarding and updating of new users' data by third parties, e.g. "Trust Anchors" (Shyft Network, 2019). A machine learning system (the Shyft Conservator) is used to confirm the validity of information collected through KYC forms, providing additional security to the entire Blockchain.
- Creation of products (e.g. asset-backed/collateralized loans and debt instruments; ETFs; hedge funds; derivatives) by financial institutions and other players, capturing a filtered target market.

Funding: Shyft is privately funded.

Platform: The Shyft Network is a combination of a centralized data attestation (the 'Shyft Bridge') and an expansive network of validation nodes that connect to the outside world (the 'Shyft Ring') - a public-facing Blockchain that is transparent, connected, and auditable. It is thus designed to improve user privacy while balancing compliance obligations. In order to protect users' personal information, Shyft extends Ethereum's codebase, adding the capability to read and write attestation data required by KYC/KYB providers. By developing a network for the secure sharing of trusted data, Shyft reduces the need for data to be duplicated. Fewer copies of user data out in the world means fewer opportunities for that data to end up in the wrong hands.

Token Model: The Shyft token is based on the Ethereum virtual machine's "Gas Equivalent," and is required to use the Shyft Blockchain. The token covers the cost of operations on the platform; transaction validation, data storage, settlement, and confirmations. Shyft Network participants could also potentially collect Shyft tokens and pay on the Shyft Blockchain for other services. In addition, the network can generate a Reputational Merit Token (RMT), intended as a reputation storehouse and incentivization mechanism, measuring positive interactions between KYC'd users and between Trust Anchor partners.

Planned Deployment: Shyft leverages existing global networks of data points, such as government institutions, telecommunications companies, exchanges, and financial service providers. Shyft recently signed an MOU with The Government of Bermuda to provide the country's Blockchain framework for KYC/AML and build interoperability into its legislation. Shyft has also partnered with Trunomy, experts in consumer consent frameworks, to implement an innovative e-ID (electronic ID) network. This network will drive global transactions and empower individuals to more easily share personal data cross-border - while adhering to the strictest KYC/AML and Anti-Terrorist Financing (ATF) compliance rules and procedures (Shyft Network, 2019).

Potential Social impact: Shyft provides a balance between risk for financial institutions, privacy of user data, and the pressing need for universal access to financial services for the 1.7 billion unbanked (World Bank, 2018a), currently prevented from accessing education, healthcare, and welfare by lack of verifiable identity. Shyft enables these individuals to access their basic human rights in a secure and automated manner, while supporting global organizations in their efforts to eradicate fraud within traditional ID systems.

Link to B4SC Model: Shyft is one of the sovereign identity and data ownership enabling shifts indicated in the B4SC Model in Chapter 1. A key potential outcome of the Shyft use case is delivering on the New Data Economy whereby individuals own their own data and are able to provide permissioned access to their data. This is part of the empowerment culture of the New World as outlined in the B4SC model.

Everest

Description: Everest is a decentralized platform incorporating a massively scalable payment solution, EverChain, with a multi-currency wallet, EverWallet, and a native biometric identity system, EverID. Everest delivers a complete solution for a new economy.

Problem: The inability to prove identity is the single most significant barrier to economic inclusion.

The Blockchain: An autonomous, distributed, encrypted, personal database for users that is self-funding on the Blockchain, with a leveraged Ethereum mainnet to show transparent (yet fast & cost-effective) transactions.

Table 3.

Organisation	Use Case	Founded	URL
Everest	Identity	2017	www.everest.org

Funding: Mistletoe funded.

Platform: Two enterprise ethereum chains. First is the "identity chain", which has pointers to off-chain storage of identity attributes; it is a proof-of-authority chain in which no one has authority, thus making it autonomous. The second chain, EverChain is a layer 2 transaction chain "above" the Ethereum mainnet. This makes it scalable, cost-effective and fast.

Token Model: Everest will use a utility token, the ID, and a USD-pegged token, the CRDT. IDs will allow entities to interact with the system, while CRDTS are the digital currency used to move value. Institutions that want access to the Everest economy or want to operate observer/transaction nodes will gain access by purchasing and holding a predetermined number of ID tokens corresponding to their role in the network. Every enrollment, verification, update, or transaction will require spending CRDTs. Everest intends to initially peg the CRDT to the US dollar, and each token will be equal to USD $0.01. There is no planned ICO for the CRDT, as it will only be used to verify identities and exchange value within the Everest ecosystem.

Development Stage: The Everest "testnet" launched in July 2018, and Everest 1.0 went live in October 2018. The firm is currently engaged in a health service project in Cambodia and a gas subsidy pilot project in Indonesia. Other possible use cases listed on the Everest website include land administration; micro-insurance; micro-financing; cash transfers; remittances; medical records; and humanitarian aid.

Planned Deployment: Indonesia was the first rollout; Samoa, Australia and New Zealand are currently getting deployed, other emerging markets include Latin America, Africa, South East Asia and the Middle East.

Expected Social Impact: Everest aims to improve transparency in the delivery of government and social services; solving de-risking and banking the un-banked. Further, they help women own land, get access to health services and reduce marginalisation (due to digital identity and a cloud wallet). They are attempting to reorganized 20% of the global economy, affecting 2-3 billion individuals.

Link to B4SC Model: Everest maps to Enabling Shifts of both Economics and Sovereign Identity with self-regulating economies and financial inclusion and is steps on the pathway to the New World.

Table 4.

Organisation	Use Case	Founded	URL
Ibisa	Financial Inclusion	2018	https://www.ibisa.network

Ibisa

Description: Ibisa is a risk-sharing service; an alternative to micro-insurance, targeting small farmers worldwide. Based on a peer-to-peer architecture supported by Blockchain and Earth Observation technology, Ibisa reduces costs typically incurred by traditional insurer-centric paradigms making protection affordable and accessible to 500 million of small-scale farmers worldwide. The service is enabled by an ecosystem of stakeholders governed by a Distributed Autonomous Organisation (Ibisa, 2018).

The Problem: Ibisa uses the latest technological developments to expand and scale the iddir traditions into a global risk sharing service. In Ethiopia, the iddir is an ancient, community-based risk sharing mechanism model that provides coverage to over 70% of farmers - this is an attractive market share for an insurance company (Aredo, 2010). However, the current practice of formal insurance doesn't scale well to micro-insurance - it incurs too many sources of incompressible costs, such as: Collecting premiums and renewing contracts for each crop season; filing, managing and evaluating claims and doing pay-outs. For policies with premiums as low as US$10-20pa, after paying all these costs there is not enough value for money left for small-scale farmers, resulting in a penetration rate of 0.5% of crop microinsurance, in all continents (Ibisa, 2018).

The Blockchain: In using Blockchain technology, Ibisa drastically reduces all claim assessment costs, is able spread operating costs across stakeholders, make monitoring and reporting to supervision authorities straightforward and automate administrative tasks in a decentralized and transparent way, reducing the risk of error. The low costs of operating insurance on the Blockchain enable Ibisa to operate a profitable business model and deliver an affordable product to low-income farmers. The peer-to-peer approach to risk sharing reproduces the model of ancestral village practices but scales globally to avoid correlated risks.

Funding: IBISA received seed funding from the European Space Agency and has the support of the Luxembourg government. Most resources are donated in-kind by the founders and team members. In September 2018, Ibisa began the process of raising Series A funds to deploy the Minimum Viable Product in Kenya, Bangladesh and India.

Platform: The components of Ibisa are;

- A set of DApps that automate global risk sharing
- DAO Governance and crypto-economics
- Last mile components: mobile money integration and identity/authentication
- EO data sources: providing not only EO data but the varied information necessary for tracking the index, assessing damage and defining coverage
- A decentralised data store that monitors operational data that could be stored off-chain

IBISA's Blockchain-specific architecture is comprised of 3 major building blocks: the risk sharing mechanism flow, the loss assessment plus indemnification entitlement flow, and the ecosystem stakeholders' revenue flow. The risk sharing mechanism flow represents the global logic for the farmers' peer-to-peer payments, mapping the process from contribution to indemnification. The loss assessment plus indemnification entitlement flow is the logic from the parametric index tracking for loss assessment. The ecosystem stakeholders' remuneration flow is the logic used to remunerate stakeholders using the 20% fee levied from farmers' premiums (Ibisa, 2018).

Token Model: Ibisa uses a utility token associated with KPIs in a Decentralised Autonomous Organisation (DAO) to incentivise good behaviour. Anyone may download a DApp to adopt a stakeholder role in IBISA but to act and receive remuneration, this person must own tokens and put them at stake while committing to a set of KPIs. At the end of each period, achievements are assessed against committed KPIs by a smart contract and all tokens at stake are redistributed among stakeholders accordingly. Ibisa is to classic insurance what bush taxis are to railways trains. Railways networks are centralised systems that serve cities in Europe well, but they are unable to provide a service to remote villages. Conversely, bush taxis are a distributed system whereby each operator is responsible for the maintenance and management of his own taxi, it takes only minimal governance to service any hamlet.

Table 5.

Organisation	Use Cases	Founded	URL
Blockscale Solutions	Property RightsLand Registration	2018	https://blockscalesolutions.com/

Development Stage: Ibisa dApps are in the development phase and demos are available. The MVP will be available for testing in 2019.

Planned Deployment: IBISA has signed Memorandums of Understanding (MOU) with several large Micro Finance Institutions and NGO's and is initiating pre-pilot activities in India, Bangladesh and Kenya to roll out the service in 2019. Other signed organizations will be part of the second wave of field deployment.

Expected social impacts: The ancestral social safety net on the Blockchain is why this concept has quickly gathered social traction with farmers worldwide.

Link to B4SC Model: Demonstrates how the enabling shifts of token economies and connecting for full stakeholder engagement may deliver empowerment and global economics in the New world.

Blockscale Solutions

Description: Blockscale Solutions has developed a proprietary Land Registry product enabled by Blockchain Technology. The first deployment of which was a proof of concept (PoC) for the city of Panchkula, in the state of Haryana, India - one of the first commercially viable Land Registries to use Blockchain Technology in this region.

The Problem: The state of Haryana, India, had concerns regarding their land registry system that they wanted to explore using Blockchain for. The current system is presumptive, i.e., it assumed that the owner of a sale deed was truly the rightful property owner – the government wanted a more conclusive, tamper-proof system to instill more confidence and trust in the system.

The Blockchain: Smart Contracts are used to govern the Land Registry, with secure storage, enforcing an autonomous and immutable rule set. These Smart Contracts live atop the Blockchain, executing a permanent transactional record. Decentralized file storage was also introduced to store all relevant documents in a secure and permanent fashion, distributed across dozens of computers to ensure integrity and accessibility.

Funding: Self-Funded

Platform: Blockscale is entirely based on distributed microservices and communication across each occurring via REST interfaces, enabling citizens to utilize their existing national identities using the Blockchain. The REST interface abstracts the complexity of the Blockchain away from end users, allowing citizens to interact with the land registry system exactly as they do today.

Token Model: Non-fungible tokens (NFT) (ERC721) are used to represent properties of the low-level asset-registry. Each property is represented by a unique NFT bound to the real-world via their metadata field which is used to store an IPFS multihash. IPFS is a decentralized file storage solution where all property data is stored that currently identifies a physical property. Therefore, the real property information may be accessed directly from the on-chain NFT registry.

Planned Deployment: Further to the Proof of Concept (PoC) in the state of Haryana, India, there are ongoing discussions with the State to develop and integrate an enterprise solution. Ultimately with the intention to deploy to full integration across the 100+ land registry locations in India. Other planned deployments are in other regions of South East Asia and South America.

Expected social impacts: A more transparent and trusted land registry system could benefit many developing countries, protecting citizens' legal and ethical interests in the transactions of land, free of corruption, manipulation or record tampering. For, many citizens are unsure if they legally own a piece of land - even with a legitimate deed of sale – or whether the vendor of a piece of land truly owns it. A Blockchain enabled solution may increase confidence in the government and protect the rights of parties in the transaction of land. In so doing, citizens of developing worlds can become more empowered and have greater control over their financial and housing interests.

Link to B4SC Model; Maps to the model via both the enabling shifts required of the Economics block with smart contracts and Government block of shifts in regulation and legislation required and works to progress further into the New World.

Table 6.

Organisation	Use Case	Founded	URL
Seso	Land Registration	2017	http://seso.global/

Seso

The Problem: Seso builds Blockchain land registry solutions across emerging economies to unlock trapped capital. Without available access to land and credit information financial institutions do not have the capabilities to efficiently provide lending. Additionally, property construction cannot meet the housing demand due this uncertainty in land ownership and credit worthiness.

The Blockchain: Seso uses the Blockchain to secure land records on an immutable registry while implementing consensus processes when transactions are processed onto the Blockchain such as mortgages, sales, and land surveys. A Seso Token will incentivizes the public to add land data onto the platform.

Platform: Seso is built on Java Script with the backend utilizing IBM Hyperledger and AWS for data storage. A public version is planned on Ethereum.

Funding: The venture is VC funded and an ICO is planned.

Token Model: Seso is preparing ERC1400 security tokens (where each token represents a share of a new property development) to equity crowdfund investment in new property developments in Nigeria. Once the development is completed and the property sold, the investors are then given their investment back, plus returns, in local currency. SESO aim to launch this in Q3 2019.

Development Stage: Seso has a current product that is being piloted in several locations and will launch a second version with the token launch in 2019.

Planned Deployment: Seso has been deployed in Nigeria and Ghana, Zimbabwe is to follow plus further expansion into Africa with existing corporate partners. Seso then plan to focus on South America.

Expected social impacts: Seso aims to unlock the US$9 trillion of trapped capital in land across the world by giving citizens the ability to secure their land and collateralize their properties by securing over 1 million land titles by 2023. This promotes global financial inclusion. Seso aims to deploy over $50 Billion of capital with strategic partners in land and property across the emerging markets (Seso, 2019).

Link to B4SC Model: This use case is driven by community needs related to economic development, legacy systems and public demand for accountability. Both operate within the space of enabling a shift to enhance knowledge and move to a trusted transparent new world.

Table 7.

Organisation	Use Case	Founded	URL
AgriDigital	Supply Chains	2015	https://www.agridigital.io/

AgriDigital

Description: AgriDigital has used Blockchain-enabled technology to create frictionless systems for the grains and cotton industries globally. Formally launching in March 2019, farmers are assured they continue to own their commodity right up until the moment they are paid, solving the problem of matching delivery to payment and opening up flexible financing options. The immutable record of ownership on the ledger means financiers are willing to lend to farmers at better rates as they have critical information about the physical state of the commodity they are financing. These records - or digital assets - can then be integrated with other technology. Using the best of emerging technologies, AgriDigital is committed to making agri-supply chains easy, simple and secure for all participants from farmer to consumer. AgriDigital builds software for the grains and cotton industries globally. The AgriDigital platform is an inventory management and trade solution for the global grains industry. Integrating with real time finance, the platform offers farmers, storage operators and traders access to a suite of trusted digital solutions. At the core of the AgriDigital vision is a truly networked and community approach to digitising agriculture.

The Problem: AgriDigital has a vision to solve three key challenges across agri-supply chains;

1. Farmers are not paid for the commodities they produce when they deliver them;
2. Buyers don't have access to flexible supply chain finance to pay farmers, as financiers lack visibility and control when financing commodities; and,
3. Consumers don't really know where their food and fibres come from restricting their ability to make informed purchasing abilities.

Agriculture is the least digitised industry, and with often limited connectivity and innovation, it hasn't been able to make the most of digital technologies, until now.

The Blockchain: Geora is the product of three years of testing Blockchain technology with some of the world's largest agribusinesses to eliminate counterparty risk by running commodity transactions on a Blockchain and allowing the supply chain to operate in confidence. Blockchain is a component of a larger digital infrastructure, one that allows users to easily access the protocol layer and ensures the information recorded truly represents the state of the physical commodity in the real world.

Geora is an open source protocol leveraging ethereum based technologies. Providing a library of smart contracts for users to access to trace, trade and finance agri-supply chains. Designed specifically to meet the needs of agriculture, Geora provides an enhanced privacy solution and fine grain data controls and permissioning.

The Platform: The AgriDigital platform integrates with Geora to create trusted digital records of physical commodities. These records, or digital assets, can then be integrated with other technology platforms to streamline data transfer and reduce human interference and associated error; and, provide a secure and shared record of an asset as it moves through multiple hands along a supply chain. As supply chains digitise, more robust and complete digital records can be created allowing other products and innovation to be overlaid. Geora provides a base protocol layer serving a community of technology companies and agribusinesses globally. Through a standard API layer, integration support and user management, Geora offers a way for applications to easily access the benefits of shared data sets and smart contracts.

Funding: AgriDigital's founders have over 80 years combined experience in the Australian agriculture industry, as farmers, business owners and traders. Having successfully exited previous agtech businesses, they brought AgriDigital to a point of launch in 2017. In September 2017 AgriDigital completed a Series A raise of AU$5.5M from Australian Venture Capital, Square Peg Capital, and is one of Australia's largest family offices with assets in food packaging

Token Model: Geora does not operate using a network token, however in creating records or physical assets Geora uses semi-fungible tokens to represent physical commodities. A standard ERC-20 token is also used to represent various currencies throughout the system, with integrations with other currency solutions to be deployed in 2019.

Development Stage: AgriDigital has been piloting Blockchain based solutions since 2016. Geora is launching publicly in March 2019 with its pilot customers.

Deployment Plans: AgriDigital serves the US and Australian grains and cotton markets, with users in over 20 countries through the platform network. Since launching in 2016, the AgriDigital platform has transacted over 5 million tonnes of grain. Geora is being used in projects globally across a range of different commodities and supply chains.

Through their pilot program, AgriDigital establishes the ability to eliminate counterparty risk by running commodity transactions on a Blockchain, allowing the supply chain to operate in confidence. Farmers are assured they continue to own their commodity right up until the moment they are paid. Solving for the problem of matching delivery to payment is enormous for removing counterparty risk along supply chains.

Blockchain opens opportunities for grain farmers and buyers to access flexible financing options. Given the ledger creates an immutable record of ownership, financiers are willing to lend at better rates as they have critical information about the physical state of the commodity they are financing. Using smart contracts, creative and innovative financing arrangements between non-traditional financiers and buyers become a real possibility.

Blockchain technology provides an immutable record of critical information about the farming, production, transport of agri-commodities. Attaching this data to the digital asset, AgriDigital and others can transfer this data securely between participants along the supply chain. In turn, this allows us to build out towards full supply chain traceability. With the power to trace commodities and create data rich digital assets, AgriDigital is addressing the growing problems of food fraud and security across global agri-supply chains.

Social Impact: In line with the Sustainable Development Goals, Geora is providing digital infrastructure to support the achievement of the Global Goals ensuring all people can access a safe and prosperous world. Digital infrastructure is allowing business like AgriDigital to deliver products to reduce inequalities (Goal 10), support responsible consumption and production (Goal 11) and build sustainable cities and communities (Goal 12).

Agriculture is a US$7 trillion-dollar industry employing over 35% of the global workforce. The challenges are enormous, with food fraud along estimated to cost a staggering US $40 billion annually. As the least digitised industry globally, there is an enormous and untapped opportunity for new technologies to radically transform agri-supply chains.

Technology platforms to streamline data transfer and reduce human interference and associated error; and, provide a secure and shared record of an asset as it moves through multiple hands along a supply chain. In line with the Sustainable Development Goals, Geora is providing the digital infrastructure to support the achievement of the Global Goals ensuring all people can access a safe and prosperous world, allowing business like AgriDigital to deliver products that reduce inequalities (Goal 10), support responsible consumption and production (Goal 11) and build sustainable cities and communities (Goal 12).

Link to B4SC Model: Maps to the model enabling shifts hyper co-collaboration and conversation and works to connect, engage and educate while building a platform for the New World.

World Wildlife Fund

Description: As part of their innovation program, WWF experiments with new approaches to solving global environmental challenges. This includes exploring emerging technologies like Blockchain. WWF works with partners and 'unusual allies' to scale solutions and accelerate both domestically and internationally. As part of this work, over the last 18 months WWF has been supporting the development of a global Blockchain strategy for WWF (World Wildlife Fund, 2018).

The Problem: The vision was to increase the sustainability of Pacific Fisheries, decrease impact and reduce worker exploitation by creating a transparent and traceable supply chain solution for the fresh and frozen supply chain. There is a disconnect between consumers and suppliers in the global seafood industry. The supply chains are opaque, rely on cumbersome paper trails and still open to worker exploitation, fraud and environmental destruction.

Over the last 30 years, WWF has been at the forefront of driving sustainable production and consumption. However, progress is failing to scale: certified sustainable production represents less than 20% of the market for most priority commodities. One of the key reasons for this has been the limits of

Table 8.

Organisation	Use Case	Founded	URL
World Wildlife Fund	Supply Chain	2017	https://www.wwf.org.au/get-involved/panda-labs

approaches to date in creating traceability and transparency in supply chains. Limited traceability prevents responsible producers from connecting with retailers/consumers who would prefer to buy ethical products and enables those behaving unsustainably to obfuscate responsibility. We have a shared ambition to see most of the world's products be sustainably and ethically produced (World Wildlife Fund, 2018)

The Blockchain: WWF were able to successfully track the fish using the Ethereum Blockchain; from being caught, to being brought on the docks, then transported to the processing plant, and then put on a plane mostly to Japan, Europe or North America.

The Platform: WWF has now developed an ambitious and potentially transformative new platform which leverages Blockchain technology and well as other emerging technologies to capture commodity data at source, store it using the Blockchain, verify the sustainability of production (using machine learning and other emerging technologies) and expose this data to consumers who want to know where their products came from. By doing this, WWF will help to transform the way that global supply chains operate, significantly decreasing environmental impact and worker exploitation.

Funding: Bootstrapped and Impact Investing.

Token Model: Not at this stage.

Development Stage: In 2017 WWF piloted the use of Blockchain for Tuna with Consensys and TraSEAble (a Fijian fishing company) to increase the sustainability of Pacific Fisheries and reduce worker exploitation by creating a transparent and traceable supply chain solution for the fresh and frozen fish market. However, during the validation phase in 2018, the project considered how to track fish using RFID tags and QR codes, and in the process tried a number of different mechanisms to improve the data on the chain.

Deployment Plans: The vision is to deploy a globally scaled platform across multiple high impact commodities, designed to enable third parties to develop their own applications and ultimately lead to rapid growth

Expected social impacts: After a successful pilot with tuna, WWF is focused on scaling for impact across multiple commodities. The scaled platform ensures sustainable production at source, digitally traces products along the supply chain, and presents sustainability in a way that changes consumer behaviour - to permit triple impact in a third of the time. There have now been implementations across three major commodities; tuna, wild caught prawns and toothfish, working in partnership with major retailers in Australia and major seafood brands like Austral (World Wildlife Fund, 2018).

Link to B4SC Model: The WWF case capitalises on the current driver of increased availability and access to technology. It is a classic example of the power of emerging Blockchain and other technologies; a traditional organisation disrupting itself to bring on Blockchain and a new world of enhanced transparency of transactions.

Flying Carpet

Description: The Flying Carpet is an Open Network for Building and Using Aerial Analytics Services, connecting analytic-hungry organisations with a pool of data scientists who compete to create world-leading analytics-extraction models from rich visual data, such as drone and satellite imagery.

The Problem: there is increasing interest in the potential to use big data and analytics for a more detailed understanding of aspects of the Earth, crops, infrastructure, people movement and to predict future events (Flying Carpet, 2019). For example, the World Bank is funding a series of big data projects including the use of high-resolution satellite data to monitor and predict movements of Internally Displaced People in Somalia and Kenya. This will improve the identification, tracking and assessment of people with a focus on high-risk and vulnerable women and children in famine and conflict-affected contexts.

The Blockchain: Flying Carpet connects data scientists who compete to create world-leading analytics-extraction models from rich visual data, such as drone and satellite imagery. Finished models are stored decentrally for future use by organisations with a minted corresponding ERC-721 NFT. Businesses can purchase analytics from models while (DAO) smart contracts can access model analytics via oracles. Model ownership NFTs – that receive all revenue each time the corresponding model is used – are held by ERC-20 Bonded curve tokens, as such these intrinsic NFTs encapsulate all future model revenue (Flying Carpet, 2019). The decentralised geospatial state determination layer that is Flying Carpet reports real-world truths to organisations or directly programming them into smart contracts via oracles. Unlike comparable geospatial data organisations, Flying Carpet distributes

Table 9.

Organisation	Use Case	Founded	URL
Flying Carpet	Big Data and Analytics	2017	https://www.flyingcarpet.network/

the network value of the analytics-extraction process across all network participants, providing specific analytics without having to rely on off-chain data sources and extraction and reporting mechanisms (Flying Carpet, 2019).

Funding: The platform is bootstrapped

Token Model: The Flying Carpet protocol, a decentralized network, deploys IoT devices to collect data in a timely and cost-efficient manner. Multiple stakeholders benefit; drone and drone charging station owners, developers who are rewarded in tokens for building machine learning applications for the network, and businesses and communities can enhance their operations and reduce costs.

Using Flyingcarpet, data scientists and service owners each capture 100% of the reward from their work. Machine learning models reward data scientists using a crypto economic incentive structure made possible by the utility token. The competition incentivization mechanism uses bounties on a live physical location heat map and a Token-Curated Registry of Opportunities (TCRO) running on the Ethereum Blockchain to collect and rank analytics-extraction opportunities. From insurance companies, to agri-companies, to governments, the Flyingcarpet network enables actionable insights through rich AI-powered analytics. The Flyingcarpet utility token, Nitrogen (NTN), is used by data scientists to stake against the models that they create and used to stake against additions to the Token-Curated Registry of Opportunities (TCRO) (Flying Carpet, 2019).

Developmental Stage: The first PoC was completed in Papua New Guinea in 2017. Working with a local coconut farmer, Flying Carpet assisted in predicting crop yields by deploying an autonomous drone to survey the 100-hectare farm.

Expected social impacts: The Flyingcarpet Network has the potential to transform services across many industries, including the energy sector, infrastructure, logistics, as well as humanitarian efforts.

Link to B4SC Model: Maps to model as it starts to engage enabling shifts required by reaching and connecting Communities progressing to the New World.

Table 10.

Organisation	Use Case	Founded	URL
GovBlocks	Government	2017	https://govblocks.io/whitepaper

GovBlocks

Description: GovBlocks uses Blockchain Technology for proactive governance in emerging markets, driven by on-chain data exchange frameworks. Using Blockchain Technology, a government can maintain an irrefutable record of any data exchange between their internal departments while securely managing citizen data. With Blockchain enabled internal data exchange, service delivery can be flipped from "pull" to "push", where citizens do not seek but instead receive services and entitlements proactively. The benefit of GovBlocks is that multiple departments can maintain their independent databases while still being able to exchange information with other departments, without requiring a centralised database and managing the associated privacy issues.

The Problem: In emerging economies, government departments work in silos and there is no facility for data exchange between them, primarily owing to issues of data sensitivity. This leads to double-handling. Lack of a common platform deprives the government of many opportunities of improving public service delivery

The Blockchain: GovBlocks is based on Ethereum with various permissioned implementations via Quorum and Hydrachain for enterprise grade deployments. Governments benefit from:

- Building scalable, permissioned Blockchain apps and eventually pushing data periodically on the public chain to achieve true immutability
- Tokenizing assets backed by physical reserves or cryptocurrencies, as the regulations evolve with time
- Choosing a technology stack that can work both for permissioned and permissionless services.

Funding: Bootstrapped

Platform: A permissioned implementation of Ethereum is proposed, however, the GovBlocks decision protocol is currently compatible with: Ethereum Public Blockchain, Ethereum Private Blockchain, Quorum (Ethereum Permissioned derivative), Hydrachain (Ethereum Permissioned derivative), RSK (rootstock) and Aion.Network

Token Model: Not used.

Expected Social Impacts; Improved institutional governance and accountability at scale.

Table 11.

Organisation	Use Case	Founded	URL
Sela	Accountability	2017	https://Sela-labs.co/

Link to B4SC Model; demonstrated the model enabling shifts of Governments and the shift from traditional to transformed that's required to progress to the New World.

Sela

Description; Sela enables the transparent execution and measurement of sustainable development projects, eliminating traditional barriers to entry for capital into the emerging world.

The Problem; Millions of people across the globe and especially in the emerging world live in extremely sub-optimal conditions due to friction and lack of transparency at various levels of developmental project execution. Sela couples distributed ledger technology with embedded Artificial Intelligence to drive transparency and accountability in economic development activities. This fusion of technology may incentivise behavioural change across segments of the value chain to improve the rate of project execution while minimizing waste, thereby activating economic development and facilitating inclusion for those who have hitherto been left behind.

The Blockchain; Distributed ledgers enable the storage and audit of files by multiple stakeholders. The Blockchain is used to track the flow of money across stakeholders in the international development value chain, reward monitor sending data through a cryptocurrency, and store hashes of data throughout a project's lifecycle. This process instils integrity in the various participants of the Sela platform.

Funding: Angel investors for pre-seed. Currently raising seed capital for the platform.

Token Model: The Sela token contributes to the governance, integrity and incentivization of the platform. The top 10% of actors of the platform are rewarded by the Sela token. These tokens can then be used to submit project proposals, up-vote or comment on project proposals and initiate loans or donations. Through this incentive mechanism, the top contributors to the network earn a share of the network they create. There is also consideration regarding the use of the token as part of prediction markets on project outcomes or maintaining curated registries of top actors on the platform.

Developmental Stage: Late early stage. There is a working minimum viable product which has been used to complete a pilot project in the Niger Delta region of Nigeria.

Planned Deployment: Pilot tests have been completed in Nigeria on a project to clean up the highly polluted Niger Delta in Nigeria. It is planned to scale this across Nigeria to other development projects. Long term plans are to partner with funding agencies like the USAID, the World bank, DFID, etc. and possibly governments across the emerging world, starting within Africa, to explore this as a way to drive transparency and accountability using technology and innovation.

Expected social impacts: Improved governance touches upon so many areas of a municipality as follows;

- Infrastructure: Roads, bridges, electricity, clean water, waste management etc.
- Environment: Vegetation, aquatic life, groundwater and air quality are few components of the environment that have been devastated over the years in the pilot community.
- Economic empowerment: cleaning up oil pollution in a fish pond which has been out of use for many years. Since the project completion, the owner has restocked the pond with fingerlings that would be ready to go to market in few months thereby creating a source of livelihood for himself and his family.
- Employment: an extension of economic empowerment is employment for workers who perform the projects and those who monitor the projects.
- Health: The UNEP study on the Niger Delta shows that benzene content in the drinking water in these communities is over 900 times the WHO standard. Ensuring this project is performed will help reduce the level of this toxicant that has contributed to reducing life expectancy in this area to about 40 years. Ensuring that hospital projects are completed will ensure that the most vulnerable in the society have access to health care.

- Education: School projects are regularly abandoned due to mis-managed funds. Sela hopes to solve this problem and ensure more children have access to education to improve literacy in the emerging markets.

Potentially, these projects will have impact on millions across the emerging world who to date suffer undue hardship due to misappropriation of development funds intended to procure the basic infrastructure needed to lead a normal life.

Link to B4SC Model: Sela demonstrates the influence of emerging economies as change agents, addressing community issues by enabling connected communities to become more important in the new world.

LAST MILE SOLUTIONS

There has been limited analysis of the costs of deploying technology at scale for last mile populations, partly because there are many barriers to reaching the poor. The first is digital access; there remain large segments of the world's poor who do not have access to electricity, internet or mobile phones. Where mobile connectivity exists, it may currently only be on 2G or 3G networks. If Blockchain-enabled solutions are to reach the most marginalised, solutions will need to be developed that overcome these access barriers.

Understanding of local sociocultural and political contexts, digital literacy, ethics, informed consent and consumer protection is a second barrier to reaching the poor. In areas of unequal development, high poverty rates, and low education access to technologies can be difficult and unaffordable, necessitating particular attention to access, relevance, adoption, quality and scaled deployment of digital technologies.

The following two case studies profile two founders working to solve these problems in two of the most difficult settings in the world; rural Papua New Guinea and Niger.

Table 12.

Organisation	Use Case	Founded	URL
IDBox	Financial Inclusion	2017	https://www.idbox.io/team.html

IDBox

Description: IDBox is a simple, low-cost device, that delivers a unique identity to enable digital transfers using a basic analogue phone and does not require electricity or access to the Internet. The core intention of IDBox is to provide last mile populations secure access to an identity which promotes financial inclusion in low infrastructure settings. This may lift the bottom 1.1 billion unbanked (World Bank, 2018) out of poverty through service provision.

The IDbox v2.0 is comprised of a screen, a linux operating system, biometric system, a solar panel, a battery, a GPS and a 2G/4G communication module. Power connectors for charging different devices (like an analogue phone or a smartphone) and solar panel connectors are positioned on the left end side of the IDbox device. It is also possible to add multi modal biometric systems such as Iris sensors or blood sensors into the IDbox device to increase security.

The Problem: The IDBox is a solution for last mile populations but could be used worldwide. It provides a network of identities that everyone can access, no one can control and cannot be shut down. The core usergroup of the IDbox device is last mile populations where the electricity grid is non-existent and/or unreliable.

Creating a decentralised identity for people in developing countries faces major challenges: low smartphone rate, no grid electricity and very little internet access. Thus, the IDbox aims to create a new way of identifying people, uniquely, securely and anonymously, cost-efficiently without need for access to the internet or power grid, permitting access to services like remittance, voting, healthcare, land registration, etc. The provision of digital identities strengthens womens' resilience in disaster areas, assists in combating trafficking and sexual exploitation across the humanitarian-development-peace nexus and support women and girls to receive humanitarian assistance.

The Blockchain: By building and storing a secure identity on the Blockchain IDBox enables the secure transfer of digital assets which may improve the life circumstances of last mile populations. Blockchain technologies and cryptocurrencies could be used to increase transparency, cut transaction costs, facilitate social investment, cash for work, enable the transfer of non-food items, or provide grants for small businesses and education.

IDbox uses cryptographic key generation with multimodal biometric systems to create a unique public key, thus the person acts as the private key and his/her biometric information are used to sign transactions for future service providers' verification processes, the generated private key and individual's biometrics are then deleted. Using a permissioned Blockchain, any organisation can run a node enabling anyone to verify transactions on the node and track transactions, without seeing the identity of individuals.

The box can be used for P2P energy trading, so people can access energy and the owner of the box can make money, people can also send remittances without a third-party company using the P2P network. A local shop can set up an exchange market in return for local money using SMS confirmation on the ID Box. All that is necessary is a crypto wallet for access to the online exchange market place that's used to exchange cash.

The process is fully secured by the transactional security offered by the Blockchain and the individuals' biometric data at the box. No one has access to the data, including IDbox. The primary point of unique access to a person's identity is an individual's phone number, the second is the wallet ID and finally, the biometric public key. Additionally, hosted on a permissioned Blockchain, only authorized users can access the network. The smart contract awarded to each population unit (i.e., a refugee camp) means any new users that are added are tracked by each smart contract's authorization key. There can be an overall smart contract per county covering all camps and every camp can have its own smart contract to track transactions, which means it is possible to track exchanges made between camps.

Development Stage: The first prototype of IDbox was built during a London Blockchain Week Hackathon in January 2017. It was based on the needs of Papua New Guinea, a Pacific country with low internet access, limited electricity and limited smartphone penetration. Since then it has been further developed, including proof of concepts and tested in an urban and a remote site in Papua New Guinea.

Token Model: The unique business model is targeted for the bottom billion, enabling everyone to access an income stream simply by being part of the Blockchain, for example, people have to pay members for access to identity and community members can trade electricity and create a micro economy in a camp or village. In addition, third party providers can provide a remuneration reward for access to identity and data if desired.

Planned Deployment: This is a scalable commercial venture, developing a production capacity from a model of 1 box per 1000 people. The scale of production depending on the number of countries using the device. It is designed for low infrastructure environments, initially PNG, Indonesia and India, but rapidly able to be deployed elsewhere.

Table 13.

Organisation	Use Case	Founded	URL
Hiveonline	Financial Inclusion	2016	https://www.hivenetwork.online/

Link to B4SC Model: Maps to the model by working to address the enabling shift of communities and more specifically generating geographically isolated shifts to reach connected communities.

Hiveonline

Description: Hiveonline is building several financial inclusion models, beginning with the Village Savings and Loans (VSLA) process. VSLAs are small businesses with mini-funds – they (80% women) input a small amount into the savings pot each week and use the pot to lend at interest.

On top of the VSLA model will be local Micro Finance Institutions (MFI) and merchants into the ecosystem, enabling women to access finance and wider markets for their goods. MFI and merchants also benefit from the reduced administration cost, reduced customer risk and more efficient markets.

Lending is funded by the VSLAs and by the microfinance institutions once the in the loop. Hiveonline operate a zero-balance system issuing stablecoins based on a fiat amount in bank, which keeps the national balance of the money flat.

They are pushing for innovation in several areas:

- Offline/asynchronous updates – many rural communities are poorly served by connectivity so in facilitating communities transacting, they synch to the wider Blockchain.
- Microservices on the platform which can permit services on custom community devices and some on personal devices
- With infrastructure providers (via the Niger Villages Intelligents programme), to provide intermittent connectivity to remote or nomadic communities via satellite. The application layer can run on handheld devices but Hiveonline are also developing feature phones (KaiOS) to allow for processing for customers who don't have smartphones

- Improved reputation system measures for non-traditional data as well as transactions (type of goods exchanged, reason for loan) plus base network information for phone records to validate customers.
- Keeping data as well as services and value close to/in the hands of the customer – the reputation system uses derived data, while the customer data belongs to the customer.

The Problem: Small businesses in developing economies largely lack access to financial services and identity, forcing them to borrow money at high rates from informal lenders or microfinance institutions. In some countries (e.g. Niger) even microfinance institutions can't reach them because of the risk of moving cash. Businesses want to reach wider markets but local supply chains are inefficient and expensive, with primary producers paying a high price.

The Blockchain: A key element of the platform is the combination of the analytical reputation system with the Blockchain records, which are used to validate that ecosystem members are meeting commitments and behaving ethically.

Funding: Hiveonline received seed funding in 2017 of $800,000 and are currently being supported by grants from CARE Denmark for the Niger build, and Techstars.

Token Model: The token model, built on Stella will have three types of token – a stablecoin, a "she token" for women paying into the fund and a "debt token" for loans. The Blockchain is used to move value, create audit trails and to store transaction data. Stablecoins are issued based on a custody fiat account, while other types of tokens are assigned a value either by the savings group (share tokens), the lending contract (debt tokens) or the market (assets).

Development Stage: The project is in build (a live version in Denmark). MVP planned for Niger in April 2019.

Planned Deployment: It is planned for deployment in Niger, Rwanda, Ghana and Kenya, currently. VSLA has 600,000 existing customers in Niger - the least developed country in the world and aims to have 60 million by 2030.

Link to B4SC Model: Is about financial inclusion and addressed the model enabling shift of Economics.

Table 14.

Organisation	Use Case	Founded	URL
Givit	Venture Philanthropy	2018	https://givitcoin.io/

Givit

Description: The Givit project is a scalable global platform which shifts the paradigm of giving from charity to venture philanthropy, all powered by digital currency. Using the concept of venture philanthropy, a new class of donors – who were previously unwilling or unable to part with funds – is engaged with the incentive of a possible return by creating a digital currency ecosystem powered by Blockchain. Givit enables anyone for the first time with the ability to aid those in need in an efficient, accessible and frictionless manner.

Funding: Funding will stem from an initial ICO, or Token Generation Event in 2019 and from capital investments from business partnerships, one of which include the largest food distributor in Latin America, Food Forward.

The Blockchain: Givit will be built on an existing POS Blockchain protocol. Givit will enable people to earn tokens and generate income by sharing their stories with the world. The GivitToken will be a utility token built upon a high speed private Blockchain. The Token will have an elastic supply, which means it will expand or contract to meet the necessary demand. The GivitToken will be used to purchase its store-of-value sister currency, GivitCoin, in well-known digital currency exchanges. Deployment of the GivitToken will take place following the TGE, with 100 million Tokens being made available to Venezuela and the remainder of the reserves becoming available to the rest of the world for purchase.

The GivitToken will be a utility token built upon a high speed Blockchain, whose operating system will add an extra layer of security and stability for its users simply because of the reliable nature of today's private digital currency trading platforms. One GivitToken will have a set value of $1 US Dollar (USD) and will be used primarily for transactional purposes, therefore it will not fluctuate. GivitCoin can be purchased with GivitToken at any time and can be subdivided into eight decimal points, which enables individuals to purchase portions of the currency with limited funds.

The Token Model: There are two types of tokens in the Givit ecosystem; the utility Token, the GivitToken, pegged to the US dollar, on an independent and private Blockchain. The GivitToken will act as the entry point for potential contributors and the direct donation to citizens of Venezuela, as well as the operating currency in the disaster relief zone in Venezuela among partners with Givit. GivitCoin is Givit's digital currency whose value will fluctuate based on real-time appreciations and depreciation movements in the crypto marketplace. GivitCoin is purchased only in exchange for GivitTokens, but will offer different opportunities, mostly in the capacity of trading and investing on the digital marketplace (Givit, 2019a).

Development stage: Givit will be introducing the utility token into Venezuela in Q2 of 2019. (Givit, 2019) Individuals can earn GivitTokens by sharing their stories on social media. Viewers will then be able to contribute to Venezuelans by buying GivitToken, distributed via airdrop to individuals who create videos telling the world their story. In Venezuela, citizens will earn GivitTokens by creating a 30-second video, or testimonial asking the world for help. Next, they upload it to Givitcoin.io, at which point Givit wrap a frame around the video reading, "Please help us in Venezuela, go to Givitcoin.io and buy GivitToken." From Givitcoin.io, the user can share their testimonial on social media, thereby "earning" a GivitToken. Venezuelans will also earn GivitTokens for 5 receiving public engagements, such as "likes" and "comments" on their videos.

Planned Deployment: Two key components are needed to facilitate transactions of digital currencies; a reliable internet connection; and a digital wallet asset to undertake the transaction. Givit's technology will initially be deployed in Venezuela and shortly thereafter to the general public around the world, primarily among communities that have ready access to smartphones and cellular data and/or an internet connection.

The Givit project has built strategic partnerships with one of the largest wireless carriers in Latin America. Through this partnership they have secured hundreds of thousands of smartphones and internet connections for the citizens of Venezuela. The internet connections will allow them to make the exchanges necessary to facilitate transactions and will also enable them to post content to the Givit Platform. Moreover, Givit is developing and building its own basic exchange wallet device BEWD), on which citizens will be able to undertake transactions and store their accrued GivitTokens. The smartphones will be the hardware used to upload and deploy content, while the Givit wallet and portal will be the software used to manage the tokens and exchanges.

The initial goal of the platform is to create a direct donor-recipient network from potential investors/contributors, to beneficiaries in disaster-stricken areas, such as Venezuela.

Expected Social Impacts: Givit plans to develop a currency ecosystem, which in turn will create a strong support to sustainably regenerate the economy's infrastructure.

In addition, as Givit's presence and support grows, the plan is to expand the token towards a sustainable global infrastructure, one that will enable communities everywhere to help themselves by generating their own income. Givit has the potential to serve every corner of the developing world, bringing millions, if not billions of dollars to individuals of those communities, many of which are unbanked and underbanked in the global financial system.

Link to B4SC Model: Maps to the model enabling shift of Economics and funding models.

COMPARISON AND DISCUSSION

In the section below, we provide a synthesis of the variables collected in the case studies and then discuss our findings and implications. Figure 2 and 3 provides a comparative snapshot of the case studies listed above.

Social Benefits

The column in Table 2 on potential beneficiaries, indicates the impact of these organisations numbers into the millions and billions, whether unbanked populations, poor farmers or individuals without identity and all projects target at least five Sustainable Development Goals.

From agriculture, to environment, to identity, to charity, the founders have demonstrated substantial vision. They see the transformative potential of Blockchain to disrupt industries and enable vulnerable groups to benefit. While this is inspiring, in way is this no easy path to chart. Scaling can be difficult, and all projects are struggling for the funding that is necessary to maintain viability. This is a common story amongst entrepreneurs that are ahead of mainstream adoption.

Challenges Ahead

In addition to funding, there are environmental challenges for Blockchain projects.

In the report of the Working Group on Social Impact, Enterprise, Economic Development and Ethics for the ADC Blockchain Summit (Thomason, 2019), a number of challenges were well articulated:

Figure 2. Comparison of identified variables

Case Study	Target	Potential Beneficiaries	Blockchain Use	SDGs	Token Use
Shyft	Unbanked populations	1.1 billion without identity, 1.7 billion unbanked (Devex, 2018)	Collects users' data off-chain, providing attestation points on chain for third-parties. Onboards and updates new users' data by third parties. 'Trust Anchors.' A machine learning system (the Shyft Conservator) confirms data validity collected by KYC forms. Creates products (e.g. asset-backed/collateralized loans and debt instruments; ETFs; hedge funds; derivatives), capturing a filtered target market.	1. No Poverty 2. Zero Hunger 3. Good Health & Well Being 5. Gender Equality 8. Decent Work and Economic Growth 9. Industry, Innovation and Infrastructure 10. Reduced Inequalities 11. Sustainable Cities and Communities 12. Responsible Consumption and Production 17. Partnerships for the Goals	Based on the Ethereum virtual machine's gas equivalent for platform costs. Participants collect tokens and pay on the Shyft blockchain for services. The network can generate a Shyft Reputational Merit Token (RMT) - a reputation storehouse and incentivization mechanism - measuring positive interactions between KYC'd users and between Trust Anchor partners.
Ibisa	Uninsured Farmers	Millions; there is a global insurance gap of US$162.5b, the majority of which comes from emerging nations (Lloyds, 2018).	Lowers the cost of insurance claim assessment. Automates the maximum number of administrative tasks. Spreads the operating costs between all stakeholders. Simplifies monitoring and reporting to supervision authorities. Undertakes parametric crop coverage.	1. No Poverty 2. Zero Hunger 3. Good Health and Well Being 5. Gender Equality 8. Decent Work and Economic Growth 9. Industry, Innovation and Infrastructure 10. Reduced Inequalities 11. Sustainable Cities and Communities 12. Responsible Consumption and Production	A utility token –associated with KPIs– as behavioural incentives for stakeholders. Anybody may download a DApp as a stakeholder role but to act and receive remuneration, they must own tokens and stake them towards a set of KPIs. At the end of each period, achievements are assessed against KPIs by a smart contract and all tokens at stake are redistributed among stakeholders accordingly.
Blockscale	Property Owners	Potentially millions	Uses the Blockchain to store and govern the Land Registry and store relevant documents in a secure and permanent fashion.	5. Gender Equality 9. Industry, Innovation and Infrastructure 10. Reduced Inequalities 11. Sustainable Cities and Communities 12. Responsible Consumption and Production 16. Peace, Justice and Strong Institutions	Non-fungible tokens (ERC721) represent properties and NFTs are bound to the real-world by metadata used to store an IPFS multihash. Therefore, the property information may be accessed directly from the on-chain NFT registry.
Seso	Property Owners	Potentially millions	Secures land records when transactions are processed onto the Blockchain such as mortgages, sales, and land surveys.	5. Gender Equality 9. Industry, Innovation and Infrastructure 10. Reduced Inequalities 11. Sustainable Cities and Communities 12. Responsible Consumption and Production 16. Peace, Justice and Strong Institutions	Created a security token for property developments, launched through a "Property Token Offering".
Agridigital	Farmers and agriculture financiers	Potentially millions	Part of a component of a larger digital infrastructure that allows users to easily access the protocol layer and ensures the information recorded truly represents the state of the physical commodity in the real world.	1. No Poverty 2. Zero Hunger 3. Good Health and Well Being 5. Gender Equality 8. Decent Work and Economic Growth 9. Industry, Innovation and Infrastructure 10. Reduced Inequalities 11. Sustainable Cities and Communities 12. Responsible Consumption and Production 17. Partnerships for the Goals	Geora does not use a network token but a semi-fungible token represents physical commodities. A standard ERC-20 token is also used to represent various currencies throughout the system, with integrations with other currency solutions to be deployed in 2019.
WWF	Supply chain producers and consumers	Potentially millions	Potentially transformative solution to transform global supply chains to drive sustainable purchase decisions, significantly decreasing environmental impact and worker exploitation.	1. No Poverty 2. Zero Hunger 3. Good Health and Well Being 5. Gender Equality 6. Clean Water and Sanitation 8. Decent Work and Economic Growth 9. Industry, Innovation and Infrastructure 10. Reduced Inequalities 11. Sustainable Cities and Communities 12. Responsible Consumption and Production 14. Life Below Water 15. Life on Land 17. Partnerships for the Goals	The competition incentivisation mechanism uses bounties on a live physical location heat map and a Token-Curated Registry of Opportunities (TCRO)

Most obstacles are political. The main obstacle is the tendency to think within existing models. There is the need for vision and to think out of the box on a very large scale. Lack of government support is slowing down the rollout and acceptance of emerging technology, as well as inertia from traditionally slow-moving institutions such as health, which is stifling the potential benefits of Blockchain technology. Despite that innovative approaches to healthcare are crucial to avoid a catastrophic waste of resources. Leadership and collaboration will be key.

Figure 3. Comparison of identified variables continued

Flying Carpet	Data-hungry organisations	Potentially millions (based on impact)	Uses a combination of Ethereum, machine learning libraries. Truebit, Golem, FOAM, open-source Flyingcarpet machine learning base classifiers (proposed), entire Flyingcarpet codebase (proposed/already open-sourced)	1. No Poverty 2. Zero Hunger 5. Gender Equality 6. Clean Water and Sanitation 8. Decent Work and Economic Growth 9. Industry, Innovation and Infrastructure 10. Reduced Inequalities 11. Sustainable Cities and Communities 12. Responsible Consumption and Production 15. Life on Land	A utility token, Nitrogen (NTN), used by data scientists to stake against created models and used to stake against additions to the Token-Curated Registry of Opportunities (TCRO) (Flying Carpet, 2019).
Sela	Donors and Government project beneficiaries	Potentially millions (based on impact)	Secures land records when transactions are processed onto the Blockchain such as mortgages, sales, and land surveys.	1. No Poverty 2. Zero Hunger 3. Good Health and Well Being 5. Gender Equality 9. Industry, Innovation and Infrastructure 10. Reduced Inequalities 11. Sustainable Cities and Communities 16. Peace, Justice and Strong Institutions	The Sela token ensures the governance, integrity and incentivization of the platform. The top 10% of actors of the platform get rewarded in the Sela token. The tokens can then be used inside the platform to submit project proposals, upvoting or commenting on project proposals and initiating loans or donating. Thus, the top contributors to the network get a share of the network they create.
GovBlocks	Donors and Government project beneficiaries	Potentially millions (based on impact)	Uses Ethereum, Quorum and Hydrachain for governments to build scalable, permissioned blockchain apps and eventually push data periodically on the public chain and tokenize assets backed by physical reserves or cryptocurrencies, as regulations evolve with time.	9. Industry, Innovation and Infrastructure 11. Sustainable Cities and Communities 12. Responsible Consumption and Production 16. Peace, Justice and Strong Institutions	Tokenized assets are not used due to uncertain regulatory treatment.
IDBox	Last mile populations	1.1 Billion without identity, 1.7 billion unbanked (Devex, 2018), 1 billion without electricity (Ritchie, 2019)		1. No Poverty 2. Zero Hunger 3. Good Health and Well Being 5. Gender Equality 8. Decent Work and Economic Growth 9. Industry, Innovation and Infrastructure 10. Reduced Inequalities 11. Sustainable Cities and Communities 12. Responsible Consumption and Production 16. Peace, Justice and Strong Institutions	Tokenised assets are not used.
Everest	Unbanked populations, internationally displaced persons and refugees.	1.1 Billion without identity, 1.7 billion unbanked (Devex, 2018),	An autonomous, distributed, encrypted, personal database for users that is self-funding on the blockchain, with a leveraged Ethereum mainnet to show transparent (yet fast & cost-effective) transactions.	1. No Poverty 2. Zero Hunger 3. Good Health and Well Being 5. Gender Equality 8. Decent Work and Economic Growth 9. Industry, Innovation and Infrastructure 10. Reduced Inequalities 11. Sustainable Cities and Communities 12. Responsible Consumption and Production 16. Peace, Justice and Strong Institutions	Everest will use a utility token, the ID, and a USD-pegged token, the CRDT. IDs will allow entities to interact with the system, while CRDTS are the digital currency used to move value. Institutions that went access to operate observer/transaction nodes will gain access by purchasing and holding a predetermined number of ID tokens corresponding to their role in the network. Every enrollment, verification, update, or transaction will require spending CRDTs. Everest intends to initially peg the CRDT to the US dollar, and each token will be equal to USD $0.01. There is no planned ICO for the CRDT, as it will only be used to verify identities and exchange value within the Everest ecosystem.
Hiveonline	Small businesses	Potentially Millions	Permissioned Stella blockchain used to move value, create audit trails and to store transaction data which are then analysed, starting with the three oro tokens and then building asset, natural capita and behaviour tokens.	1. No Poverty 2. Zero Hunger 3. Good Health and Well Being 5. Gender Equality 8. Decent Work and Economic Growth 9. Industry, Innovation and Infrastructure 10. Reduced Inequalities 11. Sustainable Cities and Communities 16. Peace, Justice and Strong Institutions	The token model has three types of token – a stablecoin, a "she token" for women paying into the fund and a "debt token" for loans. Stablecoins are issued based on a custody fiat account, while other types of tokens are assigned a value either by the savings group (share tokens), the lending contract (debt tokens) or the market (assets).
Givit	Donors & Project Beneficiaries	Potentially millions in the developing world	Givit Token is stored and used on a private blockchain.	1. No Poverty 2. Zero Hunger 3. Good Health and Well Being 5. Gender Equality 6. Clean Water and Sanitation 7. Affordable and Clean Energy 8. Decent Work and Economic Growth 9. Industry, Innovation and Infrastructure 10. Reduced Inequalities 11. Sustainable Cities and Communities 12. Responsible Consumption and Production 15. Life on Land	An unlimited number of utility tokens pegged to the USD are available, based on amount of fiat in circulation. Tokens can be used to purchase a fixed amount of Givitcoin or held as a stable store of value over local currency

Blockchain technology has technical challenges, not least platform speed and scalability, facilitating inter-chain transactions and on ramps for fiat currency. However, these are works in progress and will be solved in the due course of time. By 2025 there will be 75 billion sensors connected and emitting real time data transactions (Reinsel, Gantz & Rynding, 2018). No human system could qualify establish a system of data management for that volume of data. Blockchain could solve the IOT data real streams needs, however still predicated on the fiat bridge and the scalability and number of transactions per node.

Data format, verification, validation and evaluation, access, and participation issues risk increasing the digital divide. There is a current lack in linking the physical and the digital world, data errors from manual entry, formatting differences, and other issues risk being locked into the emerging systems (addressing the human to non-human interactions). Developers and "solution providers" with top down operating approaches may not be aware of hard-won Sustainable Development Goals and social impact frameworks, issues and ethics. Technology, built in a vacuum, and making key assumptions that get built systematically into solutions, risks creating additional problems. In addition, those working in the social impact space assume ethics are incorporated into processes based on the goal of social good. However, this can lock in inherent biases and problems, increasing marginalization and risks. An example of this incongruence is cloud storage. In poor areas there is no cloud infrastructure and no communication networks that work well - having a fully decentralized system working in areas where there is currently nothing could be the best way to show great advances in technology.

Blockchain reorganises existing power structures, it redistributes power from institutions and corporations to people and communities. Structural limits and incentives mean that those making decisions on behalf of those affected by the results of those decisions are far removed from the realities of the problem. Often the beneficiaries of the resulting policies are not consulted. This can lead to policy mismatch and low social traction, cries for transparency which can otherwise be interpreted as cries for equity. Decentralised systems bridge structural limitations and offer inclusivity - inclusivity begets transparency. The more eyes on a matter, the more audited something is. Without inclusion, power proliferates and warps democratic organisation and dissemination of resources. Blockchain is an institutional technology which allows for privatised entrepreneurial design of systems of institutional governance.

Lack of data, lack of willingness to provide data, misaligned incentives and as mentioned lack of storage and affordable computer power, are bottlenecks for development. Everything related to data should be accurate and immutable, a database is only as good as the data entered into it. Many countries do not have current, accurate or, indeed, any data on large sections of their citizenry at all. Blockchain cannot adjust for this. Aligning stakeholder interests and developing the appropriate solutions to alleviate shared problems and integrating existing initiatives for collaboration, as well as interoperability of legacy systems are priorities. Geo-political, cultural, and ethical considerations are also key in cross border efforts.

There ought to be a sense of urgency regarding conversations of moral and ethical philosophy for emerging technologies. Developing a framework for drawing out, considering and engaging in a robust conversation regarding the ethical and moral dimensions associated with emerging technologies ought not to be just limited to Artificial Intelligence and Virtual Reality. Blockchain has the potential to change our economic and trade future and, as such, is deserving of robust philosophical exploration on its own as well as on the integration with AI and Machine learning, Having a trusted data source will guarantee unbiased development of futurist outcomes tackling such an issue successfully requires understanding of the underlying philosophical underpinnings and being able to frame questions and appropriate responses - this is something that requires deep thinking and a suitable framework.

It is likely that resources to frame and guide this are beyond existing government committees and structures, so a search of reality-based and critical thinking philosophers may assist.

It is important to build emerging technology solutions that incorporate and address key ethical issues. There needs to be development of, and better use of ethical frameworks and criteria to ensure technology is building out in an inclusive, systemic way to address the issues supposed to solve. There is also a need to better incorporate diversity (gender, age, race, culture, economic and geographic) in innovation processes from problem scoping to solution building.

We believe that a transparent Blockchain makes for an ethical environment. With enough transparency, the people and the market will determine who they will support in the social impact space. Eventually, the companies and individuals with the most accountable systems will prevail.

Given that this chapter focusses on the hard to reach populations, in addition to the above, some additional considerations for greater technology adoption are highlighted:

- Capacity of existing infrastructure: Many technologies require stable electricity, mobile, or wireless networks.
- Local capacity: for deployment, maintenance, field testing, trouble-shooting, etc.
- Digital literacy of the target populations.
- The choice of technology must account for beliefs, cell-phone ownership and social media use, tailored to the problem at hand.
- Technologies can make data collection faster and easier, but they can also introduce bias. If cell-phone ownership is concentrated in certain areas or among certain demographics, SMS-based surveys will disproportionately capture those groups and may not be appropriately representative of populations in need.
- For technologies reliant upon cell-phones to track locations or population movement, care should be taken to ensure that all data is de-identified and no personal information is collected without consent.
- Depending upon the context, the use of certain technologies, such as satellite imagery or GPS tracking, can be perceived as "spying" by some populations or authorities. Ensuring local acceptance may be a problem.
- The cost of technology deployment can vary widely. The cost of satellite imagery, for example, depends upon the size of land area or resolution to be analyzed. Many mobile platforms are free, but programmers are not.
- Low legal support regarding emergent regulatory frameworks, reinforces the perception of risk.
- Unknown unintended consequences from challenging intermediary's positions in emerging markets.

Vanderwal & Hellrung (2019) examined a series of Blockchain projects specifically seeking those that are trying to connect finance to results and payment. One of the projects was the Sela project, described in this chapter. They concluded that innovation needs to be supported and financed in the global south in the reality of those environments. They also conclude that the Department for International Development (DFID), which commissioned the report, and other donors, should be active in supporting the development of standards, good practise, regulation and testing. Finally, they conclude that funding to support early stage innovators is an area where donors can play a key role.

Other challenges, highlighted by the OECD (OECD, 2016) include the design and governance of Blockchain networks; interoperability and interaction with other technologies and the policy responses to decentralisation of economic activity.

Clearly, Blockchain and Frontier Technologies are not a panacea for all socio-political problems, they are a but a tool to be used with a suite of complementary interventions to improve social impact. There remain current and emergent challenges to be resolved.

CONCLUSION

It is the firm belief of the authors, that Blockchain and other Frontier Technologies, will be an important tool for social impact, globally. While Blockchains are still in their infancy, there are emerging numbers of use cases that demonstrate it is possible to offer an inclusive future where everyone has an identity, where everyone can be connected to the economic system, where farmers get fair deals for their crops, and land registration is incorruptible.

Advances in solar, battery and digital commerce make it possible to imagine even the smallest village in Africa being able to produce and trade small amounts of energy. This is a visionary future but one that is increasingly becoming possible as technologies begin to mature. It is possible, if people connect with intention, to purposefully shape the technological tools we have, to achieve social impact at scale.

When the Sustainable Development Goals (SDGs) were created, they were a visionary leap to a future state – one where the world can be a better place for humankind. The use cases in the chapter have demonstrated what is possible when organisations try to achieve social impact using technology – however, to successfully achieve the SDGs, the global community must collectively harness the potential of technology. It is only through sharing the learning from project experimentation that it is possible to learn how to deploy this technology globally for social impact.

Chapter 7 that follows builds on this theme of experimenting for social impact by highlighting the work non-government organisations (NGOs), like the United Nations, have been undertaking using Blockchain technology. Pilot projects by NGOs have been ground-breaking – humanitarian organisations have been leaders in adopting technology for social impact – yet, as seen in Chapter 7, there is yet far to go in taking their projects to scale.

REFERENCES

Aredo, D. (2010). The Iddir: An informal insurance arrangement in Ethiopia. *Savings and Development*, *34*(1), 53–72.

Blockscale Solutions. (2018). *Home*. Retrieved from https://blockscalesolutions. com/

Cornish, L. (2018). *Insights from the World Bank's 2017 Global Findex database*. Retrieved from https://www.devex.com/news/insights-from-the-world-bank-s-2017-global-findex-database-92589

GSMA. (2018). *The mobile economy*. Retrieved from https://www. gsmaintelligence.com/

Hague, M. (2017). *How Blockchain technology can serve the have-nots*. Retrieved from https://knowledge.wharton.upenn.edu/article/Blockchain-technology-can-serve-nots/

Lloyds. (2018). *A world at risk; Closing the insurance gap*. Retrieved from https://www.lloyds.com/~/media/files/news-and-insight/risk-insight/2018/underinsurance/lloyds_underinsurance-report_final.pdf

McKinsey & Company. (2015). *How advancing women's equality can add $12 trillion to global growth*. Retrieved from https://www.mckinsey.com/featured-insights/employment-and-growth/how-advancing-womens-equality-can-add-12-trillion-to-global-growth

OECD. (2016). *Digital government strategies for transforming public services in the welfare areas*. Retrieved from /https://www.oecd.org/gov/digital-government/Digital-Government-Strategies-Welfare-Service.pdf

Reinsel, D., Gantz, J., & Rynding, J. (2018). *The digitization of the world; from edge to core.* Retrieved from https://www.seagate.com/files/www-content/our-story/trends/files/idc-seagate-dataage-whitepaper.pdf

Ritchie, H. (2019). *Number of people in the world without electricity falls below one billion.* Retrieved from https://ourworldindata.org/number-of-people-in-the-world-without-electricity-access-falls-below-one-billion

Seso. (2018). *Home.* Retrieved from http://seso.global

Shyft Network. (2019). *Shyft Network: Alphanet.* Retrieved from https://www.shyft.network/network

Stanford Graduate School of Business. (2018). *Blockchain for Social Impact.* Retrieved from https://www.gsb.stanford.edu/faculty-research/publications/Blockchain-social-impact

Thomason, J. (2019). *Report of the Working Group on Social Impact, Enterprise, Economic Development and Ethics for the ADC Blockchain Summit.* Unpublished raw data.

Vanderwal, P., & Hellrung, T. (2019). *Frontier technology connecting finance to results to payment; research study report.* Stratigos.

World Bank. (2018a). *Financial inclusion on the rise, but gaps remain, global Findex database shows.* Retrieved from https://www.worldbank.org/en/news/press-release/2018/04/19/financial-inclusion-on-the-rise-but-gaps-remain-global-findex-database-shows

World Bank. (2018b). *1.1 billion 'invisible' people without ID are priority for new high-level advisory council on identification for development.* Retrieved from http://www.worldbank.org/en/news/press-release/2017/10/12/11-billion-invisible-people-without-id-are-priority-for-new-high-level-advisory-council-on-identification-for-development

World Bank Group. (2018). *World Bank Group and GSMA announce partnership to leverage IoT big data for development.* Retrieved from https://www.worldbank.org/en/news/press-release/2018/02/26/world-bank-group-and-gsma-announce-partnership-to-leverage-iot-big-data-for-development

World Wildlife Fund. (2018). *WWF-Australia and Blockchain.* Retrieved from https://www.wwf.org.au/get-involved/panda-labs/wwf-australia-and-Blockchain

KEY TERMS AND DEFINITIONS

API: API stands for application programming interface. It is a set of routines, protocols, and tools for building software applications. APIs specify how software components should interact, such as what data to use and what actions should be taken.

Bootstrap: To self-start a project using founders' own resources.

Decentralised Application (dApp): A type of application that runs on a decentralised network, avoiding a single point of failure.

Decentralised Autonomous Organisation (DAO): An organization that is run on a decentralised network using rules encoded in smart contracts.

ERC-20: A token standard for Ethereum, used for smart contracts implementing tokens. It is a common list of rules defining interactions between tokens, including transfer between addresses and data access.

ERC-721: ERC721 is a non-fungible subset of Ethereum tokens.

FOAM: A Proof of Location protocol that empowers a permissionless and autonomous network of radio beacons that can offer secure location services independent of external centralized sources such as GPS through time synchronization.

Gas: A term used on the Ethereum platform that refers to a unit of measuring the computational effort of conducting transactions or smart contracts, or launch dApps in the Ethereum network. It is the "fuel" of the Ethereum network.

IPFS: A protocol and network designed to create a content-addressable, peer-to-peer method of storing and sharing hypermedia in a distributed file system that seeks to connect all computing devices with the same system of files.

Non-Fungible Token (NFT): A non-divisible token that cannot be exchanged like-for-like. Unique characteristics make these tokens digitally scarce.

Oracle: An oracle is a party which relays information between smart contracts and external data sources. It acts as a data carrier between smart contracts on the Blockchain and external data sources off the Blockchain. One way of keeping information private is to use oracles to retrieve private information from an external data source.

Quorum: The Quorum Blockchain is an enterprise Blockchain established by JP Morgan Chase bank in collaboration with the Ethereum Enterprise Alliance.

REST: Representational state transfer is a software architectural style that defines a set of constraints to be used for creating web services. Web services that conform to the REST architectural style, termed RESTful web services, provide interoperability between computer systems on the internet.

Rootstock (RSK): Rootstock enables users to write and run smart contracts on top of the Bitcoin Blockchain. Rootstock is a combination of a Turing-complete resource-accounted deterministic virtual machine (for smart contracts), a two-way pegged Bitcoin sidechain (for BTC denominated trade), a dynamic hybrid merge-mining/federated consensus protocol (for consensus security), and a low-latency network (for fast payments).

Chapter 7
Refugees and Humanitarian Settings

ABSTRACT

Mass migration has become one of the 21st century's greatest challenges. With an estimated 214 million people on the move internationally and forced displacement at a record high, population mobility is one of the leading policy issues of the 21st century. Women and children with no identity can be missed by national social programs in addition to the risks posed by being on the move. Developments in Blockchain can enable the tracking and delivery of in-kind aid and facilitate cash assistance programs in humanitarian settings and coordinate, collect, and analyse data in crisis to enable a timely and appropriate response. This chapter presents the ways in which Blockchain is being deployed in humanitarian and refugee settings and a series of case studies from Finland, Moldova, Kenya, and Iraq. While promising progress has been made, there remains a need for more research and evaluation as these technologies are implemented, increased user participation in design, and to ensure that privacy and security issues are addressed.

INTRODUCTION

Blockchain has the potential to disrupt a large number of industries and change the lives of many. While in its infancy, it has potential to help solve some of the world's greatest humanitarian problems; identity, migration, asylum seeking, camp management, food and remittance distribution and much more (Ardittis, 2018).

DOI: 10.4018/978-1-5225-9578-6.ch007

We live in a time of increasing global mobility; both voluntary and forced. There are 25.4 million refugees in the world and some 3.1 million asylum seekers (Harper, 2018). Wars, violence, political upheaval, religious persecution, economic instability and sociopolitical crisis uprooted record numbers of people last year; the UN Refugee Agency's annual Global Trends study (2018) finding that 68.5 million people had been forced from their homes across the world in 2017; 2.9 million more than in 2016 and the biggest increase UNHCR has ever seen in a single year (UNHCR, 2018). Mass migration has become one of the 21st century's greatest challenges. The UN have warned the death rate for refugees trying to reach Europe, particularly, is rising; for every 18 people crossing to Europe over the central Mediterranean between January and July 2018, one person died. The United States' zero tolerance on immigration policy has resulted in annual immigration arrests soaring from 110,568 in 2016 to 143,470 in 2017 (Chappell, 2018).

Of the 36 major industries that are likely to benefit from the use of Blockchain technology[1], (CB Insights, 2018) INGOs are arguably making the most headway in proof-of-concepts, using them to resolve concerns regarding institutional financial accountability, data management, personal safety and security (Coppi & Fast, 2019). Save The Children have been investigating a humanitarian passport (Shah, 2017), the Red Cross piloted Blockchain in early 2018 to test the traceability and transparency of Islamic Social Finance (The Development Circle, 2018) and the World Food Programme's *Building Blocks* programme was one of the first of its kind to facilitate cash transfers to refugees on the Blockchain. To ensure these services were possible, however, fundamentals regarding satisfying identity claims were first necessary. Indeed, a task force has been established by the European Parliament to assess the ways in which Blockchain technology could be used to provide digital identities to refugees (Ardittis, 2018).

As leaders in the adoption of Blockchain technology for social impact, what follows in this chapter is a description of humanitarian proof-of-concepts and use cases for Blockchain technology. The aspects outlined in this chapter map closely to those in the B4SC Model of Current Influences and Drivers – elements within the Communities and Technology blocks, as demonstrated in Figure 1.

The discussion below provides a clear view of why there has been a galvanizing cry for the application of Blockchain in humanitarian settings.

Figure 1. Current Influences and Drivers – Communities and Technology

COMMUNITIES	TECHNOLOGY
100 Countries With Less Than 10 Million People Are Not Part of the Dialogue	Emerging Blockchain IoT, AI, Big Data, 3D Analytics, Data Analytics
Geographical Isolation Of Countries	Rapid Technological Growth
Digitally Literate Youth	Increased Availability And Access To Technology
Social Winds of Change	Increased Mobile Penetration
ISSUES ARE: -Poverty -Economic Development -Legacy Systems -Public Demand for Accountability -Technology Empowerment	Influence And Global Adoption Of Social Media
	Cultural Barriers Changed Due To Social Media
	Cyber Security

IDENTITY

According to the World Bank (2018) there are over a billion people without a recognised identity. Including refugees, trafficked children, the homeless, and other people who slip through society without developing many institutional affiliations. The problem feeds on itself: the longer a person goes without any associations, the harder it is to provide enough of a record to create them.

The 1951 UN Refugee Convention recognises that individuals subject to the travails of war commonly have no, or little, documentation. This can make the bureaucracy involved in fleeing countries and seeking asylum troublesome. Indeed, the Norwegian Refugee Council (NRC) research found that 70 percent of Syrian refugees lack basic identification documents (Aburass, 2017). When refugees are forced to abandon their homes, many leave behind important documents such as birth certificates, marriage licences, passports and ID cards. These are nearly impossible to retrieve after leaving the country, assuming they have not already been destroyed. The loss of such important documentation makes it nearly impossible to prove one's identity (Aburass, 2017).

However, the right to be recognised as a person before the law is an inalienable human right under Article 6 of the Universal Declaration of Human Rights. A legal identity enables someone to hold other rights under law; to have a nationality and to access basic services such as health and education. By hosting and transacting unlimited amounts of valued assets through its publicly distributed ledger, identities verified on the Blockchain cannot be faked. They are time-stamped and public. This is something the UN is working towards in their project, ID2020, whereby host governments and support organisations could start issuing digitally authenticated identification documents on the Blockchain. Refugees could then use these digital documents to prove their identity and that of their families, open bank accounts, sign contracts or apply to university (Bayram, 2018).

ID2020[2] (id2020.org) is a United Nations sponsored global project comprised of an alliance of governments, NGOs and the private sector, collaborating towards resolving the issue of a secure, portable digital identity which may support refugees' eventual voluntary repatriation, resettlement or settlement efforts. According the Syrian refugees interviewed by the NRC, their documentation has been lost, destroyed or confiscated. If replacement of this documentation is impossible, for example due to the destruction of civil registries inside Syria, refugees might ultimately be at risk of becoming stateless. To provision an identity, the ID2020 project focuses on four core identity principles (Pearcy, 2018):

1. **Persistent:** The identity remains with the user from the start of life through to death.
2. **Personal:** It is unique to the user.
3. **Private:** Only the user can grant permission to use the data.
4. **Portable:** It can be accessed by the user from any location.

With the intent of satisfying the UN 2030 Sustainable Development Goal of providing a legal identity for everyone on the planet, the ID2020 alliance unveiled a prototype of the network in 2017 to help individuals such as refugees prove who they are in order to gain access to basic services such as education and healthcare (Irrera, 2017). However, this is not the only UN sponsored Blockchain-related project at the moment. UNOPS, a service and technical advisory arm to the United Nations, and IOTA announced a partnership in May 2018. The intent being to benefit UNOPS from IOTA's open-source distributed ledger and Tangle technology to improve food distribution processes and disintermediate middle-men. One reason the IOTA partnership is exciting it they use Directed Acyclic Graphs (DAGs), also known as Tangle, which operates as a mesh network. This protocol is less resource-intensive and scales much better than traditional protocols because it does not rely on every node having a full copy of the Blockchain. Instead, the Tangle protocol offloads this work to the entire network of nodes which depend on each other to verify transactions (Mathis, 2018).

There are several types of identification models: a single centralised authority which controls the system. For example, the Internet Corporation for Assigned Names and Numbers (ICANN) who is the lone administrator— and source of truth—for domain name servers online. There is a federated solution, such as Microsoft Passport, which allows users the same identity on multiple sites with a single institution (like Microsoft), that governs the identity. Then, user-centric identity models have a single account—like a Google or Facebook account, for example— that can be used to login to a number of third-party sites, like news sites or social media platforms. However, a third party brokers these identity transactions, meaning that the user sacrifices a degree of privacy in exchange for the convenience of not having to remember a host of different passwords. Finally, self-sovereign identity (SSI), gives users complete control of their own identities and related personal data, which sits encrypted in distributed storage instead of being stored by a third party in a central database (Graglia, Mellon & Robustelli, 2018).

SSI awards individuals a portable, digital credential that can be validated via zero-knowledge proof cryptography (read more about this in Chapter Two) without the recipient having to check with the authority that issued it. The concepts behind SSI have existed for over a decade, however implementing them was, until recently, technically infeasible. The arrival of Blockchain and the continuous advancement of biometrics have brought SSI from concept to reality. Blockchain functions coupled with biometrics are critical for enabling SSI, as it allows the intrinsic characteristics of the individual to be extended into the digital world (Graglia, Mellon & Robustelli, 2018).

An SSI is created using a public identifier controlled via a public/private key pair. The identity can be enriched over time by third parties adding claims to it. Data and biometric information, like facial scans, iris scans and fingerprints can be added to the identity, after which the individual can add any credentialing information like humanitarian ID or education certificates, these documents will be incorporated into the individual's SSI wallet. Equipped with an SSI and zero-knowledge proof algorithms, a user is able to demonstrate their identity, without revealing information beyond that which it is necessary to satisfy the identity test. For example, driving licenses, passports and birth certificates are common identity documents required by institutions to prove your identity. However, often they may be for a single purpose: to prove your age, address and citizenship, perhaps. Your document may, in proving your identity, reveal unnecessary information about you.

Humanitarian organisations are bound by strict privacy principles outlined in the Handbook on Data Protection in Humanitarian Action (2014). The principles of self-sovereign identity are ideal for protecting individual's identities, especially when they are on the move or multiple agencies and government bodies require proof of identity.

Advancing Blockchain research and implementation begins to mitigate the risk of future generations growing up stateless. If registration and identification procedures are not properly carried out by humanitarian organisations, people who qualify to be recognised as refugees or stateless persons—or nationals—may be subject to immigration detention and deportation to a country where they are in danger, or to illegal exploitation. Weak identification systems can make it difficult for displaced persons and their children to reunite, to repatriate after crises have ended, and to reclaim land and property that they left behind (Manby, 2016). Robust identification and registration systems for displaced people also mitigate the disruptive impacts of rapid influxes of refugees for governments and assist planning to respond to the needs of the displaced populations (Manby, 2016).

Projects like Bitnation[3], often called a start-up, but an early Blockchain project from as long ago as 2014, can help refugees or humanitarian agencies to obtain digital ID documents, which host governments can then use to verify their identity. To build trust in the Blockchain identity, Bitnation simply verifies a person's multiple social media accounts and links them to their social security number, passport and other documents.

SSI, a key-based, on-chain decentralised digital identity, which can potentially help iron out the inefficiencies associated with the issuance of government paper-based IDs, allows people to reclaim control of their own information, and provides international protection for refugees and the 'invisible population' (the stateless or those who don't have IDs) (Harper, 2018). Platforms like Blockstack[4] (blockstack.org), the Shyft Network[5] and uPort[6] agree that there's a future where someone's identity can easily be made portable (CB Insights, 2018). On Blockstack, for instance, a user will access apps atop decentralized networks, and have perfect portability of their data. uPort's open identity system allows users to register their own identity on Ethereum, send and request credentials, sign transactions, and securely manage keys & data. Tested in 2017 in the city of Zug, uPort users (and residents of Zug) were able to register their identity on the Blockchain and unlock access to government eServices like online voting and proof of residency (uPort, 2017). Aid-Tech[7] (aid.technology) provides enterprise level solutions to international NGOs, governments and corporates to help them tackle some of [the] most entrenched issues in their fields, including legal identity, financial inclusion and corruption. BanQu[8] (banqu.co) uses digital identity to lift people out of extreme poverty, connecting them to the global supply chains they participate in and the brands, organizations, and governments that power them.

The startup ExsulCoin aims to help refugees build digital identities by using Blockchain technology to establish records of their educational and professional histories, making it easier for employers to screen and hire them. ExsulCoin tested an app last year with 10 women in the Kutupalong refugee camp in Bangladesh, which houses many of the over 800,000 Rohingya Muslims who fled persecution in Myanmar. The women completed a business training module through the education app, learning how to make bracelets with Myanmar jade and market them using social media (Chaudry, 2018).

FINANCIAL INCLUSION

Without identity people are excluded from traditional financial systems. In fact, without legal proof of existence, everything from getting a job, gaining access to a bank account, finding somewhere to live, accessing education, healthcare, and voting is nearly impossible. Consequently, refugees and displaced people are deprived of protection, access to services, and their basic rights. According to the World Bank Group (2018), approximately 1.7 billion people do not use formal financial services and more than 50% of adults in the world's poorest households are unbanked (Cornish, 2018).

However, innovations in mobile technology as well as Blockchains have made substantial strides in humanitarian aid-delivery to refugees. Cash transfers on mobile networks, with identity verified on the Blockchain, are increasingly used as a mode for delivering aid (Stevens, 2018), as they are found to deliver a number of benefits to beneficiaries, the humanitarian sector and the wider ecosystem. However, in most refugee-hosting countries, mobile network operators are subject to mandatory SIM registration obligations which require customers to present an approved identity document before a SIM card or mobile money service can be activated. Without the identity documents required to pass KYC criteria in markets where humanitarian-issued IDs are not accepted for KYC purposes, asylum seekers and refugees face challenges or delays obtaining a government-issued ID or finding and connecting with their lost loved ones on a mobile phone (GSMA, 2017).

FINANCIAL INTEGRITY

NGOs and INGOs are dependent on financial aid - even from small donors. One of the inhibitors for donors, however, is lack of transparency over the path of their money. In 2017 Human Rights Watch the lack of transparency in donor funding accounted for hundreds of millions of under-delivered funds, highlighting that the main problems included the lack of information about the projects that donors are funding and their timing; and a lack of consistent, detailed and timely reporting by donors (Human Rights Watch, 2017).

Researchers hypothesise that un/under-delivered official development assistance is spent on activities in donor countries or put towards the cancellation or rescheduling of debts, instead of being used for aid. For example, more than $5bn of aid supposedly given to the Democratic Republic of Congo in 2011 was never transferred. Instead, most of this figure represented debt relief (Provost, 2013). Accordingly, international humanitarian organisations see the primary benefits of using Blockchains as methods for securing financial integrity in their process and being able to provide a trusted, transparent account of asset transfer (Coppi and Fast, 2019).

One of the first humanitarian projects piloting Blockchains began in January 2017. The U.N.'s World Food Programme (WFP) directed resources to thousands of Syrian refugees as part of a pilot project in the King Abduallah Refugee Camp in Pakistan called 'Building Blocks'. A proof of concept project, the intent was to confirm basic assumptions around the capabilities of Blockchain in authenticating and registering transactions in the Sindh province, Pakistan. The Building Blocks Blockchain platform was integrated with UNHCR's existing biometric authentication technology that allows refugees in camps to identify themselves with the blink of an eye. Taking lessons learned from this pilot project, the WFP then built and implemented a more robust Blockchain system in the Azraq refugee camp in Jordan. (World Food Programme, 2018). The codes of cryptographically unique coupons representing an undisclosed number of Jordanian dinars were sent to dozens of shops. All cashiers had to do is verify the user's identity by using the eye-scanning hardware before dispensing the cash. The transaction was recorded on the Blockchain. By October 2018, the pilot program alone, which ran for 10,000 Syrian refugees, had reportedly saved the UN $150,000 a month while eliminating a 98 percent of bank-related transfer fees. This is a noteworthy considering that organisations working in international relief can lose up to

3.5% of each aid transaction to various fees and costs and an estimated 30% of all development funds do not reach their intended recipients because of third-party theft or mismanagement (Ardittis, 2018).

The next stage of the project will see an expansion to all 500,000 Syrian refugees in Jordan receiving support from the WFP with cash transfers likely to reach close to USD1.6 billion (World Food Programme, 2018). The Building Blocks programme represented one of the largest-ever implementations of the Ethereum Blockchain for a charitable cause in recent history (O'Neal, 2018) and thanks to Blockchain technology WFP now has a full, in-house record of every transaction that occurs with local retailers, ensuring greater security and privacy for Syrian refugees.

The Start Network, which consists of 42 aid agencies across five continents, ranging from large international organisations to national NGOs, has also launched a Blockchain-based project that enables them to speed up the distribution of aid funding and facilitate the tracing of every single payment, from the donor to the recipient (Ardittis, 2018). A pilot has already been successfully tested with the UK-based charity Positive Women to reduce its transfer fees and trace the flow of funds down the chain to a project in Swaziland, resulting in zero losses at the points of delivery. Funds were sent from the UK to four Swazi schools, via a local NGO, and the saving enabled Positive Women to fund an additional three students' fees for a year (Poorterman, 2017).

The BitGive Foundation[9] (bitgivefoundation.org) also give donors greater visibility into fund receipt and use, launching a beta version of GiveTrack,[10] a Blockchain-based multidimensional donation platform that provides the ability to transfer, track, and provide a permanent record of charitable financial transactions across the globe. By leveraging GiveTrack, charities can drive stronger trust with donors.

HOUSING, LAND AND PROPERTY RIGHTS

Housing, land and property (HLP) rights, as a humanitarian concept, involve the right to a home, free from the fear of forced eviction; a place that offers shelter, safety and the ability to secure a livelihood. Projects such as Ubitquity[11] offer a Software-as-a-Service (SaaS) Blockchain platform for the storage of financial, title, and mortgage companies' documentation on the Blockchain.

Many existing HLP documents for refugees may be lost, stolen or inaccurate. For example, seventy percent (70%) of Syrian refugees interviewed by the NRC stated that their housing document was in another person's name. This may be indicative of the common practice reported by refugees of transferring ownership or passing properties down through family lines without officially changing the name on the tapu (or other document) with the Real Estate Directorate or relevant authority. The precise location of many of the refugees' HLP documents was also unclear. Only seventeen percent (17%) of refugees who reported having documentation for their property indicated that they still had this documentation with them in their country of displacement. Ten percent (10%) said they did not know where their HLP documentation was, and twenty one percent (21%) reported that their documents had been destroyed. Just over half of the HLP document holders indicated that the document was "somewhere else".

This phenomenon was particularly high in Iraq (73%) and Jordan (50%), for varying reasons. For example, refugees in Jordan reported that because they heard the Jordanian government would confiscate any Syrian documents at the border, they chose to leave them behind, either hidden somewhere or with someone in Syria. However, given the high rates of infrastructure and housing destruction inside Syria as a result of the conflict, many who left their documents "somewhere else" fear that their documents or residences may no longer exist (Norwegian Refugee Council, 2017a). Consequently, the return of IDPs and refugees to their communities of origin inside Syria will likely result in a very high number of competing claims over the use and occupancy of land and property by original owners that use of the Blockchain would be able to mediate.

EMPLOYMENT AND WORK RIGHTS

A study published in 2016 by the German Federal Office for Migration and Refugees, revealed only one in eight (13%) Syrian refugees who arrived in Germany during the 2016 migrant influx last year is now employed (Bayram, 2018; Martin, 2016). Several challenges prevent refugees from integrating into the labour market, such as learning the local language and acquiring new skills. These issues aside, many refugees are still in the process of having their asylum applications assessed, years after arrival, and therefore have limited access to work.

As a distributed public ledger capable of recording transactions securely, the Blockchain enables information to be shared widely, transparency, and transactions can be verified in almost real time. Furthermore, Ethereum's smart contracts can automatically carry out certain functions, if predefined conditions have been met. This means governments could, for example, create "Blockchain work permits" which might enable refugees to deal with employers or businesses directly and set up real-time tax payments when they receive income (Bayram, 2018).

Chronobank[12] (chronobank.io) is a full-service Blockchain project aimed at disrupting the HR/recruitment industry, with a specific focus on improving short-term recruitment for on-demand jobs (in cleaning, warehousing, e-commerce, and so on). Using a payment methodology of labour hours, their platform LaborX, means companies can hire and pay anyone from top experts from around the world, to local fruit-pickers, with cryptocurrency – instantly. This challenges the traditional model of working entirely. Workers no longer need to work two weeks in lieu before they are paid which makes it far easier for refugees to enter - and stay within - the workforce.

FORCED LABOUR

According to the International Labor Organisation (c.f, Chavez-Dreyfuss, 2018) nearly 25 million people work in forced-labour conditions worldwide, with 47 percent of them in the Asia-Pacific region. Food and beverage companies are under pressure to address the risk of forced labour in countries where they obtain sugarcane. A study released last year by KnowTheChain (KTC), a partnership founded by U.S.-based Humanity United, showed that most food and beverage companies fall short in their efforts to solve the problem.

Coca-Cola - one of 10 global companies looked at by KTC - has committed to conduct 28 country-level studies on child labor, forced labor, and land rights for its sugar supply chains by 2020. In March 2018 they partnered with the U.S. State Department, BitFury and the Blockchain Trust Accelerator to launch a Blockchain registry for workers that will help fight the use of forced labor worldwide. This is the US State Department's first involvement with technology to support social causes (Chavez-Dreyfuss, 2018).

EDUCATION

Access to education is a human right, enshrined in the Universal Declaration of Human Rights (1948), the 1989 Convention on the Rights of the Child and many other international human rights instruments. Yet millions of children and adults remain deprived of educational opportunities, many as a result of social, cultural and economic factors and many because of forced migration (UNESCO, 2018). While refugees are provided education in camps and when settled by host countries, only 61 per cent of refugee children attend primary school, compared with a global average of 92 per cent. As refugee children age, the obstacles to education increase. Just 23 per cent of refugee children are enrolled in secondary school, compared to 84 per cent globally. For higher education the situation is critical. Only one per cent of refugees attend university, compared to 37 per cent globally (UNHCR, 2018).

Education program development in third-world countries is extremely difficult, due to high-demand of human resource, inefficient paper-based administration system and poor-functioning subsidy payment systems. Amply[13] (amply.tech) is a not-for-profit project that is building a digital identity and subsidy management system on the Ethereum Blockchain for pre-schools in South Africa. By using Amply, underprivileged children can receive sovereign ID and gain access to quality preschool education and financial support.

ASYLUM PROCESSING

The potential of Blockchain is indeed not confined to the administration of funds; it can also help trace and report on all stages of key migration and asylum policy.

FUTURE DIRECTIONS

The EU has established an Asylum, Migration and Integration Fund (AMIF) for the period 2014-20, with a total of EUR 3.137 billion for the seven years. It will promote the efficient management of migration flows and the implementation, strengthening and development of a common Union approach to asylum and immigration. Blockchain could help administer this fund, both in terms of transferring funds from the European Commission to the eligible NGOs in the Member States and in terms of project managers then reporting on spending. This would help alleviate many of the recurrent challenges faced by NGOs in managing funds in line with stringent EU regulations. For, crucially, Blockchain would have the potential to increase transparency and accountability in the channeling and spending of EU funds in third countries, particularly under the and other recent schemes to prevent irregular migration to Europe (Ardittis, 2018).

Using Blockchain to manage migration would also help in cases such as Libya, where human rights abuses were feared, in crowed detention centres that were compared to concentration camps.

CHALLENGES

Applications of Blockchain technology presupposes a benevolent institution, of course. Digital identities, bank accounts and mobile phones allow corporations, donors, international agencies and local-national authorities to track people's choices and desires by how they spend their money. Such control might allow authorities and corporations to increase surveillance over refugees (Pearcy, 2018; GSMA, 2017).

It is possible for an authoritarian state to use data collected from refugees against them – or for nations of the global North which have no sympathy for the movements of refugees and immigrants towards their countries could use such information to keep refugees away, in neighbouring countries. Even in institutionally democratic countries, there are debates about mass manipulation through fake news, interference in democratic elections, the use of search engine algorithms to offer people tailored search results or expose them to different advertisements based on their preferences and choices.

As it has been possible to manipulate millions of people who are not classified as vulnerable based on the power of corporations and their technological superiority, it is also possible that this power could be used to mobilise refugees in a particular direction or discourage them from making certain decisions, putting them in a more vulnerable and dependent position (Korkmaz, n.d; Pearcy, 2018).

There remain other issues to be resolved to see this taken to scale including the capacity of existing infrastructure and costs. Some countries have regulations restricting the use of certain technologies and privacy and security has heightened focus as People caught in humanitarian crises fear having their personal information leaked or their location identified, and fears of being tracked. There is also limited evaluation and very few evaluations exist of uses of Blockchain in humanitarian contexts. Evaluation should be integrated into design and deployment.

CASE STUDY 1: FINLAND

In 2018 Finland set themselves a challenge; could they manage their 750 refugees from Syria and the Democratic Republic of Congo using Blockchain to help the newcomers get on their feet faster.

For three years now, the Finnish Immigration Service has been giving asylum seekers prepaid Mastercards instead of traditional cash disbursements, and today, the program has several thousand active cardholders. The card is linked to a unique digital identity stored on a Blockchain which maintains a full analogue of a bank account for every one of its participants. People can use their accounts to pay bills, shop or receive salaries. Every transaction is recorded in a public database maintained by a decentralised network. This enables the Immigration Service to keep track of the cardholders and their spending. And for immigrants, the account means a simple and ready-to-use banking tool, as well as the permanent ability to verify their identification to their employers (Orcutt, 2017). The Blockchain technology helps unbanked asylum seekers advance because what is typically keeping them from getting bank accounts and jobs is that they are missing a form of strongly authenticated identity.

The platform, called Moni, uses one of several public Blockchains as the means of transferring value—but in a way that to the users it seems just like using a debit card. A cardholder can pay for things at Mastercard terminals or enter a number into a Web form to make payments online. MONI takes care of the cryptographic transaction for the digital currency transaction as well as the conversion from digital currency back to fiat currency. In addition to the refugee card program, MONI's service is available to beta testers in Finland, and the company has plans to launch a consumer product soon throughout Europe. An account costs €2 per month, and the company takes a small fee each time the user makes a purchase, and for international transactions (Orcutt, 2017).

CASE STUDY 2: MOLDOVA

An estimated 40 million people were trapped as slaves last year - mostly women and girls as young as 13 - in forced labour and forced marriages. It's a lucrative business too, generating illegal profits of about $150 billion each year on a global scale (Bitcoin Exchange, 2018).

Moldova, one of Europe's poorest countries, allegedly has the highest rate of human trafficking due to widespread unemployment and poverty that drives many people to look for work internationally. Every year, hundreds of women and girls are trafficked from Moldova to Russia, Turkey, the United Arab Emirates and other nations, mainly to work as sex slaves. Consequently, Moldova has been put on the United States' watch list of countries that are not doing enough to fight human trafficking. Now, Moldova, is looking to use the Blockchain to stamp out child trafficking, with help from the United Nations. UNOPS has teamed up with the World Identity Network (WIN), a campaign group, and other U.N. agencies to launch a pilot using Blockchain to fight human trafficking and Moldova was the first country to show a concrete interest in the project (Bacchi, 2018).

Blockchain can help reduce human trafficking by giving paperless identification documents to children based on biometric data, such as fingerprints or facial scans, which would be impossible to fake. Human traffickers typically confiscate individuals' documentation (if they have any) making it nearly impossible for them to leave. Having a national database of residents' identities ultimately means agencies can protect and find them much more easily.

CASE STUDY 3: KENYA

Kenya currently hosts the seventh-largest refugee population in the world, and the second largest in Africa. By the end of April 2017, nearly 500,000 refugees and asylum-seekers were registered on the UNHCR registration system (proGres), the majority of which had fled from either Somalia or South Sudan. The refugee population is expected to remain stable soon, with new repatriations to Somalia being offset by additional arrivals from South Sudan. More than forty-five humanitarian organisations, including UNHCR and other UN agencies, government agencies, and local and international NGOs actively support refugees in Kenya under the aegis of the Kenya Comprehensive Refugee Programme (KCRP). The World Food Programme, which is part of the KCRP, has provided food assistance to refugees since 1991.

In 2015, largely as a response to national security and terrorism concerns, Kenya began the roll-out of a new national identity card that contains the card holder's biometric details, including iris and fingerprint scans. All Kenyans are legally obligated to possess the national ID once they reach the age of eighteen, and the card must be shown when accessing most public and private services, such as applying for any license or permit, paying taxes and bills, accessing formal financial services, or registering a SIM card. As of July 2016, it was projected that 26.3 million Kenyans had these identity cards, which suggests that it has almost universal coverage across the over-eighteen population (GSMA, 2017).

CASE STUDY 4: IRAQ

Iraq hosts one of the largest populations of displaced persons in the world, reaching over six million by the end of April 2017. The vast majority are internally displaced persons (IDPs) – Iraqi citizens that have been affected by the country's three decade-long conflict. It is estimated that 89 per cent of the population in Iraq lacks access to formal financial products, giving the country one of the highest rates of financial exclusion in the world. However, high mobile penetration in Iraq and across the region suggests that mobile money services, though still relatively new to the market, could help to address this gap. The first mobile money services in Iraq were launched in early 2016: Asiacell's AsiaHawala service, and ZainCash.

In sharp contrast to Kenya, the ability of MNOs in Iraq to provide services, including mobile money, to refugees enhanced by a more flexible, risk-based approach to KYC. Recognising that the vast majority of refugees are unable to present a valid passport, the Central Bank of Iraq (CBI) has granted an exception that allows refugees to open a mobile money account through a tiered KYC system. If a refugee has been fully registered on UNHCR's biometric database and has possession of a UNHCR registration certificate, they are able to use this document to open a new mobile money account, albeit one with transfer limits. This approach to KYC has allowed humanitarian agencies to adopt various electronic payment mechanisms that facilitate cash disbursement to refugees and other displaced persons. For instance, in April 2016, WFP launched a digital cash card, called a SCOPE card, to provide food assistance to IDPs and Syrian refugees across Iraq. To use this system, individuals register their identification information and fingerprints into WFP's database, which is electronically linked to the cards. A loaded SCOPE card swiped at a shop automatically connects to the database to confirm the individual's identity and, like a debit card, the cost of the purchase is deducted from the total balance and recorded on a receipt. In December 2016, WFP also launched a mobile money pilot in the Erbil governorate through mobile operator AsiaCell's hawala53 platform, leveraging the operator's extensive agent network to make the service more accessible to refugees. SIM cards with full-service functionalities were distributed to registered beneficiaries and linked to a mobile money account with the user's identification details (GSMA, 2017).

CONCLUSION

The application of Blockchains in humanitarian and refugee settings is becoming one of its strongest use cases, as humanitarian actors deploy it in camps and for people on the move. It has the potential to address digital identity, supply chains, cash transfers and remittances, integrity of donor funds flows, property registry, employment rights, human trafficking, education and asylum processing. Blockchain is more often being used in conjunction with other digital technologies including AI, IoT, big data, drones and 3D printing. The authors conclude that while promising progress has been made, there remain other issues to be resolved to see this taken to scale including the capacity of existing infrastructure and costs. Some countries have regulations restricting the use of certain technologies and privacy and security has heightened focus as people caught in humanitarian crises fear having their personal information leaked or their location identified, and fears of being tracked. There is also limited rigorous evaluation of uses of Blockchain in humanitarian contexts, iterative evaluation should be integrated into the design and deployment of the technology.

The following chapter introduces how Blockchains have been used for health care and its delivery across the world.

REFERENCES

Aburass, S. (2017). *Syrian refugee's documentation crisis.* Retrieved from https://www.nrc.no/news/2017/january/syrian-refugees-documentation-crisis/

Aid Technology. (2018). *What we do.* Retrieved from https://aid.technology/what-we-do

Ardittis, S. (2017). *Why Greece's latest refugee emergency feels like a disturbing deja vu.* Retrieved from https://www.newsdeeply.com/refugees/community/2017/12/01/why-greeces-latest-refugee-emergency-feels-like-a-disturbing-deja-vu

Ardittis, S. (2018). *How Blockchain can benefit migration programmes and migrations.* Retrieved from https://migrationdataportal.org/blog/how-Blockchain-can-benefit-migration-programmes-and-migrants

Australian Government. (2017). *2017 Foreign Policy White Paper; Soft power.* Retrieved from https://www.fpwhitepaper.gov.au/foreign-policy-white-paper/chapter-eight-partnerships-and-soft-power/soft-power

Bacchi, U. (2017). *Moldova eyes Blockchain to end child trafficking.* Retrieved from https://www.reuters.com/article/us-moldova-Blockchain-child-trafficking/moldova-eyes-Blockchain-to-end-child-trafficking-idUSKBN1DF2GQ

Bagshaw, E. (2017). *Turnbull government invests in Blockchain.* Retrieved from https://www.smh.com.au/business/the-economy/turnbull-government-invests-in-cryptocurrencybased-company-for-the-first-time-20171121-gzplb4.html

Bayram, A. (2018). *Here are three ways Blockchain can change refugees lives.* Academic Press.

Insights, C. B. (2018). *Banking is only the beginning. 50 big industries Blockchain could transform.* Retrieved from https://www.cbinsights.com/research/industries-disrupted-Blockchain/

Chappell, B. (2018). *Customs and border agency halts many 'Zero Tolerance' detentions, citing workload.* Retrieved from https://www.npr.org/2018/06/26/623484448/customs-and-border-agency-halts-many-zero-tolerance-detentions-citing-workload

Chaudhry, S. (2018). *Use Blockchain to educate and empower refugees says Exsulcoin CEO*. Retrieved from http://news.trust.org/item/20180503120421-oa2qn/

Chavez-Dreyfuss, G. (2018). *Coca-Cola, US State Department to use Blockchain to combat forced labour*. Retrieved from https://www.reuters.com/article/us-Blockchain-coca-cola-labor/coca-cola-u-s-state-dept-to-use-Blockchain-to-combat-forced-labor-idUSKCN1GS2PY

Coppi, G., & Fast, L. (2019). *Blockchain and distributed ledger technologies in the humanitarian sector*. Retrieved from https://www.odi.org/sites/odi.org.uk/files/resource-documents/12605.pdf

Development Initiatives. (2017). *Global humanitarian assistance report*. Retrieved from http://devinit.org/post/global-humanitarian-assistance-2017/#

Department of Foreign Affairs and Trade. (2016). *Humanitarian strategy*. Retrieved from https://dfat.gov.au/about-us/publications/Pages/humanitarian-strategy.aspx

Department of Foreign Affairs and Trade. (2018). *Humanitarian preparedness and response*. Retrieved from https://dfat.gov.au/aid/topics/investment-priorities/building-resilience/humanitarian-preparedness-and-response/Pages/humanitarian-prepraredness-and-response.aspx

Digital Transformation Agency. (2018). *Our projects*. Retrieved from https://www.dta.gov.au/our-projects

Graglia, M., Mellon, C., & Robustelli, T. (2018). *The nail finds a hammer; self-sovereign identity, design principles, and property rights in the developing world*. Retrieved from https://www.newamerica.org/future-property-rights/reports/nail-finds-hammer/introduction

GSMA. (2017). *Refugees and identity*. Retrieved from https://www.gsma.com/mobilefordevelopment/wp-content/uploads/2017/06/Refugees-and-Identity.pdf

Harper, C. (2018). *World refugee day; How digital identities could help a population in crisis*. Retrieved from https://bitcoinmagazine.com/articles/world-refugee-day-how-digital-identities-can-help-population-crisis/

Hempel, J. (2018). *How refugees are helping create Blockchains' new world*. Retrieved from https://www.wired.com/story/refugees-but-on-the-Blockchain/

Heston, T. (2017). *A Blockchain solution to gun control.* Retrieved from https://peerj.com/preprints/3407.pdf

Human Rights Watch. (2017). *Following the Money; Lack of transparency in donor funding for Syrian refugee education.* Retrieved from https://www.hrw.org/report/2017/09/14/following-money/lack-transparency-donor-funding-syrian-refugee-education

Irrera, A. (2017). *Accenture and Microsoft team up on Blockchain-based digital ID network.* Retrieved from https://www.reuters.com/article/us-microsoft-accenture-digitalid/accenture-microsoft-team-up-on-Blockchain-based-digital-id-network-idUSKBN19A22B

Korkmaz, E. (n.d.). *Blockchain for refugees; Great hopes, deep concerns.* Retrieved from https://www.qeh.ox.ac.uk/content/Blockchain-refugees-great-hopes-deep-concerns

Liberatore, M. (2018). *Should Australia use Blockchain to deliver humanitarian aid?* Retrieved from https://www.aspistrategist.org.au/australia-use-Blockchain-delivering-humanitarian-aid/

Manby, B. (2016). *Identification in the context of forced displacement: Identification for development (ID4D).* Working Paper. World Bank.

Martin, M. (2016). *Only 13 percent of recent refugees in Germany have found work: Survey.* Retrieved from https://www.reuters.com/article/us-europe-migrants-germany-survey-idUSKBN13A22F

Matthis, J. (2018). *IOTA, United Nations agency partner for Blockchain transparency push.* Retrieved from https://finance.yahoo.com/news/iota-united-nations-agency-partner-194006182.html

Meier, P. (2015). *Digital humanitarians: How big data is changing the face of humanitarian response.* Oakville, Canada: Apple Academic Press. doi:10.1201/b18023

Norwegian Refugee Council. (2017). *Syrian refugees' right to legal identity; Implications for return; Briefing Note.* Retrieved from https://www.nrc.no/globalassets/pdf/briefing-notes/icla/final-syrian-refugees-civil-documentation-briefing-note-21-12-2016.pdf

Norwegian Refugee Council. (2017a). *Reflections on future challenges to housing, land and property restitution for Syrian refugees; A Briefing Note.* Retrieved from https://www.nrc.no/globalassets/pdf/briefing-notes/icla/final-hlp-syrian-refugees-briefing-note-21-12-2016.pdf

O'Neal, S. (2018). *DLT in migration policy; How Blockchain can help both refugees and host nations.* Retrieved from https://cointelegraph.com/news/dlt-in-migration-policy-how-Blockchain-can-help-both-refugees-and-host-nations

Orcutt, M. (2017). *How Blockchain is kickstarting the financial lives of refugees.* Retrieved from https://www.technologyreview.com/s/608764/how-Blockchain-is-kickstarting-the-financial-lives-of-refugees/

Pearcy, A. (2018). *Could Blockchain technology help refugees prove their identity?* Retrieved from https://hackernoon.com/could-Blockchain-technology-help-refugees-to-prove-their-identity-63262fc4380c

Poorternan, A. (2017). *Start network in new partnership with disperse to test revolutionary technology.* Retrieved from https://startnetwork.org/news-and-blogs/Blockchain-experiment-humanitarian-aid

Provost, C. (2013). *Researchers find one-fifth of foreign aid never leaves donor countries.* Retrieved from https://www.theguardian.com/global-development/2013/sep/24/foreign-aid-never-reaches-intended-recipients

Shah, S. (2017). *Save the Children UK CIO to pilot a 'humanitarian passport' using Blockchain.* Retrieved from https://www.itpro.co.uk/strategy/28321/save-the-children-uk-cio-to-pilot-a-humanitarian-passport-using-Blockchain

Smith, P. (2018). *Government's 'Mind-boggling' Digital Transformation Policy Steps Out of a Time Warp.* Retrieved from https://www.afr.com/technology/governments-mindboggling-digital-transformation-policy-steps-out-of-a-time-warp-20181123-h188yu

Stevens, L. (2018). *Self-sovereign identities for scaling up cash transfer projects; designing a Blockchain based digital identity system.* TU Delft. Retrieved from https://repository.tudelft.nl/islandora/object/uuid:6cdb5450-9a81-47a9-8ffa-f9bd77c72448/datastream/OBJ/download

Sundararajan, S. (2018). *Microsoft, Hyperledger, UN join Blockchain identity initiative.* Retrieved from https://www.coindesk.com/microsoft-hyperledger-un-join-Blockchain-identity-initiative

Tassev, L. (2018). *Moldova with new crypto exchange and a token.* Retrieved from https://news.bitcoin.com/moldova-with-new-crypto-exchange-and-a-token/

The Development Circle. (2018). *Red Cross Blockchain case study – enabling transparency of Islamic social financing.* Retrieved from https://developmentcircle.org/2018/07/05/red-cross-Blockchain-case-study-enabling-transparency-of-islamic-social-financing/

UNESCO. (2018). *Right to education.* Retrieved from https://en.unesco.org/themes/right-to-education

UNHCR. (2018). *Forced displacement at record 68.5 million.* Retrieved from https://www.unhcr.org/news/stories/2018/6/5b222c494/forced-displacement-record-685-million.html

UNHCR. (2018). *Education.* Retrieved from https://www.unhcr.org/education.html

UNICEF. (2018). *UNICEF's Innovation fund announces first cohort of Blockchain investments in emerging markets.* Retrieved from https://www.unicef.org/press-releases/unicefs-innovation-fund-announces-first-cohort-Blockchain-investments-emerging

uPort. (2017). *First official registration of a Zug Citizen on Ethereum.* Retrieved from https://medium.com/uport/first-official-registration-of-a-zug-citizen-on-ethereum-3554b5c2c238

World Food Programme. (2018). *Blockchain for zero hunger.* Retrieved from https://innovation.wfp.org/project/building-blocks

KEY TERMS AND DEFINITIONS

AI: Artificial intelligence.
B4SC: Blockchain for social change model.
CSO(s): Civil society organisation(s).
HLP: Housing, land, and property.
INGO(s): International non-government organisaton(s).

NGO(s): Non-government organisation(s).
SSI: Self-sovereign identity.
UN: United Nations.
UNOPS: United Nations Office for Project Services.

ENDNOTES

[1]   Ranging from voting procedures, critical infrastructure security, education and healthcare, to car leasing, forecasting, real estate, energy management, government and public records, wills and inheritance, corporate governance and crowdfunding.

[2]   https://id2020.org/

[3]   https://tse.bitnation.co/passport/

[4]   https://blockstack.org/

[5]   https://www.shyft.network

[6]   https://www.uport.me/

[7]   https://aid.technology/

[8]   https://banqu.co/our-purpose/

[9]   https://www.bitgivefoundation.org/

[10] https://www.bitgivefoundation.org/givetrack-2/

[11] https://www.ubitquity.io/

[12] https://chronobank.io/

[13] http://www.amply.tech/

Chapter 8

Blockchain for Universal Health Coverage

ABSTRACT

In this chapter the authors provide an overview of where Blockchain is being used in high resource settings and explore its potential use in emerging health systems for universal health coverage. There is opportunity to address issues in emerging health systems through adaptation and testing of Blockchain, especially in the management of patient records and data, financing, supply chain management, health workforce management, and surveillance processes. It also has complementary relevance for identity and financial inclusion, which are vital for improving the health of the poor in emerging economies. Reference is also made to the use of Blockchain for displaced people and humanitarian settings, which is the subject of Chapter 7 of this book. There remains, however, a need for more research and evaluation as these technologies are implemented and increased user participation in design to ensure that privacy and security issues are addressed. Furthermore, greater attention to local implementation and health sector applications in low resource settings is required.

INTRODUCTION

Blockchain is increasingly seen as a technology that has potential to contribute to global health equity and universal health coverage (Till et al, 2017). Universal health coverage is defined as *ensuring that all people have access to needed*

DOI: 10.4018/978-1-5225-9578-6.ch008

health services (including prevention, promotion, treatment, rehabilitation and palliation) of sufficient quality to be effective while also ensuring that the use of these services does not expose the user to financial hardship (World Health Organisation, 2019).

A literature review of applications of Blockchain in health care (Mwashuma, 2018) concluded that Blockchain will be key in building a global health ecosystem that connects patients, clinicians, researchers, insurers and clinical laboratories. It further cited potential for Blockchain to improve patient data security, data sharing, interoperability, patient engagement, and big data analytics health information exchange, fight counterfeit drugs, and improve research processes and AI based diagnostics. Additionally, an article in the reputable British Medical Journal (Till et al, 2017) posits that Blockchain could remake global health financing and contribute to global health equity and universal health coverage. Blockchain is demonstrating its potential to re-architect many incumbent business models, removing friction and improving data sharing in a highly secure environment while leveraging existing IT infrastructure (Brodersen et al, 2016).

The basic features which underpin the technology help demonstrate why the approach may suit health sector transformation, especially. Firstly, Blockchain enables a distributed database, where each party on a Blockchain has access to the entire database and its complete history. No single party controls the data or the information and every party can verify the records of its transaction partners directly, without an intermediary. In this system, peer-to-peer transmission is supported, with communication occurring directly between peers as opposed to through a central node. Each node stores and forwards information to all other nodes (Iansiti & Lakhani, 2017). With health systems in emerging settings often decentralized, they face constant challenges both to centralize information (national reporting) and to share information across disparate nodes (sharing information on patient treatment at different health service sites). Distributed databases are, by design, intended to address these issues.

Secondly, Blockchain technology enables transparency with pseudonymity, where each transaction is visible to anyone with permissioned access to the system, but where users can choose to remain anonymous or provide proof of their identity to others. Once a transaction is entered in the database recording on the database is permanent, chronologically ordered, and available to all others on the network. Finally, transactions can be tied to computational logic and programmed. Blockchains offer properties of decentralization, transparency, and immutability that can potentially be leveraged to improve healthcare interoperability. Programmable Blockchains have generated interest as a potential solution to key challenges such as inefficient clinical report delivery and fragmented health records.

This chapter begins with a brief overview of how Blockchain is being used and developed in high resource health care systems, then explores the potential in emerging economies for health care and related areas, given that many determinants of good health are social - such as the conditions in which people are born, grow, live, work and age

Blockchain for health care fundamentally reaches towards Empowerment in the New World as represented in the B4SC model in Figure 1.

FOCUS OF BLOCKCHAIN IN HEALTH CARE

Key challenges in healthcare include identity management, provenance, credentialing, health record management, bundled payments, medical device security and interoperability. An overview by GitHub (2018), a major repository of open source code, found significant activity in health care data infrastructure, electronic and patient health records, and health care analytics, medical device and IoT security, identity, supply chain, and digital medicine and care delivery. Blockchain technology is helpful in "verifying the integrity of patient data shared across different organizations, can create immutable audit trails for data governing health care business processes and maintain the integrity of data collected in clinical health trials." For example, Gem is

Figure 1. The New World; Empowerment

using Blockchain technology "to provide data transparency, change-auditing and fine-grained access control to health records."

Blockchain technology has the potential to address interoperability challenges present in health IT systems. It can become the technical standard to enable individuals, health care providers, health care entities and medical researchers in securely sharing electronic health data. This section examines some of these key areas of Blockchain health system innovation.

Patient Management, Service Delivery and Information

The longitudinal management of patient information, and access to patient information, within a health system, is an ongoing challenge. Within the literature, patient data management systems, including data infrastructure, patient records and analytics, emerges as important applications. The notion of historical patient care influencing present decisions fits well into the Blockchain model, where the identity of a present event is dependent on all past events (Peterson et al, n.d). In a patient-centered care model, use of distributed ledger approaches, enabled by the Blockchain, grants patients easier access to and control over sharing their own medical data, and enables different providers access to personal medical records or prescription history (Zhang et al., n.d; Rabah, 2017). Distributed ledger approaches may have a unique ability to bring cohesion to an otherwise disparate and overly complicated system of delivering data across the healthcare spectrum (Brodersen et al, 2016).

The Estonian eHealth Authority is the commonly cited example of a real-world application of Blockchain technology in healthcare. In 2005, the Estonian Ministry of Social Affairs launched a new e-health concept by phasing in four projects: Electronic Health Records, digital images, digital registration and digital prescription. The implementation of these projects aims to create a unified national health information system, linked with other public information systems and registers (European Commission, n.d). At the center of the system is the electronic health record, for which the Estonian ID card is used to authenticate and provide digital signatures. Access to this record is regulated by law, with access only enabled to licensed attending medical professionals (Saluse et al, 2010). The Estonian eHealth Authority collaborated with Guardtime, a cyber-security provider that uses Blockchain systems to ensure the integrity of data, to secure the over one million healthcare records of its citizens (Brodersen et al, 2016; Heston, 2017).

Access to complete medical records is essential in order to adapt the treatment and provide personalised care and sharing information among the medical community is a major challenge. Blockchain can provide a structure for data sharing as well as security. It allows the patient to control the access he gives to his medical records. The patient defines through a smart contract the condition on which his data can be accessed on the Blockchain. In fact, all this will be done through an API and the patient will set the conditions on his profile.

Interoperability is a major challenge for health systems and is often focused on data exchange between organisations (hospitals, insurers etc.). Blockchain can enable patient-driven interoperability, where health data exchange can be patient-mediated and patient-driven. Currently patient data is held at multiple points in the system and no one has the complete picture. This has benefits for operational efficiency, duplication in clinical interventions, overall health system cost, waste, and improved clinical care, by facilitating improved access to relevant, longitudinal clinical data at the point-of-care (Catalini, 2018). Examples include the "Healthcare Data Gateway" (Yue et al, 2016); and MedChain (http://medchain.us/, n.d.) a permissioned network of medication stakeholders that facilitate medication-specific data sharing between patients, hospitals, and pharmacies.

One Australian start-up is attempting to accelerate the transition to digital health by building the country's first Blockchain based digital health platform. Secure Health Chain was developed in the regional New South Wales town of Wollongong by three Doctors who became fed up with the slow rate of progress. Patients describe this as their 'health passport' and no longer need to choose between portability and security. Patients are now able to carry a 'single-source of truth' with up to date health information in their back pocket, with the peace of mind that it is protected by the superior encryption power afforded by Blockchain technology (secure.health.io)

Clinical Trials and Surveillance

Blockchain may also support better a surveillance process through its 'community of trust' structure. It may, for example, support the 'trusted community' of research, gathering researchers and patient communities, social network data flows, with features of individual granularity, decentralisation and security and with transparent interactions to ensure easier and more transparent analysis (Benchoufi & Ravaud, 2017). For both surveillance and clinical research, it may be an opportunity for clinical research: it may help in structuring more transparent, checkable methodology and help check clinical

Table 1. Applications of Blockchain in clinical trials

Issue	Blockchain Solution
Selective reporting of data from trials	The study protocol, including planned analysis and clinical outcomes can be hashed to a text file. Any change to the original file, would result in a completely different hash.
Data falsification, data "beautification" and data invention	Data Integrity is ensured by the cryptographic validation of each transaction. Each transaction with Blockchain is time-stamped. This information is publicly transparent; any user owns a copy of the proof of the time-stamped data.
Problems including missing data, endpoint switching, data dredging, and selective publication	Blockchain can prove the existence of documents describing pre-specified endpoints in clinical trials. Blockchain smart contracts provide a technological solution to the data manipulation problem, by acting as trusted administrators and providing an immutable record of trial history.
Consent	Blockchain enables data user's control or differential privacy, data sharing. The Estonian e-Health authority has just implemented a Blockchain solution enabling storage of a million health records, letting patients control data access through a "Keyless Signature Infrastructure" (E-Estonia, n.d)
Collection of Consent	It is possible to build a Smart Contract that will be executed with the only condition that patients will only be included when their consent has been obtained.
Ensure All Steps are Completed	Blockchain, can also chain together different clinical trial steps so that each step depends on its predecessor. Blockchain Smart Contracts, and can enforce the level transparency, traceability and control over clinical trial sequences.
Blockchains provide a notarization functionality	Through posting a cryptographic hash of a text, data, or general-purpose file to a Blockchain database, it can be proven that this file or text existed at a certain time point. Lab books could post digests to a *Blockchain* system to make them immutable by means of time-stamped entries and study design can be pre-registered to a *Blockchain to* prevent the alteration of study design after the experiment.
Data Sharing	Through Blockchain databases, data can be stored and shared. Cryptography can assure that the data is only available to permissioned people. For subject anonymity, this can be organized with cryptography.
Clinical Health Data Exchange and Interoperability	Blockchain data exchange systems are cryptographically secured and irrevocable. This would enable seamless access to historic and real-time patient data and eliminate the cost of data reconciliation.
Many clinical trials go unreported, and investigators often fail to share their study results	Blockchain-enabled, time-stamped immutable records of clinical trials, protocols and results addresses outcome switching, data snooping and selective reporting, thereby reducing the incidence of fraud and error in clinical trial records.
Clinical Trials	Blockchain represents a powerful solution to ensure the integrity of clinical trials data from start to finish. It can generate a higher level of trust and increase in data transparency' and the consensus mechanism prevents modification and Blockchain networks make it easy and safe to use data by multiple parties in ways that ensure privacy and integrity.

trial integrity (Benchoufi & Ravaud, 2017). Table 1 summarises a number of potential applications for Blockchain in clinical trials.

Medical Supply Chain Integrity and Provenance

Provenance – tracking of assets across a supply chain – has emerged as an early application area for Blockchain (Rabah, 2017). The benefit of using Blockchain in healthcare supply chains could take place across the entire supply chain spectrum, extending from drug companies and manufacturers, as well as improvement to pharma clinical trials and longitudinal health research for the patient. Distributed ledger approaches have something strong to offer to supply chain management, which should be tested for emerging health systems. Blockchain technologies help with two main issues when it comes to drug traceability: first, it allows companies to track their products down the supply chain, creating an airtight circuit, impermeable to counterfeit products. Second, it also allows stakeholders, and especially labs, to take action in case of a problem by identifying the exact location of their drugs.

Health Payment Systems

The strength of Blockchain lies in its development as a financial technology, especially for payments and money transfers. There is also an emerging development of distributed ledger approaches and Blockchain for health financing and insurance. The literature shows that there are several aspects worth considering across the health payment systems.

There is interest within the health insurance sector about the potential for Blockchain-driven approaches to improve health insurance payments, systems and management (Deloitte, 2016). Firstly, within the health payment process, the distributed ledger process can use smart contracts across parties that enable automatic adjudication of claims and direct payment processes and reduce the number of intermediaries that exist today which lead to more streamlined transactions (Randall, Goel, Abujamra, 2017). Deployment of a Blockchain application that utilizes a smart contract and verifiable ledger of all service and payment activities could further reduce fraud and overpayment in health systems (Randall, Goel, Abujamra, 2017).

Secondly, Blockchain has the potential also to be used for the automated validation of claims, which may increase the efficiency and security of the payment process. The software can store encrypted patient identifiers, health plan information, and provider claims within a Blockchain that is shared by payers and providers, enabling near real-time automatic claims processing, eligibility verification, and preauthorization (Angraal et al, 2017). Facilitating claim settlement by reducing bureaucracy and introduce bill management to reduce fraud and speed up payment may be achieved more efficiently by creating consortia of health providers and insurers as part of a 'permissioned' chain (Makridakis et al, n.d).

Human Resource Management

One of the great promises of Blockchain technology is that it can serve as a decentralized, permanently unalterable storage alternative for all types of information, making the technology a prime tool for certification of digital data and identities (Makridakis et al, n.d). This could include health provider identities and may potentially be extended to include validated credentials. While many different tools can periodically authenticate the user, health regulators and financiers must ensure that health care provider's claims are true, given surrounding fraud, waste, and abuse have become of paramount importance to both providers and payers (Brodersen et al, 2016). There are already applications tested in high resource systems to manage health workforce credentialing for flexible workforce deployment, which could usefully be further developed for deployment of health workforce in emergencies, disasters and outbreaks; or in regions where there is health workforce migration and movement.

Blockchain Potential in Emerging Markets for Universal Healthcare

Many of these solutions described are designed for high resource health settings - for example, UK or US health systems. Their practical application in emerging health systems is less clear. The following section explores how Blockchain technology could be a transformative accelerator enabling many of these interventions to reach the poor. Much of its content is from Jane Thomason's 2017 article, "Blockchain: An Accelerator for Women and Children's Health?"

Unacceptably high rates of maternal and child deaths still prevail in Asia and Africa and The Global Strategy for Women's, Children's and Adolescents' Health and Global Investment Framework for Investing in Women's and

Children's Health identify the evidence based interventions in the 74 high burden countries that together account for more than 95% of maternal and child deaths worldwide. These interventions could prevent more than 147 million child deaths, 32 million stillbirths and save more than five million maternal lives between 2013 and 2035. These include immunisation; breastfeeding and improved nutrition; training and supervising health workers; strengthening the supply chain; better collection of data through improving health information systems; allocating resources to supporting good governance through informed and transparent decision making; and investing in health financing mechanisms that reduce barriers to essential care and protect people from financial distress (Thomason & Lopez, 2013). Many of these interventions can be enabled or accelerated using Blockchain.

Identity

As raised in Chapter Seven, a legal identity is a fundamental human right and is a prerequisite for financial inclusion, access to services, movement of people and a multitude of things we take for granted. Still, many millions of people worldwide do not have a legal identity (World Bank, 2018). The potential to confer a permanent, immutable record of identity in the Blockchain owned by individuals could be game changing. Without identity, poor women and children may be denied access to government services, finance and fundamental human rights. Blockchain can be used to ensure women and children's access to these services and enable health rights.

Identity data is held immutably on a Blockchain, the web of trust "hardens" the data over time, the identity data remains in the ownership of the individual and individuals give permissions on who can see what data for what purpose and for how long. It's a transformative concept. Blockchain records can be used to establish an identity where no state identity exists or can be used.

Supply Chains for Distribution of Vaccines and Medical Supplies

Getting quality medicines to the poor is critical to their efficacy. Blockchain offers the capacity for purchasers to see every part of the journey their product took before arriving in their hands. It also enables supply chain companies to identify attempted fraud more easily, because once a block is on the

Blockchain, it cannot be altered. IBM offers a service which allows customers to test Blockchain solutions to track high value items on supply chains. This service is being used by Everledger (2017) to promote transparency into the diamond supply chain and UK firm Provenance is working to enable companies to be more transparent about where their products are made and by whom and environmental impacts.

Take also the example of the Port of Rotterdam (Port of Rotterdam, 2019), which implements a Blockchain supply chain solution. Each participant in a supply chain ecosystem can view the progress of goods through the supply chain, understanding where a container is in transit. They can also see the status of customs documents, or view bills of lading and other data. Detailed visibility of the container's progress through the supply chain is enhanced with the real-time exchange of original supply chain events and documents. No one party can modify, delete or even append any record without the consensus from others on the network. This level of transparency helps reduce fraud and errors, reduce the time products spend in the transit and shipping process, improve inventory management and ultimately reduce waste and cost. The solution enables the real-time exchange of original supply chain events and documents through a digital infrastructure, or data pipeline, that connects the participants in a supply chain ecosystem. This promotes sustainable transport by integrating shipping processes and partners and establishing evaluation frameworks through increased transparency and trusted access. This has clear relevance for health supply chains.

Drug counterfeiting is a major problem in the pharmaceutical industry. It is estimated that 10% to 30% of the drugs sold in developing countries are counterfeit (World Health Organisation, 2017). The main characteristic of Blockchain technology that is useful in drug traceability is security. Each new transaction added to a block is immutable and timestamped, making it easy to track a product and make sure the information cannot be altered. Blockchain offers a supply chain solution which allows end-to-end track and trace. If efficacious drugs are not provided, patients' health and lives are at risk. Blockverify is working to prevent the counterfeiting of drugs which cause thousands of lives to be lost. Blockchain can be used to confirm that vaccines are genuine, not out of date and the vaccine record can be linked with individual ID record to confirm vaccine delivery. It could also be used to unlock payment to providers as well as provide incentive to parent (i.e. confirmed vaccination allows access to other service/benefit) through use of cryptocurrencies (Blockverify, n.d). These solutions need to be tested in emerging markets and applied for health supply chains.

Data and Health Records

Blockchain technology has the potential to address the interoperability challenges currently present in health IT systems and to be the technical standard that enables individuals, health care providers, health care entities and medical researchers to securely share electronic health data (Linn & Koo, n.d). Blockchain is based on open standards and provides the necessary data security, while also assuring patient identity and verification of services covered by insurance and rendered by providers. Blockchains offer a solution that not only enables secure data exchange but that places a person's health records more within their reach and control, rather than being fragmented and oftentimes inaccessible to the patient in some far-removed central database. There is even the potential for patient-owned longitudinal health records, based around patient ID. Medical histories on a Blockchain cannot be lost or altered without the patient's permission and the patient can have access via a mobile app.

Hard to reach populations including long distance truck drivers, female sex workers and men remain the residual drivers of the HIV epidemic, regardless of the significant decline in the number of new infections. For example, in South Africa estimates from 2014 and 2016, indicate long distance truck drivers have an HIV prevalence of 56 percent and female sex workers to have an HIV prevalence of 90.6 percent (Georgetown University, 2017; Klapper, 2017).

Thomason and Wier (2018) posit that innovative Blockchain technology solutions could improve continuity of care, data access, improved targeting for programming and design, portable identities, reliable supply chain, fund movement, interoperable records that allow populations to access services across clinical facilities, and privacy. This would allow drivers to access linked services across multiple countries. Together with biometrics, Blockchain can protect identity and enable access to services. One means of ensuring continuity of care for these populations would be the provision of a unique digital identity, which could be linked to an electronic personal health record in clinics and care points along trucking routes, enabling patients to confidentially access care in multiple locations.

However, moving weak systems for patient records and health data from their current, protected status onto open, anonymised public ledgers will require a reorientation of process, thought and law in many countries. In emerging health systems Blockchain may offer the potential to leapfrog to a better data system, but this needs to be tested.

FINANCIAL INCLUSION

Addressing poverty is a critical aspect to achieving universal health coverage (UHC). The poor of the world need assistance with cross-border and internal payments, and multiple successful initiatives (e.g., mobile money) have contributed to increased financial inclusion for this population. Blockchain's unique characteristics allow financial institutions to tailor their products and services to promote ease of use for the unbanked and underbanked. A company from the Philippines, Coins.ph, offers a good example of Blockchain's potential. Situated in the country ranked third in the world for receiving remittances, totaling approximately 30 USD billion a year, Coins.ph provides Filipino users a mobile, Blockchain-based platform to allow them to send money at a more affordable and faster rate. Blockchain allowed Coins.ph to build an application to facilitate fund transfers without reliance on existing bank infrastructures and to be more agile in their services at a more affordable price (Georgetown University, 2017).

Current remittance processes are slow and expensive. Digital currency remittances can move funds from remitter or donor to recipient almost instantaneously with low transaction costs. CASHAA is operating in India and Nigeria and transmits remittances at no cost to the consumer. Experience from Bangladesh shows that women actually prefer to receive payments by phone, rather than cash (Klapper, 2017). In order to be possible this will rely on the confirmation of the identity of the recipient, emphasizing the criticality of solving the identity piece. With Blockchain enabled digital currencies and identity – financial inclusion can be provided to the two billion unbanked in the world (Kunt et al, n.d). Blockchain would reduce the transaction costs for remittances, providing the unbanked access to financial systems and ensuring that funds intended for the poor actually reach them.

CASH TRANSFERS

UHC has traditionally relied on donor funded programs. This is both unsustainable and insufficient. As poverty declines the remaining poor are likely to be split between middle-income countries and fragile states (Summer, 2013). Traditional poverty alleviation efforts will not work in countries where aid is already becoming irrelevant as domestic resources grow. Mobilization of domestic financing and private financial flows will be critically important. Traditional development assistance will not be core to solving global development problems in the future. There will also be an increasing importance of non-aid sources of financing from high-income to developing countries: non-concessional loans from development banks (multilateral and national) for development investments focused on growth and job creation and transfers from high-income to developing countries in support of global public goods (Birdsall, 2013).

With two-thirds of the 1.1 billion unbanked owning smartphones, decentralised finance offers a world of opportunity to the poor. Using only a telephone on a 2G or 3G service, anyone can connect directly to the network to access financial services without using a third party - money can be sent directly, from person-to-person – even in remote locations. Credit is more easily available and at cheaper rates. As global remittance fees can span anywhere between 7.1 and 9.4 per cent, major efforts at reducing poverty include chipping away at the dominance of large financial actors using decentralised networks (World Bank, 2018) as M-Pesa has done in challenging Western Union. As cash transfers have been found to improve the social determinants of health (Owusu-Addo, Renzaho & Smith, 2018), Blockchains are considered able to reduce the severity of poverty and create empowerment opportunities through financial inclusion.

Blockchains are low-cost, relatively easy to implement and they prevent accidental or deliberate financial loss during transactions. Consequently, they have been found highly valuable by non-government organisations, using them to create and store digital identities for displaced people and enable cash transfer programs cost-effectively. Findings from pilot studies by organisations such as the United Nations and the International Federation of the Red Cross have been satisfactory; indicating savings of thousands of dollars in third-party transaction fees and efficiently delivered cash to beneficiaries in scalable programs. These pilots are novel innovations that have been successful in samples of, on average, 2000 people. However, while almost every government in the world is researching Blockchains, it may be several years before we see their implementation at a national level.

In Sierra Leone, Blockchain is being used for identity and cash transfers using Kiva Protocol and Hyperledger. Xavier Michon, Deputy Executive Secretary of the United Nations Capital Development Fund, has declared that the Sierra Leone cash transfer system "could serve as a model for both developing and developed nations in the future," (cf O'Neal, 2018). Sierra Leone have been working with the World Bank and the UNCDF to modernise the financial records of its citizens since 2016. In that time, it has managed to digitize the records of over 5 million of its 7.1 million citizens. The Kiva protocol establishes a digital identity and digital wallet for (socially underwritten) loans and transfers against that loan. The established identity and credit history builds a lending profile for borrowers that makes future borrowings from national banks easier. This project is supported by the Sierra Leonean government, beginning in 2019 and to be rolled out nationwide until 2022 for 6.24 million people.

The Red Cross is using permissioned Multichain for Cash Transfers with RedRose and M-Pesa mobile. 2100 Kenyan households were chosen for a pilot Blockchain open-loop cash transfer programme run by the Red Cross. This was the first of its kind – humanitarian organisations typically use closed-loop payments like-vouchers. Personal information was uploaded to a RedRose data management program, integrated with the mobile money provider M-Pesa, using a Multichain Blockchain. Findings indicated an efficient process with 2,090 beneficiaries receiving their money in three days. This is the only open-loop Blockchain solution that has shown it can be scalable.

TRACKING DONOR FUNDS THROUGH SMART CONTRACTS

In "Unchain the Block: Speed, transparency and efficiency in donor fund flows" (Thomason, 2019), Thomason and Wier (2019) make the case that if Blockchain were applied to cash transfers for the $177.6 billion given by donors in developing countries, there could be savings realized of an additional $15 billion that donors can spend on services.

Using smart contracts, Blockchain can ensure that donor funds reach intended recipients in a transparent way without middlemen and leakage along the way. Aid delivery can be tracked with transparently recorded "weigh-stations" showing location in supply chain and ultimate delivery. A smart contract could unlock a delivery payment when a service is delivered to intended recipient (using a Blockchain enabled identity). A Blockchain record can support donor funds by providing a specific record of care achieved through the funding.

HUMANITARIAN AND REFUGEE SETTINGS

Chapter Seven discussed at length the applications of Blockchain in humanitarian and refugee settings, so it is only summarized here. Digital technologies can add value to refugees and displaced people in multiple ways and are already being harnessed both by humanitarian agencies and people on the move. Many displaced populations rely on cellphones as an absolute necessity, sometimes prioritizing phones over food or shelter.

The process of migration can increase vulnerabilities to chronic and noncommunicable diseases or cause life-threatening complications. Most migrant women face poorer pregnancy and birth outcomes. Under 13 interventions as part of the European Strategy and Action Plan regarding the health of refugees, the WHO (2018) recommends cooperative mechanisms for the universal, inclusive, provision of indiscriminatory care for migrants and refugees. This can be enabled using new distributed technologies that can provision a globally recognised, secure, portable digital identity and corresponding health record that enable health providers and government body's access to medical records and legal documentation.

Blockchain technologies are being used by non-government organisations to provide digital identities to internationally displaced women and children as the foundation for service delivery in refugee camps in Syria, Jordan and Pakistan. Coupled with protocols such as proposed standards like Fast Healthcare Interoperability Resources (FHIR), which breaks down data silos by securing and distributing medical records, it is possible to create a portable, permanent identity for women and children, with sharable medical records, that indicate vaccination status, past medical treatments and current medical conditions, easing the process of seeking medical treatment across borders and gaining asylum. [1]

CHALLENGES

As for many technologies and new business processes, there are several challenges for emerging health systems which may be associated with Blockchain use. These are not necessarily distinct to Blockchain applications; however they are worth highlighting to provide a sense of balance and risk assessment. For example, as discussed by Brodersen et al. (2016), there may be regulatory and legal challenges because Blockchain technologies offer a new socio-political paradigm for doing business, few legal and regulatory frameworks are in place to govern their use. Regulatory sandboxes are useful settings within which to test new technology approaches. As for most systems which collect individual data, distributed access to the data set does comes with the risk for potential compromise or reidentification (Angraal, 2017). Storage of large amounts of information 'on the chain' is a considerable challenge, and ways in which data is stored off the chain for health application need to be established.

The transition to patient-driven interoperability will require new processes around security protocols, privacy configurations, electronic consent, and governance. Permissioned, member-only Blockchain consortia can minimize public exposure, with data storage off-chain, with on-chain focused around permissions or other meta-data, along with patient-friendly applications ecosystem of intermediaries to manage public keys and permissions.

Longer term issues of building local digital capacity, education of governments and donors, and building partnerships and conversations with ecosystems that have not historically interacted remain important issues to address, and there is a need for development of taxonomy and standards, governance and how to protect the vulnerable. The challenges need to be provided in realizing a production grade Blockchain system to address these issues. In healthcare, privacy and sensitive of data is significant concern.

CONCLUSION

There is a surprising amount of literature related to the application of distributed ledger approaches and Blockchain technology. However, much of this literature focuses on the potential of the approach for high resource health systems, and very little on the application in emerging health systems.

There is evident potential and opportunity to address issues in emerging health systems through lateral adaptation and testing of distributed ledger approaches using Blockchain from well-functioning health systems. Areas of focus could be the management of patient records and data, health payment systems, supply chain management, health workforce management and surveillance processes.

Much more needs to be reviewed in terms of country implementation and experiences for the health sector application, however, health system innovation should not exist in a vacuum. The distinct advantage of considering Blockchain approaches is that it is well-tested in other sectors. Supply chain management and provenance is an area of clear focus, with benefits for management of supply chain systems in emerging health settings. Its proven application in the financial sector, for improving efficiency and effectiveness of payment systems through use of smart contracts, and its emerging use in health insurance systems in high functioning health systems, is worth exploring for its application in emerging health reimbursement systems. There remains a need for more research and evaluation as these technologies are implemented, increased user participation in design and to ensure that privacy and security issues are addressed.

To be most effective in a health system, a Blockchain must be an addition to the healthcare ecosystem, and not invalidate or minimize existing, precious, technology investments. For emerging health systems, Blockchain is best viewed as a tool in the healthcare toolbox- one that may overcome some of the challenges of current service models have. From this perspective, distributed ledger approaches and Blockchain systems could be tested for use in emerging health systems, especially if focused on reaching the most vulnerable. Blockchain's potential for social impact is yet to be realized, with limited but growing use cases in developing countries.

The focus of the global community needs to move from the underlying technology to exploring use cases – and looking for solutions that can scale. There are many practical questions to be answered in settings with little internet access and electricity. However, for Blockchain to help move the world toward health equity, the global health community, the global financial community and the global tech community must work together to help shape this process.

ACKNOWLEDGMENT

An earlier version of this chapter was significantly contributed to by Anneke Schmider.

REFERENCES

Angraal, S., Krumholz, H. M., & Schulz, W. L. (2017). *Blockchain technology applications in health care. In Circulation: Cardiovascular Quality and Outcomes*. Dallas, TX: American Heart And Stroke Association.

Behlendorf, B. (2017). The potential for Blockchain technology in Health IT. *Healthcare Information and Management Systems Society*. Retrieved from http://www.himss.org/news/potential-Blockchain-technology-hit

Benchoufi, M., & Ravaud, P. (2017). Blockchain technology for improving clinical research quality. *Trials*, *18*(1), 335. doi:10.118613063-017-2035-z PMID:28724395

Birdsall, N. (2013). *'The Future of Aid'- 2030: ODA no more (global policy)*. Retrieved from https://www.cgdev.org/article/future-aid-2030-oda-no-more-global-policy

Blockverify. (n.d.). *Blockchain based anti-counterfeit solution*. Retrieved from http://www.blockverify.io/

Brodersen, C., Kalis, B., Leong, C., Mitchell, E., Pupo, E., & Truscott, A. (2016). *Blockchain: Securing a new health interoperability Experience*. Retrieved from https://www.healthit.gov/sites/default/files/2-49-accenture_onc_Blockchain_challenge_response_august8_final.pdf

Catalini, C., & Gans, J. S. (2016). *Some simple economics of the Blockchain* (working paper no. 2874598). Retrieved from SSRN website: https://papers.ssrn.com/sol3/papers.cfm?abstract_id=2874598

Deloitte. (2016). *Blockchain in health and life insurance. Turning a buzzword into a breakthrough*. Retrieved from https://www2.deloitte.com/us/en/pages/life-sciences-and-health-care/articles/Blockchain-in-insurance.html

Demirguc-Kunt, A., Klapper, L., Singer, D., & Van Oudheusden, P. (2011). *The Global Findex Database 2014: Measuring financial inclusion around the world*. Retrieved from http://documents.worldbank.org/curated/en/187761468179367706/The-Global-Findex-Database-2014-measuring-financial-inclusion-around-the-world

E-Estonia. (n.d.). *Healthcare*. Retrieved from https://e-estonia.com/solutions/healthcare/e-health-record/

European Commission. (n.d.). *An Electronic Health Record for every citizen: A global first Estonia*. Retrieved from ec.europa.eu/regional_policy/en/projects/best-practices/estonia/1435/download

Everledger. (n.d.). *Home*. Retrieved from https://www.everledger.io/

Georgetown University. (2017). *Blockchain and financial inclusion: The role Blockchain technology can play in accelerating financial inclusion.* Retrieved from https://digitalchamber.org/assets/Blockchain-and-financial-inclusion.pdf

Github. (2018). *Where are the healthcare-related Blockchains?* Retrieved from https://github.com/acoravos/healthcare-Blockchains

Heston, T. (2017). *A case study in healthcare Innovation* (working paper No AUTHOREA_213011_3643634). Retrieved from SSRN website: https://papers.ssrn.com/sol3/papers.cfm?abstract_id=3077455

Iansiti, M., & Lakhani, K. (2017). The truth about Blockchain. *Harvard Business Review.* Retrieved from https://enterprisersproject.com/sites/default/files/the_truth_about_Blockchain.pdf

Klapper, L. (2017). Why women workers and managers prefer electronic wage payments in Bangladesh. *World Bank Development Research Group.* Retrieved from https://www.betterthancash.org/news/blogs-stories/why-women-workers-and-managers-prefer-electronic-wage-payments-bangladesh

Linn, L., & Koo, M. (n.d.). *Blockchain for health data and its potential use in health IT and health care related research.* Retrieved from https://www.healthit.gov/sites/default/files/11-74-aBlockchainforhealthcare.pdf

Makridakis. (n.d.). *Blockchain: Current achievements, future prospects/challenges.* Retrieved from https://www.researchgate.net/profile/Spyros_Makridakis/publication/320728728_Blockchain_Current_Achievements_Future_ProspectsChallenges_and_its_Combination_with_AI/links/59f824990f7e9b553ebf048a/Blockchain-Current-Achievements-Future-Prospects-Challenges-and-its-Combination-with-AI

O'Neal, S. (2018). *Ahead of traditional banking: How Africa employs Blockchain for financial inclusion.* Retrieved from https://cryptoleadingnews.com/news/ahead-of-traditional-banking-how-africa-employs-Blockchain-for-financial-inclusion/

Owusu-Addo, E., Renzaho, A., & Smith, B. (2018). Cash transfers and the social determinants of health; A conceptual framework. *Health Promotion International.* doi:10.1093/heapro/day079 PMID:30272155

Peterson, K., Deeduvanu, R., Kanjamala, P., & Boles, K. (n.d.). *A Blockchain-based approach to health information exchange networks*. Mayo Clinic. Retrieved from https://www.healthit.gov/sites/default/files/12-55-Blockchain-based-approach-final.pdf

Rabah, K. (2017). Challenges & opportunities for Blockchain powered healthcare systems: A review. *Mara Research Journal of Medicine and Health Sciences*, *1*(1), 45–52.

Randall, D., Goel, P., & Abujamra, R. (2017). Blockchain applications and use cases in health information technology. *Journal of Health & Medical Informatics*, *8*(3), 276. doi:10.4172/2157-7420.1000276

Saluse, J., Aaviksoo, A., Ross, P., Tiik, M., Parv, L., Sepper, R., . . . Enni, K. (2010). *Assessing the economic impact/net benefits of the Estonian Electronic Health Record system DIGIMPACT Final Report*. Retrieved from http://www.praxis.ee/fileadmin/tarmo/Projektid/Tervishoid/Digimoju/Digimpact.pdf

Summer, A. (2013). The donors' dilemma: Emergence, convergence and the future of aid: An introduction. *Global Policy*. Retrieved from https://www.globalpolicyjournal.com/blog/17/10/2013/donors'-dilemma-emergence-convergence-and-future-aid-introduction

Thomason, J. (2017). Blockchain: An Accelerator for Women and Children's Health? *Global Health Journal*, *1*(1), 3–10.

Thomason, J. (2019). *Unchain the block: Speed, transparency and efficiency in donor fund flows*. Retrieved from https://www.linkedin.com/pulse/unchain-block-speed-transparency-efficiency-donor-fund-thomason/?published=t

Thomason, J., & Lopez, A. (2013). Civil registration and vital statistics – everybody's business but nobody's business. *Lancet*, *381*(9874), 1275–1276. doi:10.1016/S0140-6736(13)60838-7 PMID:23582394

Till, B.M., Peters, A.W., Afshar, S., & Meara, J.G. (2017). Blockchain technology to global health equity: Can cryptocurrencies finance universal health coverage? *BMJ Global Health, 2*(4).

WHO. (2018). *Health of refugees and migrants; regional situation analysis, practices, lessons learned and ways forward*. Retrieved from https://www.who.int/migrants/publications/EURO-report.pdf

World Bank. (2018). Migration and development brief 29. *Knomad*. Retrieved from https://www.knomad.org/publication/migration-and-development-brief-29

World Health Organisation. (2016). *The global strategy for women's, children's and adolescents' health. (2016-2030).* Retrieved from http://www.who.int/life-course/partners/global-strategy/global-strategy-2016-2030/en/

Yue, X., Wang, H., Jin, D., Li, M., & Jiang, W. (2016). Healthcare data gateways: Found healthcare intelligence on Blockchain with novel privacy risk control. *Journal of Medical Systems*, *40*(10), 218. doi:10.100710916-016-0574-6 PMID:27565509

Zhang, P., Walker, M., White, J., & Schmidt, D. (n.d.). *Metrics for assessing Blockchain-based healthcare decentralized apps.* Vanderbilt University. Retrieved from https://www.dre.vanderbilt.edu/~schmidt/PDF/IEEE-Healthcom-2017.pdf

Zhou, Y., Ancker, J. S., Upadhye, M., McGeorge, N. M., Guarrera, T. K., Hegde, S., ... Lin, L. (2013). The impact of interoperability of electronic health records on ambulatory physician practices: A discrete-event simulation study. *Informatics in Primary Care*, *21*(1), 21–29. doi:10.14236/jhi.v21i1.36 PMID:24629653

ENDNOTE

[1]   For security, medical records would not be stored on the Blockchain but transactions allow providers remote access to data.

Chapter 9
Donors and International Organisations

ABSTRACT

In this chapter the authors examine the response of the international development community to Blockchain and frontier technologies. It considers multilateral, bilateral organisations, and non-government organisations, and their role in curating the design and implementation of these technologies. The authors conclude that the global development community need to be active regarding the digital future. International development organisations have a key role to play in building the evidence on how technology can contribute to making development co-operation more effective, impactful, and inclusive. There is a widespread view that Blockchain and frontier technologies offer an important opportunity to accelerate progress towards the SDGs. It is time for international development organisations to lean in and help shape the new technologies as they rapidly accelerate and galvanise a more systematic and joined up international development approach to the digital future.

INTRODUCTION

In the decentralised, anti-government, anti-bank, libertarian conceptualisation of Blockchain, global institutions were not front and centre in thinking nor engagement. However, as the technology matures, and there become an increasing array of use cases relevant to international development, broad scale implementation of Blockchain for social impact will be slower and quite

DOI: 10.4018/978-1-5225-9578-6.ch009

possibly less than optimal without the support of the international development community. Broadly speaking, the international development ecosystem institutions currently includes the UN system, global development banks, other multilaterals such as OECD, bilateral donors, global funds, academia and international civil society organisations (CSO). These are powerful institutions and can accelerate, ignore or slow the large-scale execution of digitisation for social impact. They also have an important role to play in education and production and dissemination of evidence of effectiveness. Therefore, it is important to review where major global players sit in relation to digitisation and social impact.

Given that these technologies are new, the public discourse has largely been shaped by social media and blogs. While there are now peer reviewed journals emerging such as Journal of the British Blockchain Association and Frontiers in Blockchain, most of the public narrative to date has been shaped by social media. Devex, the largest global platform for development practitioners is a good place to start. It is often seen as the place to go for the latest breakthroughs in international development. In 2016, Devex published a blog on Blockchain and its potential for international development (Mendoza, 2016) highlighting that "With potential to change the trajectory of crises, such as famines or the spread of diseases, the innovative use of data will drive a new era for global development." This has been followed by a series of posts further elaborating on the applications of Blockchain for international development. Thomason (2017) posted on Devex, 7 ways to use Blockchain for international development (Thomason, 2017), in this post she profiles financial services, remittances, peer to peer energy trading, supply chain, land registry, identity and funds tracking. She concluded: "The international development community needs to start thinking about the ways Blockchain technology can transform how we do our work" In 2018, Devex further posted on what development practitioners need to know about Blockchain (Arkin, 2018), the five key points highlighted were: charities are accepting digital currencies as donations; payments and money transfers are the fastest moving sectors; the Bermuda approval of first crypto currency regulations; China is exploring as part of its 'One Belt One Road' initiative; and financial inclusion is a real opportunity.

Increasingly, universities and academia are also engaging in Blockchain, universities such as Nicosia, Princeton, Universidad Europea Madrid, Duke, UCLA and Oxford offering courses on Blockchain. Carla LaPoint (Pointe, 2017) has produced and ethical framework for the implementation of Blockchain. Stanford University (2017) has produced a report on Blockchain and social impact, which concluded that early data suggest that Blockchain can provide incremental (65% of initiatives) or transformative (25% of initiatives) solutions to the world's toughest challenges.

The British Blockchain Association has been a leader in trying to galvanise the academic community to build the scientific evidence base for Blockchain, by launching a peer reviewed journal the Journal of the British Blockchain Association, which includes articles on all aspects of Blockchain. The British Blockchain Association is also convening the first scientific conference on Blockchain in London in 2019. Another peer reviewed journal, Frontiers in Blockchain (www.frontiersin.org/Blockchain#, n.d.) was launched in 2018, and has a specialty section for Blockchain for Good. This academic and scientific work is important to build legitimacy and the evidence base and provide a reference point amidst the hype.

MULTILATERAL ORGANISATIONS AND REGIONAL BODIES

From among the international development institutions leadership seems to be emerging from the OECD and the World Bank. The section below summarises the publicly available information on the work of international organisations.

OECD

The OECD moved fast to explore how Blockchain would impact on its work. In May 2018, it convened a Workshop on Digital Financial Assets, bringing together regulators, government, policy makers and industry to discuss (1) Digital Financial Assets: Main challenges for monetary policy and the financial system; (2) Digital Financial Assets: What are they? Opportunities and challenges for firms; (3) Main challenges for regulation, taxation and AML /CTF (OECD, 2018). Some key conversations from the OECD workshop included creating a shared rulebook, more governed by sound principles (such as protection of consumer rights and establishment of common standards) than an effort to proscribe every aspect of behaviour and every use case. A desire to establish a practical framework for thinking, rather than cut-and-paste of existing regulation applied to traditional financial assets, and bearing in mind the need for investor protections and that the poor and the dispossessed could benefit from certain applications of Blockchain, and a desire to create an environment that promotes that. Digital identity, particularly self-sovereign digital identity, can bring a billion people into the identity system if deployed across the right type of Blockchain and enhanced with multimodal nextgen biometrics.

The OECD Blockchain Policy Forum, in 2018 was attended by 1,000 people, with 18,000 watching the livestream from 200 countries. The discussions explored how international development institutions can scale strategies, what mechanisms they do within their respective agencies and share among donors and partners.

Thomason (2018) highlighted some of the use cases discussed at the OECD Blockchain Policy Forum in 2018:

- **Identity:** Opportunity to rapidly establish and scale an advanced digital identity system leveraging today's technological advances.
- **Financial inclusion:** Digital currencies and large scale roll out of mobile money systems could fuel rapid widespread access to financial services that was not available before.
- **Land and assets registration**: Through digitization of assets, people would be able borrow to improve their livelihoods and an immutable digital record (once established) means that ownership is unambiguous.
- **Payments**: Digital payments provide benefits of traceability and efficiency in disbursement.
- **Supply chains of medicines**: Advances in logistic chain management leverages both digital and data analytics to not only improve the tracking and authenticity of medicines.
- **Energy**: The provision of access to affordable electricity through the introduction of off-grid renewable energy technologies, especially based on solar photovoltaic, has the potential to dramatically improve the lives of the poor.
- **Economic growth**: Digitization accelerates economic growth and facilitates job creation
- **Voting:** Overcoming identity obstacles in cost effective ways is also a key to resolving some of the deep-seated problems of democratic processes.
- **Government Efficiency**: Adapting and utilizing digital technologies in government operations can drastically reduce the cost of the government sector, as well as the efficacy of service provision and social impact.

- **Financial protection:** Financial inclusion for poor families enabled by remittances and mobile/ digital payments
- **Direct health incentive payments:** Antenatal attendance, specific treatment attendance, immunization
- **Improved government responsiveness**: Blockchain based polling for social accountability
- **Provenance:** for drug supplies and agricultural value chains
- **Speed, transparency and efficiency in donor fund flows**: Donors distribute their funds through systems that are costly, cumbersome, and porous. Blockchain can enable the international development community can increase the impact of the dollars it spends on aid.

Thomason (2018) reported that the five key takeaways from the OECD Policy Forum were:

1. **Bold leadership is needed:** International institutions have a role in supporting governments to prepare for and create policy and regulatory frameworks that foster, and do not hamper, digital innovation. International institutions can also promote principles and standards for digital development throughout the aid system, to ensure that more digital products and services reach, empower and improve the lives of poor people, particularly those at risk of being left behind. Structural policies should also facilitate innovation and entrepreneurship to foster innovation and technology diffusion, ensure that competitive conditions prevail and avoid erecting barriers to cross border digital markets.
2. **The digital talent pool is too shallow**: There is a global shortage of two main types of talent: (i) high level policy specialists who also have an up to date knowledge of frontier technologies to advise international institutions and governments; and (ii) developer talent (entrepreneurs, programmers, designers, and engineers) who can build and maintain the digital systems that governments will depend on. Software talent is now said to be more important to companies than actual cash.
3. **New models of finance and procurement will be needed:** These are new technologies and there is limited funding to support the commercial scaling of social impact prototypes. Taking successful use cases to scale will likely require new forms of financial and institutional partnerships. International banks, investors, and development finance institutions can play a role in expanding the reach of Blockchain into emerging markets.

Blockchain also enables new forms of finance including crowd funding and dynamic funding mechanisms from private finance markets. Tax mechanisms and incentives allow Blockchain to encourage the private sector to invest in Blockchain, for example, through tax credit schemes where credit flows back to investor. More funding is needed in social impact capital to support the development and testing of new technologies for development, that have longer time horizons, lower financial returns but higher social returns financing. Some donors are experimenting with new forms of partnership for technology, but traditional procurement mechanisms will need review.

4. **International development institutions should experiment and shape** Within existing programs, international institutions can support testing and conducting pilots and find space for opportunities to digital solutions in aid programmes. They can identify the most promising use cases for development purposes. International development institutions can help match make technology companies to existing problems and find solutions already being implemented elsewhere in developing countries and support them to work with local entrepreneurs to mould their technology to fit culture and context of each country. There is an acute need build the evidence base on the impact of the Blockchain use cases and share. There is also a need for new approaches to evaluation that account for the shorter feedback loops of technological experimentation and the need for ongoing data gathering and analysis during design, testing and rollout of a technological solution

5. **Exponential collaboration:** Many participants spoke of Blockchain collaboration as developing a new global economic system. If we are to realise the promise of a digital future which lifts people out of poverty and creates positive social impact, we must connect many different worlds and we collaboration with governments; NGOs; development partners; industry, and research institutions.

Prior to the OECD Policy Forum, the OECD DAC convened a roundtable on *"Harnessing the potential of digitalisation and disruptive digital technologies for development co-operation;"* (Development Assistance Committee of the OECD, 2018) where representatives from civil society, government and multilateral institutions joined in conversations on how donors could harness the potential of digitalisation and frontier technologies (including Blockchain, AI, machine learning, IoT, and big data) to deliver maximum development impact. In addition to DAC members, participation included representation from GSMA, OECD STI Director, UNCTAD, CONCORD, Abt-Associates and the World Bank.

It was again emphasised that digital skills and knowledge within development agencies and the risk of digitalisation being something specific with flagship projects, rather than mainstreaming it as a cross-cutting enabler. Donors will need to engage in strategic foresight and testing plausible futures to envision the different scenarios going forward and to address the fragmentation of silos within governments.

The roundtable discussions concluded that most DAC members have policies supporting digitalisation as part of their development co-operation but are struggling in the implementation of digitalisation. There is a need for examples of good practice, exchange of experiences and guidance when it comes to competence and skills development, as well as when it comes to mainstreaming and working across government and agencies. GSMA noted that as we are in the digital era, we need a clear rationale for development actors, donors/governments to come in, such as where there is market failure. Digital strategies should be mainstreamed in existing programming. This is an opportunity to seize digital upside. UNCTAD noted that we must look at the front-runners. Digitisation for development is about more than technology, and the DAC has a critical role to play in catalysing more attention to the digital dimension in development assistance strategies.

This roundtable explored how donors could mainstream digitalisation and frontier technologies within development co-operation, from providing an enabling environment through policy, aligning policy goals with digitalisation strategies to how development assistance is delivered on this ground. Some key themes that emerged from discussions included:

- The need for DAC members to have comprehensive digital strategies;
- Understanding the risks for developing countries, for instance digital exclusion;
- The need to improve digital literacy in partner countries and digital competence within donor organisations;
- Digitalisation, like innovation, means supporting experimenting, allowing failure and partnering with new actors;
- How to scale solutions and how to tailor interventions to the local context.

APEC

The Asia-Pacific Economic Cooperation (APEC) is a regional economic forum established in 1989 to leverage the growing interdependence of the Asia-Pacific. APEC's 21 members aim to create greater prosperity for the people of the region by promoting balanced, inclusive, sustainable, innovative and secure growth and by accelerating regional economic integration. Bridging the digital divide among APEC economies has been a major theme of APEC 2018. In the lead up to APEC, there was a high-level group of APEC Central Banks and financial inclusion and digital experts at the *Asia Pacific Financial Inclusion Forum - The Inclusion Imperative: A Call to Action* on 27-28 June Tokyo (FDC ADB Institute, 2018). The Central Banks represented included Papua New Guinea, Bangladesh, Myanmar, Chile, Cambodia, Thailand, Nepal, Vietnam Lao PDR, Mongolia, Sri Lanka and Indonesia, as well as the IMF and the Japan Financial Services Agency.

Michelle Curry of the Foundation for Development Cooperation spoke of issues of improving cross border credit data sharing, data protection, reducing cost and friction in remittances and protection against indebtedness. A key recurring theme was that access to a bank account does not drive usage. Conversations were formed around: Leveraging digital and mobile platforms and distributed ledger technology to monetise non-traditional assets and reduce cost of remittances and the critical role of women in economic inclusion. Broad based discussions were held on the structural reforms needed to achieve economic inclusion, in a region where 50% of people don't have bank accounts. These included:

- Regulatory reforms
- Low cost access to financial products and services
- Regulatory sandboxes
- Credit data bases
- Universal ID systems to facilitate KYC
- Economic inclusion
- Reduce barriers to employment
- Education
- Social transfers
- Reduce barriers to gender equality
- Land registries
- Portable pension schemes and micro pensions
- Asset monetisation schemes

Two key ingredients dominated the conversation for closing the financial inclusion gap and these were the role of women in economic inclusion and that digital and distributed ledger technology has significant but unrealised potential. It was noted the profile and market potential of women consumers remains largely unexplored in SE Asia and that global changes in technology have potential to bring new opportunity to women and that improved access to financial services can play a catalytic role in advancing women's inclusion in economic markets.

It was also concluded that Blockchain had potential to solve some of the financial inclusion challenges. Remittances were a focus, but also opportunities with mobile money and digital currencies, as well as land registration and tokenisation of assets. In some quarters there was deep seated concern about the risks of technologies and how regulators can keep up with the conversation. Concerns about consumer protection from speculative cryptocurrencies, veracity of Initial Coin Offerings and risks to privacy and informed consent were aired. A key issue that emerged was that education of Central Banks and Governments will be vital and building a bridge between those creating the new technologies and those regulating them. (FDC, 2018)

British Commonwealth

As part of the Commonwealth Business Forum from 16-18 April 2018, London, UK, was a session titled Developing the Digital Economy: Disruption, Big Data and A.I. In her LinkedIn post on the Forum Thomason (2018) summarised some of the key messages (Thomason, 2018). The role of government was vital to driving innovation through: Political leadership – setting policies to attract talent to each country; investors, academics and developers; Ensuring access to talent. Creating visa policies and incentives to attract entrepreneurs, programmers, designers, engineers and UX designers and enhancing curricula in schools so that core digital skills are taught to all from a young age. Government can also play a role in attracting finance – such as government backed bonds with matched funding and venture capital incentives to back tech companies and developing infrastructure – including physical spaces, broadband, plus underpinning policies, data, trading arrangements, policies on data and making trading available.

Data was discussed at every turn from making anonymized data available for health research, to data portability, to paying people for access to their data, to data as part of digital infrastructure, data rules in a digital economy, data protection, and sophisticated rules about private data. Figuring out how data is used and protected is a central problem to be resolved.

Regional bodies like the Commonwealth and APEC can support emerging economies through sharing knowledge, access to talent and talent development, investment in transformation of education. A welcome recommendation was put forward to develop a digital commonwealth initiative from all countries to share agenda and knowledge.

World Bank

The World Bank have increasingly been active in Blockchain. In 2017, the World Bank opened a Blockchain Lab (Stanley, 2017). The Lab will serve as a forum for learning, experimentation and collaboration on distributed ledger technology. The Blockchain lab will bring together internal and external participants to work on Blockchain use cases of significance to the bank's member countries. Core focus areas include land registry, digital identity, aid distribution and financial infrastructure.

The World Bank also launched bond-i (Blockchain operated new debt instrument), the world's first bond to be created, allocated, transferred and managed through its life cycle using distributed ledger technology. The two-year bond raised A\$110 million, marking the first time that investors have supported the World Bank's development activities in a transaction that is fully managed using the Blockchain technology (Bank, 2018).

Asian Development Bank

The Asian Development Bank (ADB) has been active in exploring the potential for Blockchain in Asia, including on energy, trade, fintech, financial inclusion, governance, insurance and public procurement. The ADB estimates that Blockchain can close the trade finance gap.

The global trade finance gap currently stands at $1.5 trillion, or 10% of merchandise trade volume, and is set to grow to $2.4 trillion by 2025, the Asian Development Bank calculates. But a new study shows that this gap could be reduced by $1 trillion if DLT is used more broadly. The largest opportunities could come from smart contracts, single digital records for customs clearance. They would help mitigate credit risk, lower fees and remove barriers to trade. (World Economic Forum, 2018)

UN

Various UN bodies are exploring Blockchain for improving processes and achieving the SDGs, including UNICEF, UN Women, UNHCR and UNCEFACT. UNCFACT (United Nations Centre for Trade Facilitation and Electronic Business) have produced a White Paper examining how Blockchain can enhance international supply chains and its impact on standards and gaps in standards. The White Paper concluded that there are several areas that UNCEFACT could contribute to including: a reference architecture specification; process modelling in support of smart contracts; inter-ledger interoperability framework, resource discovery framework; trade data semantics framework and Blockchain application data needs.

UNICEF

In December 2018 UNICEF invested in several start-ups in emerging markets; the Mexico-based OneSmart, ensures integrity of several critical municipal services. OneSmart (os.city)[1] provides governments with the citizen-centric data necessary to support improved social outcomes. For example, the delivery of state-provided social services to children and young people or interrogating the (bureaucratic) misappropriation of funds in emerging markets. With a modular platform, institutions can pick from applications that enable city listening, the improvement of trust and transparency or open urbanisation, giving governments the real-time insights necessary to build proactive, responsive cities. Utopixar[2] (utopixar.com) will deliver a social collaboration tool for communities and organisations to facilitate participative decision-making and value transfer (UNICEF, 2018).

BILATERAL ORGANISATIONS

DFID (UKAid)

DFID UKAid has long been interested in innovation and digitalisation, although has been less public on Blockchain. It recently funded a report conducted by GSMA and funded by UK Aid GSMA (2017) (GSMA, 2017) which concluded that "Blockchain-enabled platforms that leverage mobile money services could provide a more convenient, cost-effective and transparent way for humanitarian organisations to transfer entitlements to refugees, and for donors to transfer project funds across international borders. The high uptake of mobile money services in developing markets – particularly among the segments of society which are targeted by development aid – suggests that operators should explore opportunities to link into and support these platforms. In doing so, they are likely to find new, exciting ways to support the delivery of aid, expand their customer base and generate new sources of revenue".

USAID

The USAID Primer on Blockchain (USAID, 2018) is aimed to equip international development agencies and partners to assess whether and how DLT might apply to their work. It provides a set of key questions to consider for assessing relevance of DLT to development challenges; a basic summary of the technical aspects of DLT; and an illustrative list of DLT applications being tested across a range of sectors. USAID also conducted a regional training on "Demystifying Blockchain and its Uses for International Development" (USAID, June 18-20 Bangkok, Thailand, 2018).

Danida

Denmark has been something of a fast mover in examining the potential for Blockchain in international development, including in appointing the world's first tech ambassador. In its report "Hack the Future of Development Aid (Ministry of Foreign Affairs of Denmark et al, 2017) based on a series of #Hacks, it proposes that there are key opportunities for Blockchain including: Innovate aid money with cryptocurrency; turn rights into code on the Blockchain; and disrupt the aid model. The report notes "technology will not wait" and cites innovations that are happening in Nigeria, Kenya, Rwanda, Sierra Leone and South Africa. It concludes that to stay relevant development agencies need to hack the way aid is designed and delivered.

KfW

KfW the German Development Bank will carry out a six-month pilot in Burkina Faso to explore the potential of Blockchain. (Kramer, 2018) The trial will use the TruBudget Blockchain for contract design, tendering, and payment on projects. This will allow stakeholders to view processes in real time. If the trial proves successful, the Blockchain project's open-source protocol will be made available to others without cost. This would be a valuable demonstration of transparency in the use of aid funds, one of the key uses cases for Blockchain in international development.

CIVIL SOCIETY ORGANISATIONS (CSOs)

Mercy Corps has been an early thought leader in this space, publishing two white papers, on Blockchain and humanitarian applications (Luchetta, 2017). and another comparing Blockchain platforms (Mercy Corps, n.d.). These are both practical down to earth and well-informed thought leadership pieces for international development. Mercy Corps continues to experiment with Blockchain in its international programs.

The CSO Partnership for Development Effectiveness publication "Digital for Development" (CONCORD Europe and FOND Romania, 2018) notes that "the possibility of creating a free and fair world has never looked so achievable" with the advent of digitisation. The report concludes that digital technologies have a central role to play in the SDG agenda and that it is critical that CSOs understand how digitisation can be used for development and can help steer the agenda.

In February 2018 the International Development Research Centre Ottawa, Canada convened a global meeting on Harnessing the Power: CRVS Systems For 2030 Global Agendas (International Development Research Centre, 2018). The conference discussed the importance of breakthrough innovations to remove systemic failures and gaps, and to create a sustainable permanent system able to play a significant role in the economy and governance of the country. As part of the event, two labs were conducted on Blockchain and CRVS. The report notes that participants considered the uses of public and private Blockchains and how the technology offered solutions in low infrastructure environments. Many potential use cases were identified, including identity, supply chain, registries, financial inclusion and remittances. To achieve successful implementation and scale up however, participants agreed that there would need to be a shift in thinking that accepts the concept of decentralization. To enable this shift, dialogues need to be established between the tech community and the international development community to further explore its application in-country. Involvement from the international development community will ensure the evolving technology is designed to solve real problems. Small investments in proofs of concept may yield big results. Actions and recommendations from the conference on Blockchain and CRVS (International Development Research Centre, 2018) were to:

- Produce a white paper on Blockchain, CRVS and Digital Identity, including consideration of legal and regulatory issues that countries will face.
- Facilitate regulatory sandboxes so countries can have technical demonstrations and co-design opportunities in a safe environment.
- Develop a register of Blockchain and identity projects in developing countries to keep abreast of technology developments affecting civil registration and ID systems.
- Facilitate learning exchange around legal and regulatory challenges – enabling countries with experience of Blockchain to share knowledge with others.

These recommendations more generally show the ways in which international organisations and donors can play a vital role. This is discussed further below.

KEY CONSIDERATIONS FOR DONORS AND INTERNATIONAL ORGANISATIONS

While the potential of digital transformation is clear, it will take the bold leadership of government, international development institutions, industry, academia, CSOs and the whole eco-system to achieve. There remain cultural and institutional barriers to harnessing this potential. The World Economic Forum (World Economic Forum, 2018) highlights five inhibitors to digital transformation, and these are relevant to adoption of Blockchain by international agencies. These are:

- Lack of collaboration for societal gains – incentives are not in place to generate social benefits
- Regulation and protection of consumer interests – innovation is taking place at a far greater speed than regulation. New models will be needed.
- Cannibalisation of existing revenue schemes – continued preference by incumbents on 'evolutionary' change rather than 'revolutionary' change and completely new business models

- Skills for tomorrow's workforce – digital skills gaps are increasing
- Technology adoption rates – the establishment is still sceptical of technological advances and do not stop technologies when they become available.

Collaboration for Social Gains

Borrowing the term "hyper-collaboration" from industry and considering it in the context of global social impact, Thomason (2018) added "Co" to create Hyper co – collaboration (Hc^2) – because social impact and global commons issues require a greater level of cooperation and shared interest than industry collaboration. These will be new collaborations for ecosystems that don't normally collaborate or converge. To create major global Hc^2 around issues such as gender equity, financial inclusion or climate change and green energy, it will take horizontal and vertical collaboration among industry, technologists, governments, international institutions, researchers, NGOs, funders, and impacted communities. Imagine a global Community Token Economy of these various ecosystems, governed and incentivised and investing through token economics.

Thomason hypothesises that to realise the promise of a digital future which lifts people out of poverty and creates positive social impact, will require the connection of many different worlds proposes Hyper co – collaboration (Hc^2) for a digital enabled and better future (Thomason, 2018), UK Consultancy (Consultancy.UK, 2017) describe hyper-collaboration as based on the belief that it is innovation ecosystems, not individual companies, which will deliver the novel solutions the world is waiting for. Innovation ecosystems bring together diverse and complementary capabilities from across the globe. They outline several attributes:

- **Collaboration exists between "non-obvious" partners** as well as universities, research institutes, customers and suppliers.
- **There are often dozens, potentially even hundreds, of collaborating partners**, rather than just a handful.
- **Collaboration is often enabled by digital** and other rapidly evolving technologies (such as cloud computing in biotechnology). Digital technologies may also enable "convergence" across industries to create truly novel solutions around particularly important and robust market needs.

- **There are multiple levels and means of collaboration**, ranging from super-strategic alliances through to joint ventures and grass-roots "intrapreneurship."
- **Players and relationships evolve rapidly.** Start-ups mature, initiatives may fail and strategic interests will often diverge.
- **There is availability of (open-source) data** and a culture of sharing information and intelligence within a fit-for-purpose IP framework.

Thomason (2018) poses 5 sets of immediate collaborative efforts to pave the way for digital transformation. This is represented by the Hyper Co-Collaboration block in the enabling shift section of the B4SC Model.

The 5 sets are detailed below.

Collaboration to Help Shape the Technology

Technologists are often working in a vacuum advancing technology, with a limited understanding of different social, institutional, infrastructure and cultural contexts. For technology to work, it must be scaled to suit the context. Governments and international institutions can help shape the application of technology for maximum social benefit and protect the interests of the poor and vulnerable. Collaboration to understand the political economy for implementation is especially important as intermediaries will be removed and the implications of this change will be a key aspect to integrating this change into public sector work. Researchers can help by developing rapid cycle analytics to monitor the impacts of technology adoption and advice on

Figure 1. Enabling Shifts Requires; Hyper Co-Collaboration

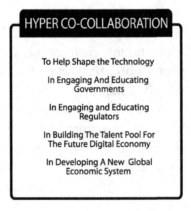

the policy environment and regulatory environment being contemplated by governments. NGOs and communities can report on their user experience and industry can partner to see how to scale technologies commercially.

Collaboration in Engaging and Educating Governments

The deployment of Blockchain applications will continue to accelerate with or without government and international agency support. Governments and international institutions need more knowledge, to understand the benefits and pitfalls of this new technology and issues surrounding implementation and scale. They need to be able to learn from other countries experience and understand how to deploy it for social benefit and develop plans for expanding digital capability and ambition. Who teaches policy makers Blockchain and frontier technologies? It must be the technology industry building bridges between the technology ecosystem and governments and international institutions will be part of building the needed platform for successful adoption of transformational technologies.

Collaboration in Engaging and Educating Regulators

Regulators are interested in safety and soundness of the financial system and consumer protection and that Know your Customer (KYC) and Anti Money Laundering (AML) are adhered to. They are cautious about the risks of technologies and consumer protection from speculative cryptocurrencies, veracity of Initial Coin Offerings and risks to privacy and informed consent. Many are adopting a regulatory sandbox approach to test in a safe environment. At the OECD on 5 July 2018, there was a meeting among OECD regulators and industry. An outcome was the desire to develop joint principles-based approach to digital financial assets that are recognized across borders. This kind of collaboration and dialogue between industry and regulators needs to continue.

Collaboration in Building the Talent Pool
for the Future Digital Economy

There is a global talent shortage of developers and specialists working on Blockchain, AI and associated technologies. Traditional education approaches will never meet the future, let alone current needs. In developing countries, there are vast numbers of young people who through innovative training approaches could be taught digital skills. Building mutual benefit collaborations with industry to develop new forms of training e.g. gamification and fast track learning that can be global and virtual will be an essential part of building capability for a digital future.

Collaboration in Developing a New Global Economic System

Blockchain has potential to lead to a new global economic system. Community Token Economies (see Chapter 2 for further details) to address global commons problems are already emerging – although we have yet to see them at scale.

Regulation, Ethics and Protection of Consumer Interests

Innovation moves faster than regulation. Furthermore, Blockchain regulation will need to operate across international boundaries, so new forms of global governance and regulation will be needed. At a government level, international institutions can support governments to revise regulations to encompass digital and cross industry collaboration and digital services and platforms and to be updated on global efforts to collaborate on regulation and standards.

Considering legal issues that will impact upon international agencies views about Blockchain, Jenny Leung of Coindesk (Leung, 2018) highlights two important ones. The first is in relation to data protection, especially with the recent issuance of GDPR (European Union, 2018) which has given rise to tensions between Blockchain and the GDPR, the rules around the right to erasure, right to rectification and the principle of data minimization. The second is as Blockchain projects become more geographically decentralized, anonymous and/or censorship resistant, domestic regulators must tackle breaches of their laws by facilitating global coordination or, perhaps, harmonization of their securities, commodities, money transmitter, and tax laws. Leung (2018) further reports that a number of different organisations including IOSCO, CPMI, G20 and FSB, OECD, and the EU Blockchain Partnership (launched by the EU Commission) all initiated discussions about how domestic regulators participate in global collaboration and keep up with rapidly changing technology landscape. She suggests that it may be years before real progress is made due to the differing approaches and attitudes of regulators and governments around the world.

La Pointe (La Pointe, 2017) was early to identify that code is not neutral and that intentionality of design is crucial with Blockchain. She notes the risks where while Blockchain can be an instrument of democracy, it can also be used by governments and others to exert and consolidate power over people; crypt-economic systems could contribute to greater equity but could also create exploitative systems. The Blockchain Ethical Design Framework focuses on ethical intentionality, with key issues of how governance is created, how identity is defined, how inputs are verified, how access if granted, how ownership of data is verified and how security is set up and assured. This provides a valuable starting point for international institutions to support government and industry to establish an ethical approach to design and understand the relationship between design and human outcomes.

Evolutionary or Revolutionary?

There is a lot to do and it needs to be done fast. The pace of technological change is exponential (Kurzweil, 2001). Evolutionary approaches are being disrupted by technology and changing social attitudes. The iPhone is just over 10 years old. The rise to prominence of companies such as Airbnb and Uber emphasises the importance of identifying sectors potentially at risk of similar disruptions. In eight years, Airbnb now advertises three times more beds than the world's largest hotel chain and Uber which launched in 2011 has become the largest passenger transport network (Le Jeune, 2016).

The international development community, being largely government financed tends to be conservative and risk averse. The powerful elites who run these organisations have a lot invested in maintaining the status quo and are more likely to stand back rather than lean in. To date, the Danes have been closest to seeing Blockchain as revolutionary with their "Hack the Future" report. There is a strong inertia impacting on the traditional 'development set'. This is likely to change with the emerging prominence of China and India disturbing the equilibrium and engaging in more revolutionary innovation. As highlighted in Chapter 4 of this book, innovation often originates in developing countries. Users are likely to be far better at finding innovative solutions to problems than aid agencies.

A revolution will also be needed in finance and procurement models of international agencies. The current procurement models of many international organisations are not well shaped for co-development of technology. They tend to be shaped for obtaining goods and services, through contracts. Interested organizations submit a proposal in response to a Request for Proposals. Alternatively, they are the transfer of funds to another party for the implementation of programs that contribute to the public good. There are procurement models such as Grand Challenges, which have been utilised by

Canada and USAID e.g. A $30 million grand challenge calling on innovators to submit ideas to combat Zika and "the disease threats of tomorrow." New models will be needed, and models that allow for blended finance and major private sector collaboration. Working with the private sector will be an essential part of digital transformation and closer cooperation with industry in the development of standards and regulation. Examination is also needed of financial models and financial sustainability for technology.

Revolutionary and agile approaches to evaluation tools will be needed, with much shorter feedback loops and ongoing data gathering and analysis during design, testing and rollout of a technological solution.

Digital Skills

Globally, digital skills are in short supply. Indeed, it has been reported that Software developers are now more valuable to companies than money (Gaybrick, 2018). Rania Elshiekh and Laurie Butgerit (Elshiekh & Butgerit, 2017).) have published a review of surveys empirical studies which tackled gamification to encourage computer science students and help them in learning coding or improving their coding skills. They found improved performance, motivation, overcoming online disadvantage like isolation, lack of motivation, and lack of interactivity and concluded that gamification is successful, and engagement is a valuable indicator of students' academic achievements. For example, large Blockchain companies like EOS are developing their own coder trading programs using gamification. This is a real opportunity for emerging economies, to build digital talent for the growing market of the digital economy. International Development organisations need to skill up themselves but would also be of great service if they commissioned work on what rapid are training methods being deployed globally for digital training.

Accelerating Technology Adoption

When technology benefits consumers, it will be adopted. Understanding that most people prefer the known to the unknown, it is important to consider user experience and culture. Social media will play a powerful role in user adoption. The world population is 7.6 billion and the internet has 4.1 billion users. Close to half the world's population (3.03 billion people) are on some type of social media, the majority of this accessed via smart phones (Hatch, 2018). Millennials are connected, fast-acting, and will adopt the new technologies that can quickly impact their lives for the better.

There are five enabling shifts required to accelerate technology adoption as indicated in the B4SC Model in Chapter One:

1. The first is the increasing mobile and internet penetration that makes access to technology ubiquitous.
2. The second is user experience and user benefit, when people see the benefit, they will adopt the technology
3. The third is an understanding of the move to the new data driven economy owned and permissioned by individuals
4. The fourth is a connected eco-system with all stakeholders building hyper-co-collaboration for social impact
5. The fifth is that international institutions support and provide models for global and national governance and enabling standards and regulations.

WHAT ROLE CAN DEVELOPMENT AGENCIES PLAY?

Development agencies can work to overcome cultural and institutional barriers to harnessing digital potential. The World Economic Forum (World Economic Forum, 2018) identified five ways in which governments and policy makers can maximise digital impacts: Revise regulations to encompass digital and cross industry collaboration and digital services and platforms; Prioritise data security; Empower individual relevance and develop new skills for the jobs of the future; Develop new incentive structures to enable societal value creation and; Localise efforts as the impact of digitalisation will be substantial at a local level.

Some of the key roles that donors and international organisations can play include:

1. Proactively support emerging economies to leapfrog and rapidly move to a digital future and build digital as a sector of the economy.
2. Suggest appropriate monitoring and benchmarks for things like: internet speed and minimum internet penetration; internet access and usage; rural inclusion and mobile network coverage.
3. Support the development and scaling of digital "global goods" and open source systems
4. Support momentum toward country-led strategies digital health roadmaps, data use partnerships, and building the digital eco-system.

5.   Help define new partnerships and financing models for technology.
6.   Convene policy discussions on topics like enabling regulatory framework; the development of technologies which address public good, economic policies to stimulate growth in the digital age, with the government sector demonstrating leadership in digital adoption.
7.   Provide a coordinated Information Clearing House to build the evidence and share it and digital platforms can play an essential role in the roll-out of digitalisation where experiences can be shared, collaboration and joint investments can be triggered, common approaches to regulatory problems be explored, and means for re-skilling of the workforce be further exchanged.
8.   Promote good practice, share information and strengthen capacity-building on human resources development in the digital age in cooperation with relevant partners.
9.   Share policies to facilitate innovation and entrepreneurship to foster innovation and technology diffusion, ensure that competitive conditions prevail and avoid erecting barriers to cross border digital markets.

The global development community has a vital role is setting a bold leadership agenda for digital transformation. The World Economic Forum (World Economic Forum, 2018) identified five key enablers to maximise the return on digital: Agile and digital savvy leadership; Forward looking skills agenda; Data access and management; Ecosystem thinking and Technology infrastructure readiness. These are all domains, where the global development community can contribute.

The global development community need to be active and at the table of the digital future. The DAC are focussing on understanding how technology can contribute to making development co-operation more effective, impactful and inclusive. They are exploring: a systemic approach to digitalisation; creating an enabling environment for digitalisation and operationalising a digitalisation strategy. Frontier technologies offer an important opportunity to accelerate progress towards the SDGs. It is time to lean in and help shape the new technologies as they rapidly accelerate. It is time to galvanise a more systematic and joined up international development approach to the digital future.

CONCLUSION

Digital disruption has the potential to enable transformation and reshape business models faster than at any time in history. The World Economic Forum predicts that the introduction of digital services will be one of the most important factors in transforming health care over the next decade. Despite the relative slowness among many development agencies in embracing digital transformation, there is increasing evidence and interest among development agencies in embracing digital development agendas.

The UN Secretary General established a high level panel on Digital Cooperation to raise awareness about the transformative impact of digital technologies across society and the economy, and contribute to the broader public debate on how to ensure a safe and inclusive digital future for all, taking into account relevant human rights norms. The WHO Director General announced that he was establishing a Department of Digital Health to "harness the power of digital health and innovation by supporting countries to assess, integrate, regulate and maximise the opportunities of digital technologies and artificial intelligence."

Many development interventions could be delivered faster, more efficiently, or more effectively by leveraging digital technologies. Smartphones, and cloud computing, offer significant opportunities to apply frontier technologies to improve outcomes in developing country settings. As outlined in Chapter 4 on emerging economies, the number of unique mobile subscribers will reach 5.9 billion by 2025, equivalent to 71% of the world's population. The global population is getting younger and many live in emerging economies. The emerging markets are home to 85% of the global population, where nearly 90% of people under 30 reside. Adolescents live digitally, this provides a fertile ground for the uptake of digital technologies. There are five characteristics of emerging economies that will accelerate digital transformation: the size and scale of the market, the youth bulge; mobile penetration; persistent and urgent challenges and governments which are agile and increasingly and pro-digital.

International agencies are under increasing pressure to make the best use of resources and account for aid dollars. A drive for transparency and accountability has become more important, and the publishing of "timely transparent harmonised and open high-quality data" can be aided by digital means and bring increasing transparency, accountability and efficiency over improving aid delivery.

REFERENCES

Arkin, F. (2018). *What you need to know about Blockchain in 2018.* Retrieved from https://www.devex.com/news/what-you-need-to-know-about-Blockchain-in-2018-93007

Butgereit, L. (2015). Gamifying a PhD Taught Module: A Journey to Phobos and Deimos. In P. Cunningham & M. Cunningham (Eds.), *IST-Africa 2015 Conference Proceedings.* IIMC International Information Management Corporation. Retrieved from https://ieeexplore.ieee.org/document/7190516/authors#authors

CONCORD. (2018). *Development going digital?* Retrieved from https://concordeurope.org/blog/2018/10/01/report-digitalisation-development/

Consultancy UK. (2017). *The growth of hyper-collaboration in an innovation-driven world.* Retrieved from https://www.consultancy.uk/news/14577/the-growth-of-hyper-collaboration-in-an-innovation-driven-world

Development Assistance Committee of the OECD. (2018). *Harnessing the potential of digitalisation and disruptive digital technologies for development cooperation.* Paris: OECD DAC.

Elshiekh, R., & Butgerit, L. (2017). Using Gamification to Teach Students Programming Concepts. *Open Access Library Journal, 4*(8). doi:10.4236/oalib.1103803

European Commission. (2018). *2018 reform of EU data protection rules.* Retrieved from EU: https://ec.europa.eu/commission/priorities/justice-and-fundamental-rights/data-protection/2018-reform-eu-data-protection-rules_en

Graglia, M., Mellon, C., & Robustelli, T. (2018). *The nail finds a hammer; self-sovereign identity, design principles, and property rights in the developing world.* Retrieved from https://www.newamerica.org/future-property-rights/reports/nail-finds-hammer/introduction

GSMA. (2017). *Blockchain for Development: Emerging opportunities for mobile, identity and aid.* Retrieved from https://www.gsma.com/mobilefordevelopment/resources/Blockchain-development-emerging-opportunities-mobile-identity-aid/

Hatch, C. (2018). *Be in the know: 2018 social media statistics you should know.* Retrieved from https://www.disruptiveadvertising.com/social-media/be-in-the-know-2018-social-media-statistics-you-should-know/

HM Treasury FCA, Bank of England. (2018). *Cryptoassets Taskforce: final report.* London: Her Majesty's Treasury. Retrieved from https://assets.publishing.service.gov.uk/government/uploads/system/uploads/attachment_data/file/752070/cryptoassets_taskforce_final_report_final_web.pdf

International Development Research Centre. (2018). *Harnessing the Power: CRVS systems for 2030 global agenda.* Ottawa: International Development Research Centre. Retrieved from https://crvssystems.ca/sites/default/files/inline-files/WebVersion_CRVS_Innovations_Conference_Outcomes_Report.pdf

Kramer, M. (2018). *German bank tests Blockchain for development in Africa.* Retrieved from https://www.ethnews.com/german-bank-tests-Blockchain-for-development-in-africa

Le Jeune, S. (2016). The sharing economy report. *Schroders.* Retrieved from https://www.schroders.com/hu/sysglobalassets/digital/resources/pdfs/2016-08-the-sharing-economy.pdf

Leung, J. (2018). *7 legal questions that will define Blockchain in 2019.* Retrieved from https://www.coindesk.com/7-legal-questions-that-will-define-Blockchain-in-2019

Luchetta, C. (2017). *A Revolution in Trust: Distributed Ledger Technology in Relief & Development.* Retrieved from https://www.mercycorps.org/research/revolution-trust-distributed-ledger-technology-relief-development

Mendoza, N. (2016). *Blockchain and bitcoin: Global development game changers?* Retrieved from https://www.devex.com/news/Blockchain-and-bitcoin-global-development-game-changers-88672

Mercy Corps. (n.d.). *Block by Block; A comparative analysis of the leading distributed ledgers.* Retrieved from https://www.mercycorps.org/sites/default/files/Block%20by%20Block%20-%20DL%20Comparative%20Analysis_0.pdf

Ministry of Foreign Affairs of Denmark et al. (2017). *Hack the Future of Development Aid.* Copenhagen: Sustainia. Retrieved from http://um.dk/~/media/UM/English-site/Documents/Danida/Goals/TechVelopment/Hack%20The%20Future%20December%202017v2.pdf?la=en

OECD. (2018). *Workshop on Digital Financial Assets.* Paris: Unpublished Draft Workshop Report.

Pointe, C. L. (2017). *Blockchain ethical design framework social impact.* Washington, DC: Beeck Centre Georgetown University. Retrieved from http://beeckcenter.georgetown.edu/Blockchain-ethical-design-framework-social-impact/

Stanford Graduate School of Business. (2018). *Blockchain for Social Impact. Moving Beyond the Hype.* Retrieved from https://www.gsb.stanford.edu/sites/gsb/files/publication-pdf/study-Blockchain-impact-moving-beyond-hype.pdf

Stanley, A. (2017). *End poverty restore trust: World Bank dives into Blockchain with lab launch.* Retrieved from https://www.coindesk.com/end-poverty-restore-trust-world-bank-dives-into-Blockchain-with-lab-launch

Thomason, J. (2017). *Opinion: 7 ways to use Blockchain for international development.* Retrieved from https://www.devex.com/news/opinion-7-ways-to-use-Blockchain-for-international-development-90839

Thomason, J. (2018). *Hyper Co-Collaboration for Global Social Impact.* Retrieved from https://www.linkedin.com/pulse/hyper-co-collaboration-global-social-impact-dr-jane-thomason/

United Nations Centre for Trade Facilitation and Electronic Business. (2018). *White Paper on technical applications for Blockchain to United Nationsl Centre for Trade Facilitation and Electronic Business deliverables.* Retrieved from https://www.unece.org/info/media/news/trade/2018/uncefact-whitepaper-on-Blockchain-for-trade-facilitation-open-for-comments-until-21-july/doc.html

USAID. (2018). *Primer on Blockchain.* Retrieved from https://www.usaid.gov/digital-development/digital-finance/Blockchain-primer

USAID. (2018). *Demystifying Blockchain for international development.* Retrieved from https://uncdf-cdn.azureedge.net/media-manager/documents/91125?sv=2017-07-29&sr=b&sig=Co4BjTYkD8Z14YvaOm IZ3SDWfc%2BTh8jsOkvzuPIHFe4%3D&se=2019-05-25T02%3A53%3 A01Z&sp=r&rscd=attachment%3Bfilename%3D10-10-18_Frontiers%20 Event.pdf

World Bank. (2018). *World Bank prices first global Blockchain bond, raising A$110 million.* Retrieved from https://www.worldbank.org/en/news/press-release/2018/08/23/world-bank-prices-first-global-Blockchain-bond-raising-a110-million

World Economic Forum. (2018). *Digital Transformation Initiative Unlocking $100 trillion for Business and Societ from Digital Transformation.* Retrieved from http://reports.weforum.org/digital-transformation/wp-content/blogs.dir/94/mp/files/pages/files/dti-executive-summary-20180510.pdf

World Economic Forum. (2018). *Blockchain could enable $1 trillion in trade, mostly for SMEs and emerging markets.* Retrieved from https://www.weforum.org/press/2018/09/Blockchain-could-enable-1-trillion-in-trade-mostly-for-smes-and-emerging-markets/

KEY TERMS AND DEFINITIONS

APEC: Asia-Pacific Economic Cooperation.

Digital Divide: A gulf of understanding between those with access to technology and those without, or with restricted access.

DFID: Department for International Development (a branch of the UK government).

Hyper Co-Collaboration (Hc^2)**:** Enhanced social impact and global commons cooperation and shared interest. A new form of collaboration for ecosystems that don't normally collaborate or converge.

KfW: Kreditanstalt für Wiederaufbau. A German, state-owned, development bank.

OECD: Organization for Economic Cooperation and Development (OECD).

UN: United Nations.

ENDNOTES

[1]   http://os.city/

[2]   http://www.utopixar.com/

Chapter 10
The Emerging Future

ABSTRACT

This chapter draws together the various chapters of the book, summarising the high-level points from each. It highlights how Blockchain and other frontier technologies will be an important tool for social impact globally. A renewed focus and promise on emerging economies is highlighted as they now have a way to access knowledge, talent, capital, and to share their talent and ideas and to seek global investment in ways that were not possible before. Some of the policy and governance challenges which will emerge from Blockchain economies are raised as well as the need for more research and discovery. It reinforces the links to the Sustainable Development Goals (SDGs) and the ways that Blockchain and frontier technologies can exponentiate impact towards the SDGs and should be a focus of governments, international institutions, and indeed, the entire ecosystem.

INTRODUCTION

The decision to write this book was based on an acute awareness of the rapidly changing landscape of technological innovation, and the relative paucity of credible information available to government, industry and the community on progress and impact. This is a purposeful effort to fill some of that gap. It is by nature incomplete, as advances are made daily and the book will therefore be outdated fast. However, it is information from a snapshot in time when the authors have gathered and distilled available knowledge and have presented it in plain English to build understanding and share knowledge.

DOI: 10.4018/978-1-5225-9578-6.ch010

It was also intentional, as it is the firm belief of the authors, that Blockchain and other Frontier Technologies will be an important tool for social impact, globally. It is now possible, with technology, to envision a world where everyone has an identity, where everyone can be connected to the economic system, where farmers get fair deals for their crops, and land registration is incorruptible. It is conceivable that anyone in the world can now become educated. Emerging economies now have a way to access knowledge, talent, and capital and to share their talent and ideas and to seek global investment in ways that are accessible to entrepreneurs and small businesses. New forms of self-regulating economies are emerging and Blockchain may be the platform for solving problems of the global commons through distributed autonomous communities, incentivised through token economics to collaborate, invest and collaborate on global problems like climate change.

The Sustainable Development Goals (SDGs) were an aspirational visionary leap to a future state where the world can be a better place for humankind. However, they will not be achieved without harnessing the potential of technology. Nor will they be reached alone. There is a clear social impact link between SDG 1 (no poverty), 2 (zero hunger), 3 (good health and well-being), 4 (quality education), 5 (gender equality), 8 (decent work and economic growth), 9 (industry, innovation, and infrastructure), and 16 (peace and justice, strong institutions). It is the authors' firm conviction that investigating how Blockchain and Frontier Technologies can exponentiate impact towards the SDGs should be a focus of governments, international institutions and indeed the entire eco-system. This book is intended to help stimulate that conversation.

OVERVIEW

Beyond the initial introduction and basics of blockchain, in each of the chapters, the book outlines progress and work being done across the world in the context of the B4SC model. The B4SC model frames the current influences and drivers, the enabling shifts required and the predicted social changes that are possible in the future. The authors hope that people will find the model a useful start to a conversation and that others will challenge it, build upon it and make it better.

Much of the focus on Blockchain has been overshadowed by the hype and rise of crypto-currencies and Initial Coin Offerings (ICOs) - this is not the focus of this book. The authors examine the use of Blockchain technology beyond cryptocurrency, and how it is being developed across the world. It is increasingly on the policy agendas of many countries.

Chapter 3 examines how blockchain will enable governments to create increased public value and broad public sector modernisation (with greater openness, transparency, engagement with and trust in government) through the integration of digital technologies and user preferences in service design and delivery of direct personal services and in shaping public policy outcomes, whilst also achieving efficiency and productivity gains. Digitalization can enhance the efficiency and competitiveness of businesses, the current technological improvements can also improve efficiency and effectiveness of government functions, thereby enhancing sustainable economic and civic growth.

Blockchain has direct application to enhance economic growth through financial inclusion; social accountability and improved effectiveness and efficiency of government institutions; smart connected government leveraging algorithmic decision making and execution; open and networked service delivery and citizens as censors though transparent communications channels. As part of this digital transformation journey, many governments around the world are looking at how Blockchain can be applied to enable economic growth better services to citizens. Blockchain offers the benefits of security and reduced cyber threat; immutability where it is no longer possible to delete, alter, rewrite or manipulate data on the Blockchain; savings in time and cost; reduced operating costs; and real time reporting of data and transparency. Future focussed states are pivoting and embracing ambitious digital transformation agendas.

Chapter 4 discusses some of the initial front moves made by small states who can pivot more nimbly, and emerging market innovators. Their trail blazing is setting a high bar for the traditional states to follow. Focussing on the potential social impact of Blockchain, the authors discuss the evolving capacity and potential for innovation to come from emerging markets. They explore why technological innovation for social impact seems to be moving fastest in emerging markets and small economies. While most of the development and implementation of blockchains has taken place in Western countries, arguably its greatest potential yet resides in emerging markets such as Argentina, Brazil, Chile, China, Colombia, Czech Republic, Egypt, Greece, Hungary, India, Indonesia, Korea, Malaysia, Mexico, Morocco, Qatar, Peru, Philippines, Poland, Russia, South Africa, South Korea, Taiwan, Thailand, Turkey and United Arab Emirates. The authors expect rapid developments in use cases from these countries in the coming years.

There are five characteristics of emerging economies that will enable the transformation of these economies. The first and most compelling reason is the sheer size and scale of the market. There are more smart phone users, there are more people, and there are more people under 30 years of age - the digitally literate demographic. Mobile penetration is growing rapidly and currently stands at more than two thirds of the global population. GSMA (2019) predicts that the number of unique mobile subscribers will reach 5.9 billion by 2025; equivalent to 71% of the world's population. Growth will be driven by developing countries, particularly India, China, Pakistan, Indonesia and Bangladesh, as well as Sub-Saharan Africa and Latin America. Another driver is that emerging markets simply have big problems to solve which stimulates innovation. Small States have traditionally been disadvantaged by isolated geography and limited access to knowledge and scarce human resources. Technology can help them overcome some of these barriers. Finally, governments are increasingly agile and in Mauritius, Kenya, UAE, and Bermuda for example are driving the technology innovation agenda.

Chapter 5 explores the use of blockchain in the world's rapidly growing cities. Emerging technology can help improve city services to its citizens. Digitisation using blockchain, will potentially help citizens feel more secure and create efficiency and improved services to cities. City governments may benefit from building digitally trustable processes for such areas as registries, social accountability, health care, welfare payments, mobility, identity, supply chains, voting, and universal services. The transparency and decentralisation intrinsic to the Blockchain often challenges the fundamental structures of centralised governments. For cities, these are opportunities to develop urban, physical and political structures that can improve the speed, transparency, and security of cities around the world. Blockchain has potential to be a technology enabling decentralised neighborhood scale co-creation, collaboration and citizen engagement activities. Blockchain technology, if embedded into the design of cities, can provide a digital layer of trust, hitherto rarely experienced in cities.

In Chapter 6, the authors explore the potential application of the Blockchain to reduce poverty and inequality through a selection of case studies. The window to global inclusion and economic participation is identity. The opportunity to rapidly establish and scale an advanced digital identity system leveraging today's technological advances has potential to unlock many barriers faced by the poor, as well as facilitate greater economic growth through ease of transactions. Once a person has an identity, they can potentially have access to a range of essential services like financial credit, health care and education.

The roll out of digital money systems could fuel rapid widespread access to financial services that was not available before. This could have tremendous impact on economic livelihoods of the large segments of rural populations that are unbanked. Government and donor payments often do not reach their intended recipients. Utilization of digital payments, and potentially smart contracts that automate payments conditional on certain variables, can reduce the amount of leakage in social welfare payments. Digital payments provide benefits of traceability and efficiency in disbursement. Smart contracts through digital transactions ensure funds reach intended recipients in a transparent way without middlemen and leakage along the way.

Many poor people own land and assets, but due to insufficient and unverifiable records, are not able to access value of their assets. Through a government led digitization of assets, people could borrow to improve their livelihoods and an immutable digital record (once established) could determine that ownership is unambiguous.

Health facility supply chains are crucially important to ensure the authenticity and quality of life saving medicines. Poor-quality medicines are a major public health threat, particularly in settings with a weak regulatory environment. Advances in logistic chain management leverages both digital and data analytics to not only improve the tracking and authenticity of medicines, but also ensure consistency of availability and quality.

The case studies in Chapter 6 provide a spectrum of use cases in various stages of development that demonstrate how, in a tangible way, Blockchain - often coupled with other technologies - has the potential to solve real problems faced by the poor and vulnerable.

Chapter 7 examines blockchain and mass migration, one of the 21st century's greatest challenges. Approximately 70 million people were forced from their homes across the world in 2017 (UNHCR, 2017). When people are forced to abandon their homes, many leave behind important documents such as birth certificates, marriage licences, passports and ID cards. These documents are nearly impossible to retrieve after leaving the country, assuming they have not already been destroyed. Blockchain can solve this problem, and associated others, for displaced people. Humanitarian and refugee settings is one of the most active areas for blockchain experimentation, and arguably its strongest social impact use case, as humanitarian actors deploy it in camps and for people on the move. It has the potential to address digital identity, supply chains, cash transfers and remittances, integrity of donor funds flows, property registry, employment rights, human trafficking, education and asylum processing. The chapter concludes that while promising progress has been made, there remain other issues to be resolved to see this taken to scale including the capacity of existing infrastructure and costs, regulations restricting the use of certain technologies and privacy and security has heightened focus as people caught in humanitarian crises fear having their personal information leaked or their location identified, and fears of being tracked and the need for further rigorous evaluation of uses of Blockchain in humanitarian contexts.

Chapter 8 reviews how Blockchain can contribute to global health equity and universal health coverage, re-architecting many incumbent business models, removing friction and improving data sharing in a highly secure environment while leveraging existing IT infrastructure. Initially, it examines the applications in high infrastructure settings including in the management of patient records and data, financing, supply chain management, health workforce management and surveillance processes, and then discuss their application in low resource settings. As discussed elsewhere, Blockchain also has complementary relevance for identity and financial inclusion, which are vital for improving the health of the poor in emerging economies.

Chapter 9 considers how donors and international organisations can play a crucial role in advancing the responsible adoption and scaling of technology. The landscape of donor engagement with Blockchain is discussed as well as the ways in which donors can support and enable with the responsible adoption and scaling of Blockchain. Policymakers need to be able to make an informed assessment of the technology, its impacts on public outcomes and its future direction. This is where donors and international organisations can help. The authors conclude the key roles that donors and international organisations can play include:

1. Establish and promote appropriate monitoring and benchmarks for: internet speed and minimum internet penetration; internet access and usage; rural inclusion and mobile network coverage.
2. Proactively support emerging economies to leapfrog and rapidly move to a digital future and build digital as a sector of the economy and develop country-led strategies digital health roadmaps, data use partnerships, and building the digital eco-system.
3. Convene policy discussions on topics like enabling regulatory framework; the development of technologies which address public good, economic policies to stimulate growth in the digital age, and profile leadership in digital adoption

4. Provide a coordinated Information Clearing House to build and disseminate evidence and digital platforms can play an essential role in the roll-out of digitalisation where:
    a. experiences can be shared,
    b. collaboration and joint investments can be triggered,
    c. common approaches to regulatory problems be explored,
    d. means for re-skilling of the workforce be further exchanged,
    e. strengthen capacity-building among economies
    f. models to facilitate innovation and entrepreneurship to foster innovation and technology diffusion, ensure that competitive conditions prevail and avoid erecting barriers to cross-border digital markets can be shared,
5. Support the development and scaling of digital "global goods" and open source systems, and
6. Help define new partnerships and financing models for technology.

EMERGING THEMES

Not Enough Is Understood

There is clearly potential in the technology, and there is a place for a global effort to purposefully curate and shape technology as a tool for good. Technological innovation is taking place rapidly and globally. Not enough is known about the possible impact of the new data economy, nor of the operation of global distributed autonomous communities, or how self-sovereign identity would manifest. Is it possible to build self-regulating economies that are responsible and distributed and where participants are incentivised to contribute to the economy in a positive and collaborative way towards a common purpose? The technological tools exist. Many questions remain to be answered.

What happens in the new data economy, when individuals - instead of corporations - own their own data and permission others to use it? While it is technologically possible, will traditional institutions, who currently own the data, allow it to happen? Medical records are currently dispersed among, hospitals, clinics, insurers and doctors – how can an individual access them, let alone take control over them?

How do governments and international institutions get up to speed with the pace of technological change? Currently several countries, including Serbia, Mauritius and Bermuda, are finding their own advice from experts and industry opinion leaders, to move faster in their technological innovation journey.

Blockchain seeks to decentralises finance and makes borders irrelevant. Blockchain will blur the jurisdictional boundaries of economic activity. Can governments regulate digital, borderless economies?

How do you build bridges between players who have not traditionally worked together and connect governments, development agencies, tech entrepreneurs, industry, academics to find common ground and build collaboration? There is a need for close and careful monitoring to see how this manifests and to share this information with the many who are interested.

Consumer Protection, Especially in Resource Poor Settings

Deployment of Blockchain in resource-poor settings requires a strong understanding of local social, cultural, and political contexts in order to be effective. It will also require users to have sufficient levels of both digital literacy and health literacy. Additional challenges are validation and quality, affordability and commercialization; ethics, privacy, confidentiality, data security, open source systems, informed consent and data ownership apply in particular to resource-poor settings.

Design and Governance of Blockchain Networks

Blockchain economies will demand a rethinking of governance. In particular, the enforcement of accountability through technical specifications and smart contracts, will require a deep understanding of the objectives of the network and decision rights, incentives and accountabilities. Beck et al. (2018) outline how governance in the blockchain economy may depart radically from established notions of governance and suggest a research agenda focussed on decision rights, accountability and incentives.

The blockchain economy demands a reassessment of established notions of governance. How exactly governance will change in the emerging blockchain economy is however still little understood. Nevertheless, the promise of the blockchain economy is dependent on the implementation of effective governance mechanisms, which are, in turn, dependent on a thorough understanding of the phenomenon. (Beck et al., 2018)

There Are Risks

Risks of authoritarian states, persecution and unintended consequences. Risks of bad actors using digital identities, bank accounts and mobile phones that allow authorities to track people's choices. Such control might allow authorities to increase surveillance over vulnerable or persecuted populations. An authoritarian state could use such data collected from refugees against refugees – or nations of the global North which have no sympathy for the movements of refugees and immigrants towards their countries could use such information to keep refugees in neighbouring countries.

Data, Data, Data

It's all about the data. Data is relevant at every turn from making anonymized data available for health research, to data portability, to paying people for access to their data, to data as part of digital infrastructure, data rules in a digital economy, data protection, and sophisticated rules about private data.

Governments Need to Be a Catalyst

Political leadership is needed, setting policies to attract talent; investors, academics and developers; enhancing curriculum in schools so that core digital skills are taught to all from a young age. Government can help attract finance – such as government backed bonds with matched funding and venture capital incentives to back tech companies and accelerate infrastructure – including physical spaces, broadband, plus underpinning policies - data - trading arrangements - policies on data and making trading available. Government can set an enabling business environment for digital innovation.

RECOMMENDATIONS

To accelerate technology adoption will require key enabling shifts, as elaborated in the B4SC Model in Chapter one:

1.   Increasing mobile and internet penetration, making access to technology ubiquitous.
2.   User experience and user benefit; when people see the benefit, they will adopt the technology.
3.   An understanding of the move to the new data driven economy owned and permissioned by individuals.
4.   A connected eco-system with all stakeholders building hyper-co-collaboration for social impact.
5.   International institutions support and provide models for global and national governance and enabling standards and regulations.
6.   Collaboration for societal gains – incentives are not in place to generate social benefits and to develop new incentive structures to enable societal value creation.

To see the benefits of Blockchain at scale will require the enabling shifts as outlined indicated in the B4SC Model to be into place. As it is by those occurring that the "new digital world" will emerge. These include the conversations, hyper-co-collaboration, government engagement, self-sovereign identity, connected communities and the economic shifts to decentralised, self-regulating economies.

FURTHER RESEARCH

As outlined above, not enough is known about what the impact and implications of Blockchain will be in the future. A research agenda is needed through strategic foresight, to look to the future and identify research questions that need to be addressed to enable equitable and responsible deployment. Many of these are suggested in the preceding section. To protect consumers, there is also a need for ethical principles for the responsible, validated and equitable deployment of these technologies to be further elaborated. Finally, what governance mechanisms will be required for global, regional and national level, to support the development of leadership and cooperation approaches to help bridge the fragmented and divergent ecosystem of Blockchain solutions and programs. The scientific community can contribute a great deal by studying implementation and providing validated operational research on what happened and why. The world needs to be in learning mode, as technology exponentiates and impacts across the world in various ways daily. Sharing this kind of knowledge will be a vital role to help policy makers understand how to face the future. Policymakers need to be aware that the benefits of innovation arising from blockchain, and related technologies are not a given – and that the technology faces many issues and questions need to be answered.

CONCLUSION

This book is a contribution to a growing body of knowledge about how innovators are developing applications for Blockchain, specifically around social impact. It highlights the central role of emerging markets as catalysts for social innovation because this is where the problems are greatest and where there is greatest potential to leapfrog. There are innovators and technologists working across the world on implementing Blockchain to solve many of the Sustainable Development Goal problems. This book provides the reader with an introduction to blockchain and the potential applications of the technology to improve lives of the poor and disadvantaged. It is by nature, inadequate and will be out of date the moment it is released. This is a point in time of the development and application of Blockchain and the authors have gathered the available knowledge and learnings for greater sharing and as a contribution to the knowledge base. There is more to do, questions that remain unanswered and research that is needed. Nevertheless, time and technology wait for no one and this book is a contribution to the thinking about how Blockchain and other frontier technologies can be tools for social change and improve inequality and inequity in the world.

REFERENCES

Beck, R., Müller-Bloch, C., & Leslie King, J. (2018). Governance in the Blockchain economy: A framework and research agenda. *Journal of the Association for Information Systems, 19*(10).

GSMA. (2019). *The Mobile Economy*. Retrieved from https://www.gsma.com/r/mobileeconomy/

UNHCR. (2017). *Global trends; Forced displacement in 2017*. Retrieved from https://www.unhcr.org/5b27be547.pdf

About the Authors

Jane Thomason is a Frontier Technology and social impact thought leader, recognised in Forbes Magazine (2018) as Blockchain's Leading Social Development Evangelist, and The Introducer (2019) as a Blockchain women leader, Jane is a pioneer for Blockchain & digital technologies for social impact, education and empowerment of women. She is focussed on emerging economies and how Frontier Technologies can accelerate poverty reduction and improve service delivery. In 2018 she was awarded Top 10 Digital Frontier Women and UN Decade Of Women Quantum Impact Champion. She has held Board and CEO roles in tertiary hospitals and health care sector in Australia and globally. She founded an international development company in 1999, built it to $50 m revenue, merged with Abt Associates and led to achieve a tripling of revenue and diversification to $250m with 650 staff. She resigned as CEO in March 2018 to commit full time to a global digital transformation agenda. She has 30 years' experience in emerging economies in public health, poverty and inequality. She holds multiple appointments including Global Adviser on Digital Transformation Abt Associates, Digital Transformation Adviser to the Partnership for Maternal, Neonatal and Child Health, Digital Transformation Sub-Committee Chair, Kina Bank Papua New Guinea, Founding Member, British Frontier Technology Industry Association, Fellow of the Australian Digital Commerce Association and Section Chief Co-Editor Blockchain for Good: for Frontiers in Blockchain. Jane is adviser to Blockchain start-ups with social impact applications and is currently working with start-ups to develop Blockchain use cases in emerging economies. She is a regular hackathon judge and mentor including London Blockchain Week, London Fintech Week, Consensys and EOS Global Hackathons. She believes that the next wave of transformational innovation will be from emerging economies and has potential to reduce inequality and improve services to the poor.

Sonja Bernhardt OAM holds a BA, GDBA and an MBA, she is CEO and Director of ThoughtWare a software house in Australia. Never one to 'retire' Sonja has taken her life long technology interest to present emerging technologies on cruise ships. She is also a popular ABC Radio technology commentator, as well as a published author. Sonja, personally and her business is the recipient of many awards. Throughout her career Sonja has served on technology related committees for the United Nations, APEC (Asia Pacific Economic Cooperation), Ministerial Advisory Boards, as well as prestigious national and state-based organisations.

Tia Kansara is a multi-award-winning entrepreneur and economist. The youngest to ever receive the Royal Institute British Architects honorary fellowship, she is the co-founder of Kansara Hackney Ltd, the first ISO-certified sustainable lifestyle consultancy, and CEO of Replenish Earth Ltd, a cause and a collective action to protect the global commons. Hailed amongst the Top 100 most influential leaders in Tech by the Financial Times and Inclusive Boards, her clients include Coca Cola, Bloomberg, the European Commission, Forbes, Formula One, MIT, and Siemens.

Nichola Cooper is PhD candidate at the University of the Sunshine Coast researching the future of trust in decentralised economies. She is Head of Research for NewVote and a Senior Research Analyst for Blockchain Quantum Impact.

Index

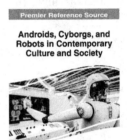

Ensure Quality Research is Introduced to the Academic Community

Become an IGI Global Reviewer for Authored Book Projects

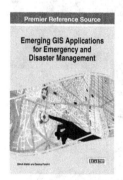

The overall success of an authored book project is dependent on quality and timely reviews.

In this competitive age of scholarly publishing, constructive and timely feedback significantly expedites the turnaround time of manuscripts from submission to acceptance, allowing the publication and discovery of forward-thinking research at a much more expeditious rate. Several IGI Global authored book projects are currently seeking highly qualified experts in the field to fill vacancies on their respective editorial review boards:

Applications may be sent to:
development@igi-global.com

Applicants must have a doctorate (or an equivalent degree) as well as publishing and reviewing experience. Reviewers are asked to write reviews in a timely, collegial, and constructive manner. All reviewers will begin their role on an ad-hoc basis for a period of one year, and upon successful completion of this term can be considered for full editorial review board status, with the potential for a subsequent promotion to Associate Editor.

If you have a colleague that may be interested in this opportunity, we encourage you to share this information with them.

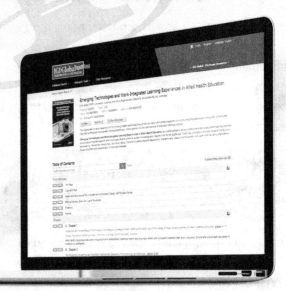

Printed in the United States
By Bookmasters